René Descartes, Henry Augustus Pierson Torrey

The Philosophy of Descartes, in Extracts from his Writing

René Descartes, Henry Augustus Pierson Torrey
The Philosophy of Descartes, in Extracts from his Writing
ISBN/EAN: 9783337073534
Printed in Europe, USA, Canada, Australia, Japan
Cover: Foto ©Thomas Meinert / pixelio.de

More available books at **www.hansebooks.com**

Series of Modern Philosophers
Edited by E. Hershey Sneath, Ph. D.

THE
PHILOSOPHY OF DESCARTES

IN

EXTRACTS FROM HIS WRITINGS

SELECTED AND TRANSLATED

BY

HENRY A. P. TORREY, A. M.
Marsh Professor of Philosophy in the University of Vermont

NEW YORK
HENRY HOLT AND COMPANY
1892

COPYRIGHT, 1892,
BY
HENRY HOLT & CO.

THE MERSHON COMPANY PRESS,
RAHWAY, N. J.

PREFACE.

THE following translations from the philosophical writings of Descartes are made, with one exception, from the French text of Cousin's edition of the collected works in eleven volumes. The extracts from the "Principles" are translated from the Latin text of an Elzevir edition of the *Opera Philosophica*, Amst., 1677. No selections have been made from the mathematical writings, as not coming within the scope of the series. For the same reason, as well as for want of space, the more specifically physical views of Descartes are not fully represented. Much, perhaps, will be missed, but, on the other hand, portions of writings which, to the translator's knowledge, have not hitherto appeared in English, have been introduced. It is perhaps unnecessary to add that in making his selections the translator has derived much aid from the great historians of philosophy, particularly, Kuno Fischer, Erdmann, and Ueberweg, and from the recent treatise of Liard. In the revision of certain portions of the work, Professor Veitch's version has been consulted with advantage.

CONTENTS.

	PAGE
BIBLIOGRAPHY	v
LIFE AND WRITINGS	1
THE PHILOSOPHY OF DESCARTES AND ITS INFLUENCE	15
SELECTIONS FROM DESCARTES' WRITINGS ARRANGED IN PARTS	37–345

    Part First.—METHOD............................37–104
        The Discourse Upon Method.—Parts I, II, III...... 37
        Rules for the Direction of the Mind................ 61

    Part Second.—METAPHYSICS........................107–204
        Meditations on the First Philosophy................ 107
        Principles of Philosophy, Part I................... 191

    Part Third.—PHYSICS............................207–272
        The World, or Essay Upon Light................... 207

    Part Fourth.—PHYSIOLOGY........................275–287
        The Tract on Man.......................... 275
        Automatism of Brutes............................ 281

    Part Fifth.—PSYCHOLOGY........................291–326
        The Passions of the Soul......................... 291

    Part Sixth.—ETHICS 329–345
        On the Happy Life............................... 329
        On the Summum Bonum........................ 342

INDEX 347

BIBLIOGRAPHY.

I. *Works of Descartes published during his lifetime.*

1. *Essais philosophiques*, which consisted of *Discours de la Méthode* pour bien conduire sa raison, et chercher la vérité dans les sciences; plus *la Dioptrique, les Météores*, et *la Géométrie*, qui sont des essais de cette Méthode. Leyde, 1637. Published anonymously.

R. Cartesii *Specimina Philosophiæ* sive dissertatio de methodo recte regendæ rationis, Dioptrice et meteora ex gallico latine versa (par Étienne de Courcelles) et ab autero emendata. Amst., Elzev., 1644.

Geometria a R. Descartes, gallice edita, cum notis Florim. de Beaune, latine versa et commentariis illustrata a Fr. a Schooten. Lugd. Bat. J. Maire, 1649.

2. Renati Descartes *Meditationes* de prima philosophia, ubi de Dei existentia et animæ immortalitate ; his adjunctæ sunt variæ objectiones doctorum virorum in istas de Deo et anima demonstrationes, cum responsionibus auctoris. Paris, 1641.

Second edition of the same, with changed title and Bourdin's objections with replies added, published under the author's superintendence. Amst., Elzev., 1642.

French version of *Meditationes* by the Duc de Luynes; of the *Objectiones et Responsiones* by Clerselier; the whole revised by the author. Paris, 1647.

3. Renati Descartes *Principia Philosophiæ*. Amst., Elzev., 1644.

Principes de la Philosophie écrits en latin par René Descartes, et traduits en français par un de ses amis [the Abbé Picot]. Paris, 1647.

4. *Epistola Renati Descartes ad celeberrimum virum Gisbertum Voëtium*, in qua examinantur duo libri nuper pro Voëtio Ultrajecti simul editi : unus de confrater-

nitate Mariana, alter de philosophia Cartesiana. Amst., Elzev., 1643.

5. *R. Descartes notæ in programma quoddam* sub finem anni 1647 in Belgio editum cum hoc titulo : explicatio mentis humanæ sive animæ rationalis, ubi explicatur, quid sit et quid esse possit. Amst., Elzev., 1648. These "*notæ*" appear in the "Lettres," Œuvres (Cousin), t. 10, p. 70. A Monsieur .... [Régius] Remarques de René Descartes sur un certain placard imprimé aux Pays-Bas vers la fin de l'année 1647.

6. *Les passions de l'âme.* Amst., Elzev., 1650.

II. *Posthumous works.*
   1. Edited by Clerselier.
      1. *Le monde*, ou traité de la lumière. Paris, 1677. (First published [not by Clerselier] in 1664.)
      2. *Traité de l'homme.* Paris, 1646. *De la formation du fœtus*, published in connection with the preceding.
      3. *Les lettres de René Descartes*, 3 vols. Paris, 1657-1667.
   2. Not edited by Clerselier.
      1. *Opera postuma Cartesii*, Amst., 1701, containing, with others, two works published for the first time, viz.: *Regulæ ad directionem ingenii.* (*Régles pour la direction de l'esprit*, Œuvres [Cousin ed.] t. 11, pp. 201-329), and *Inquisitio veritatis per lumen naturale* (*Recherche de la vérité par les lumières naturelles*, Œuvres [Cousin], t. 11, pp. 333-376).
      2. *Compendium musicæ.* Utrecht, 1650.
      3. *Traité de la mécanique* composé par M. Descartes, de plus l'abrégé de la musique du même auteur, mis en français. .... N. Poisson, Paris, 1668.

III. *Collected works.*
   1. *Opera philosophica.* Elzevir, Amst., 1644 (Editio tertia, 1656), 1670, 1672, 1674, 1677.

2. *Opera omnia*, 1st ed. 8 vols. 1670-83. 2d ed. 9 vols. 1692-1701 and 1713. Elzevir, Amst. See Brunet.

3. *Opera omnia*. Frankfort, 7 vols. in 4to, 1697. See Bouillier, t. 1, p. 36.

4. *Œuvres de Descartes*, Paris, 1724, 13 vols. in 12mo. "Fort incomplète." Bouillier.

5. *Œuvres de Descartes*, publiées par Victor Cousin, 11 vols. in 8vo. Paris, 1824-26. (The most nearly complete edition.)

6. *Œuvres philosophiques*, Garnier, 4 vols. in 8vo. Paris, 1835.

7. *Œuvres inédites de Descartes*. Foucher de Careil, Paris, 1859-60.

8. *Œuvres de Descartes*, nouvelle édition precédée d'une introduction par Jules Simon. Paris, 1868.

[The above titles have been collected mainly from the bibliographical notices of Kuno Fischer (*Descartes and his School*, p. 298, trans.) ; Ueberweg (*Hist. of Philos.*, Vol. ii, p. 42, trans.); Bouillier (*Hist. de la Philos. Cartésienne*, t. 1, p. 36), and Brunet (*Manuel du Libraire*).

For an interesting account of the lost writings see Kuno Fischer, *Descartes*, p. 300.]

Works Relating to Descartes.

1. *Renati Descartes Principia Philosophica more geometrico demonstrata* per Benedictum de Spinoza. Amst. 1663.

This volume contained as an appendix his Cogitata Metaphysica, the earliest published work of Spinoza.

2. *Censura philosophiæ Cartesianæ*, Paris, 1689, and *Nouveaux Mémoires pour servir à l'histoire du Cartésianisme*, Paris, 1692, both by (Bishop) Daniel Huet.

3. *Voyage du Monde de Descartes*, par P. G. Daniel. Paris, 1691.

The same, *Iter per Mundum Cartesii*. Amst, 1694. Containing also, *Novæ Difficultates a Peripatetico propositæ*, etc.

4. *Dictionnaire historique et critique, Pierre Bayle.* 1695-97, 1702, 2 vols. 1740, 4 vols. Engl. trans. London, 1736.

5. *Le Cartésianisme, ou la veritable rénovation des sciences.* Bordas-Demoulin. Paris, 1843.

6. *Fragments de Philosophie Cartésienne: Fragments de Philosophie Moderne,* par V. Cousin. Paris, 1852 and 1854.

7. *Histoire de la Philosophie Cartésienne,* par F. Bouillier. 2 vols., Paris, 1854. (The principal authority on the subject.)

8. *Descartes, ses Précurseurs et ses Disciples,* par E. Saisset. Paris, 1865.

9. *Descartes,* par L. Liard. Paris, 1882. (A remarkably fresh and interesting presentation of the speculations of Descartes in the light of contemporary science and philosophy.)

10. *Descartes* (in Blackwood's Philosophical Classics), by J. P. Mahaffy. Edin. and Phila., 1881.

11. *Commentaire sur les Méditations de Descartes, par Maine de Biran* (Found in Bertrand's *Science et Psycologie: nouvelles œuvres inédites de De Biran.* Paris, 1887). See *Mind,* vol. 12, p. 625.

12. *The Fundamental Doctrines of Descartes.* By H. Sedgwick (in *Mind,* vol. 7, pp. 435, *seq.*)

13. *The Method, Meditations and Selections from the Principles of Descartes,* translated from the original texts, with introductory essay, historical and critical, by J. Veitch. Edin. and Lond. (1st ed. 1850-52), Tenth edition, 1890.

("The extracts from the Principles correspond to what is found in the edition of Garnier." Two earlier, now rare, English versions are mentioned by the author: The Method, Lond., 1649; The Meditations, W. Molyneux, Lond., 1680. See preface.)

14. A translation of the Meditations appeared in the *Journal of Speculative Philosophy,* vol. 4, 1870, and of the introduction to the Meditations, in the same Journal, vol. 5, April, 1871, both by Wm. R. Walker.

Among the historians of philosophy who have

treated of Descartes at length should be mentioned especially :
Kuno Fischer : *Geschichte der neuern Philosophie.* Mannheim, 1854, *seq.* New editions of the earlier volumes have since appeared. The third and revised edition of the first volume, containing Descartes, has recently been translated into English by J. P. Gordy, Ph. D., under the title, *History of Modern Philosophy*, by Kuno Fischer, *Descartes and his school.* New York, 1887. Kuno Fischer also has translated into German the principal philosophical works of Descartes. Mannheim, 1863.

Titles of numerous essays on Descartes, mostly German, may be found in Ueberweg's full bibliography (Hist. of Philos., vol. ii, p. 43, trans.). In addition may be mentioned the following recent monographs :

P. J. Schmid : *Die Prinzipien der menschlichen Erkenntniss nach Descartes.* (Promotionsschrift), Leipzig.

Hartmann: *Die Lehre des Cartesius De Passionibus Animæ und des Spinoza Dè Affectibus Humanis dargestellt und verglichen.* W. Ohlan, 1878.

B. Gutzeit: *Descartes' angeborene Ideen verglichen mit Kant's Anschauungs-und-Denkformen* a priori. Bromberg, 1883.

B. Trognitz : *Die mathematische Methode in Descartes' philosophischem Systeme.* Saalfeld, 1887.

P. Plessner : *Die Lehre von den Leidenschaften bei Descartes.* (Inaugural Dissertation.) Leipzig, 1888.

Wm. Wallace : Article on *Descartes* in the *Encyclopædia Britannica*. Ninth edition.

Neuf lettres inédites à Mersenne. See notice in *Mind*, Oct. 1891 (vol. 16, p. 555).

WORKS ON THE LIFE OF DESCARTES.

Descartes : *Discours sur la Méthode.*
A. Baillet: *La vie de Mr. des Cartes.* Paris, 1691, abridged, 1693.
Thomas: *Éloge de René Descartes.* Paris, 1765 (Dis-

cours qui a remporté le prix de l'Académie française en 1765). Especially the Notes to the above.

J. Millet : *Histoire de Descartes avant* 1637 (Paris, 1867), *depuis* 1637 (Paris, 1870).

Kuno Fischer : *Hist. of Mod. Philos., Descartes and his school* (trans.), pp. 165-297.

J. P. Mahaffy: *Descartes.* pp. 7-143.

C. G. J. Jacobi : *Ueber Descartes' Leben.* Berlin, 1846.

LIFE AND WRITINGS.

RENÉ DESCARTES (De Quartis)* was born March 30, 1596, at La Haye, in the province of Touraine. His father, Joachim Descartes, was a councilor of the parliament of Bretagne. His mother, Jeanne Brochard, was the daughter of a lieutenant-general of Poitiers. She was of a delicate constitution, and transmitted to René, her third and last child, the germs of consumption, of which disease she died a few days after his birth. Like Newton, the feeble boy seemed destined to an early grave, but careful nursing saved him. The wise father would not suffer the eager mind in the frail body to be overtaxed. Allowed to carry on his studies, but only as play, the reflective turn of the boy's mind asserted itself in constant inquiries into the causes of things, and before he was eight years old his father began to call him his "little philosopher." In 1604 René was sent to the college of La Flèche, in Anjou, recently established by Henry IV. in the royal palace, under the care of the Jesuits, and designed to be the foremost school for the education of the nobility. The impression made upon the young mind of the philosopher by the studies there pursued is vividly conveyed in his own words in his *Discourse on Method*. He finished his course at La Flèche in

* Thomas, *Notes sur l'Éloge*. *Œuvres de Descartes* (Cousin), t. i, p. 81.

1612, when he was sixteen years of age. Among his schoolmates one, eight years older than himself, Marin Mersenne, was destined to be his lifelong friend. The point of chief interest is this : the mind which was to lay the foundation for modern philosophy there became interested, not in learning merely, but in *knowledge*, in the nature of knowledge itself, and in what can be clearly and distinctly known, as distinguished from what is obscure and confused. Hence the fascination of mathematics.

In the year 1613 his father sent young René to Paris to see life. For two years he spent most of his time in amusements, then for two years more shut himself up in seclusion and pursued his studies. At last, weary of the city and convinced that he would learn more by mingling with the world at large, in 1617, at the age of twenty-one, he enlisted as a volunteer in the army of the Netherlands. He joined the garrison in Breda, under the Prince Maurice of Nassau. During two years' stay there, while an armistice prevailed, he found leisure to cultivate mathematics, and made the acquaintance of a celebrated mathematician, Beeckman, for whom he wrote his *Compendium Musicæ*, the earliest of his works now extant. From the army of the Netherlands he went to Bavaria and enlisted in the service of Maximilian at the beginning of the Thirty Years' War, and afterward in that of the Emperor Ferdinand II. He took part in several campaigns in Bohemia and Hungary, but finally quitted the service and ended his military life soon after the battle of Neuhasel, in July, 1621. He was then twenty-five years of age. Intervals of peace favored the philosopher during his career as a soldier. Diplomatic negotiations interrupted the movements of the Bavarian army, they went into winter quarters, and Descartes was stationed at Neuburg, on the Danube, during the winter of 1619-20. During that period, left undisturbed to his reflections, he made a memorable discovery.* It produced so profound an impression upon his mind that he put down in his diary the exact date. "On the tenth of November I began to make a wonderful discovery."† It was probably "his first glimpse of the principles of the fundamental science, or *mathesis universalis*," ‡ to the development of which he thereafter devoted his life. He saw the possibility of solving geometrical problems by algebra, and laid the foundations of analytical geometry. But the *inventum mirabile* meant for Descartes a great deal more than this. He thought he had discovered the key to unlock all the mysteries of nature. He thought that by considering all physical change as matter in motion he could subject the whole realm of nature to mathematical demonstration. § But his thought went even further than this. He conceived mathematical knowledge as the type of all knowledge. Its criterion of certainty, clear and distinct intuition, its analytical method, he would apply to the cogni-

---

* See *Discourse on Method*, part ii.
† "Intelligere cœpi fundamentum inventi mirabilis." Kuno Fischer's *Descartes*, trans., p. 194.
‡ Erdmann, *Hist. of Philos. Modern*, trans., p. 9.
§ " In the words of his epitaph, written by his intimate friend Chanut, with whom he had often talked over his mental history: 'In his winter furlough, comparing the mysteries of nature with the laws of mathematics, he dared to hope that the secrets of both could be unlocked by the same key.'—In otiis hibernis Naturæ mysteria componens cum legibus Matheseos, utriusque arcana eadem clave reserari posse ausus est sperare." Mahaffy's *Descartes*, p. 27.

tion of every branch of human inquiry. He would thus lay new foundations for philosophy. After quitting the army Descartes spent the next five years mostly in travel, then for three years he lived in seclusion in the suburbs of Paris. It was probably during these years that he wrote out the first sketch of his doctrine of method, *The Rules for the Direction of the Mind* (*Regulæ ad Directionem Ingenii*).

In 1629, at the age of thirty-three, the philosopher sought and found a country and a mode of life most favorable to the prosecution of his design.* Acting upon the maxim, *Bene vixit, bene qui latuit*, he went secretly to Holland, where in a favorable climate he enjoyed during twenty years the desired seclusion, and there produced that series of remarkable works which gave a new direction to speculative thought and laid the basis of modern philosophy.

The philosophical works of Descartes appeared in the following order. The *Discourse upon Method* was the first. It was published anonymously at Leyden, June 8, 1637, in connection with the *Dioptric*, the *Meteors*, and the *Geometry*. The volume was entitled: " Discourse on the Method of Rightly Conducting the Reason, and Seeking Truth in the Sciences, also the Dioptric, the Meteors, and the Geometry, which are essays in this Method." The whole work was known also as " The Philosophical Essays." " Written," says Mahaffy,† " in the popular tongue of Europe, and with a clearness and simplicity rarely equaled even in

---

* " I desire quiet. I have guided my life thus far according to the motto *Bene vixit, bene qui latuit*, and I intend to continue to do so." Letter to Mersenne, January 10, 1634, *Œuvres*, t. vi, p. 243.

† *Descartes*, p. 70.

French prose—the best prose in modern Europe—it [the Discourse of Method] produced an electric shock throughout the learned world, which no other work of the kind ever did in the history of philosophy." Descartes himself thus justifies his use of his native tongue rather than Latin, the tongue of the learned, as a vehicle for his scientific thought. " And if I write in French, which is my vernacular, rather than in Latin, the language of my teachers, the reason is that I believe that those who make use of their simple natural reason will be better judges of my opinions than those who believe only in the ancient books ; and as for those who combine good sense with learning, whom alone I desire for my judges, they will not, I am sure, be so partial to the Latin as to refuse to attend to my arguments because I present them in the vulgar tongue." *

In explanation of the title of the work, Descartes, writing to his friend Mersenne, says, " I do not call it Treatise upon method, but Discourse upon method, which is the same as Preface or Announcement of the method, to show that I have no intention of unfolding it, but only of talking about it ; for, as may be seen from what I say of it, it consists rather in practice than in theory ; and I call the treatises which follow essays in this method, because I contend that the things they contain could not have been discovered without it, and one may learn from them the value of it. As also I have inserted in the first discourse something in metaphysics, in physics, and in medicine, to show that it applies to all sorts of matters." † In a letter to a friend of Mersenne, he says further, " I think I have

* *Discours de la Méthode*, p. 6, ad fin. *Œuvres*, t. i, p. 210.
† *Lettres*, *Œuvres*, t. vi, p. 138.

shown that I employ a method by which I might explain equally well any other matter, provided I could make the necessary experiments and had the time to consider them."* Regarding the *Method* of Descartes, Saisset has very well said : " It ought not to be forgotten that in publishing the *Method*, Descartes joined to it, as a supplement, the *Dioptrics*, the *Geometry*, and the *Meteors*. Thus at one stroke he founded, on the basis of a new method, two sciences hitherto almost unknown and of infinite importance—Mathematical Physics and the application of Algebra to Geometry ; and at the same time he gave the prelude to the *Meditations* and the *Principles*—that is to say, to an original Metaphysic, and the mechanical theory of the universe." †

Next appeared, in 1641, his most important work, the *Meditations*. It was published first at Paris with the title, "*Meditationes de prima philosophia, ubi de Dei existentia et animæ immortalitate.*" A second edition was published in Amsterdam by Elzevir in 1642, with the title somewhat changed, "*Meditationes de prima philosophia, in quibus Dei existentia et animæ humanæ a corpore distinctio demonstrantur.*" ‡ The Meditations are six in number, with the following titles : The First ; of the Things which may be Doubted. The Second ; of the Nature of the Human Mind ; and that it is more easily known than the Body. The Third ; of God ; that He exists. The Fourth ; of Truth and Error. The Fifth; of the Essence of Material Things, and, for the second time, of the Existence of God. The Sixth ; of the Existence of Material

* *Lettres, Œuvres*, t. vi, p. 306.
† Veitch, *Descartes*, Introd., p. xii.
‡ See K. Fischer, *Descartes*, p. 247.

Things, and of the Real Distinction between the Soul and the Body of Man. In a somewhat unique way the writer endeavored to forestall criticism. Before the work was printed, he sent copies of it in manuscript, through Mersenne and other friends, to several of the most learned men of the time, soliciting their objections. Seven sets of objections were thus collected, to all of which Descartes made elaborate replies. These objections, with the replies, were added to the work, which was then published. The first set of objections were those offered by a certain Caterus, a Catholic theologian of Louvain, and relate principally to the proof of the Divine existence; the second and sixth are reports of objections collected by Mersenne from various persons, and concern the question of the immortality of the soul and the logical defects in the arguments; the third are from the English philosopher Thomas Hobbes, who objects, among other things, to clear conception being made the test of truth; the fourth were those of Antoine Arnauld, the celebrated Jansenist of Port Royal, who questions Descartes' originality in respect to his *Cogito, ergo sum,* finds the distinction between soul and body too sharply drawn, detects a logical circle in the attempt to prove the divine existence by the clearness of the idea of God, and the reality of what we clearly conceive by the Divine veracity, and also finds difficulty in harmonizing Descartes' view of substance and accident with the doctrine of Transubstantiation. The fifth set of objections were those of the French philosopher, Pierre Gassendi, who, from a materialistic point of view attacked the idealism of the new philosophy. To these six series of objections, published with Descartes' replies in the first edition of the Meditations, there were added, in the second edition, those of the Jesuit Father Bourdin, a scholastic theologian who sought to overthrow the new doctrine by attacking the method itself; of greater importance were the criticisms of the writer who styles himself *Hyperaspistes*, and of Henry More, the Cambridge Platonist, whose objections were not embodied in the work, but were published, with Descartes' replies, among his letters of the years 1640 and 1648.*

The Meditations, originally written in Latin, were translated into French by the Duc de Luynes, and the seven sets of objections and replies by Clerselier. Descartes revised the translations and changed some passages in the Latin text.† The French version was published in Paris, 1647.

The important treatise, *The Principles of Philosophy*, followed. It was written in Latin. The first edition, bearing the title, *Renati Descartes*‡ *principia philosophiæ*, was printed by the Elzevirs in Amsterdam, 1644. The treatise has four parts: Part I, Of the Principles of Human Knowledge. Part II, Of the Principles of Material Things. Part III, Of the Visible World. Part IV, Of the Earth. The first part is a repetition, with slight additions, of the thoughts contained in the Meditations. The manner of the whole work is dry and scholastic, as compared with the free and flowing style of his other writings, but it was intended to present in a more exact form a complete summary of his system.

* *Œuvres*, t. viii, p. 242, t. x, p. 178.
† See K. Fischer, *Descartes*, p. 299. Professor Veitch has collated the French in his translation, which is from the Latin text.
‡ He objected to the Latinizing of his name.

LIFE AND WRITINGS.   9

The remaining parts contain the substance of his suppressed treatise, *De Mundo* (*Le Monde, ou Traité de la Lumière*). A French version was made by one of Descartes' friends, the Abbé Picot. It was approved by the author, who says of it in a letter to the Abbé, which is printed as a preface to the work: "The version of my Principles which you have taken the trouble to make is so elegant and so finished that I am led to hope it will be read by more people in French than in Latin, and that it will be better understood."*

The last work of Descartes, published in the lifetime of the author, was the Treatise on the Passions (*Traité des Passions de l'Âme*). It was written in French, for the Princess Elizabeth of the Palatinate, in 1646, but not finished until 1649. At the solicitations of his friends the treatise was published the following year, by the Elzevirs, at Amsterdam, by whom also a Latin version was brought out shortly after the author's death. The scope of the treatise is indicated in these words: "My design has not been to expound the passions as a preacher, nor even as a moral philosopher, but solely as a natural philosopher (*en physicien*)."† He seeks to exhibit the passions as due to the union of body and soul and as mental phenomena resulting from the motions of the animal spirits.

The motto, *Bene vixit, bene qui latuit*, which Descartes had adopted for his life, whether dictated by prudence or timidity, or both, is characteristic of the man. He lived at a time when it was dangerous to

* *Œuvres*, t. iii, p. 9.
† *Réponse à la Séconde Letter, Les Passions. Œuvres*, t. iv, p. 34.

express new truth openly. He had to encounter, or evade, the opposition of theologians, both Catholic and Protestant. He chose, when it was possible, to avoid a quarrel. He stood in fear of the Inquisition. With the fate of Galileo before his eyes, he suppressed his treatise *De Mundo*. He thought it necessary to do this, even although in that treatise he had presented his views as a mere hypothesis of what would happen in an imaginary world.

"But because I have endeavored to explain my principal discoveries in a treatise which certain considerations prevent me from publishing, I cannot make them understood better than by giving here a summary of its contents. .... I designed to comprehend in it all that I thought I knew, before writing it, concerning the nature of material things. But just as painters do, who cannot represent on a flat surface equally well all the aspects of a solid body, and therefore choose one of the more important, which they set in full light, and the rest in shadow, so I, fearing I could not get into my essay all I had in my mind, undertook merely to set forth quite fully what I thought about light ; then, as occasion was presented, to add something about the sun and the fixed stars, because light proceeds almost wholly from them ; of the heavens, because they transmit it ; of the planets, the comets, and the earth, because they reflect it ; and, in particular, of all bodies which are upon the earth, because they are either colored or transparent or luminous ; and, finally, of man, because he is the spectator of all.

"But, in order to put all these things a little into the shade, and to be able to say more freely what I thought about them, without being obliged either to accept or to reject the opinion received among the learned, I resolved to leave this whole present world to their disputes, and to talk only of what might happen in a *new* one, if God should create, somewhere in imaginary space, enough matter to compose it, and should set in motion in various ways and without order the different parts of this matter, so that it should form a chaos as confused as ever poets could feign, and thereafter affording it no more than his ordinary assistance to nature, leave it to act according to the laws which he has established." *

But the philosopher soon discovered that to present his views even under the guise of a mere hypothesis would not afford him sufficient shelter. The doctrine of the earth's motion, a necessary part of his theory, was not tolerated at Rome, even as an hypothesis. The sentence of condemnation against Galileo, who defended the Copernican theory, contained these words: "*quamvis hypothetice a se illam proponi simularet.*" Writing to his friend Mersenne in November, 1633, Descartes says: "I have just been inquiring at Leyden and at Amsterdam whether Galileo's *System of the World* was not there, for it seemed to me I had heard that it had been printed in Italy the past year. They told me that it was true that it had been printed, but that all the copies of it were immediately burned at Rome, and that he had been sentenced to do penance; which made so deep an impression upon me that I almost resolved to burn all my papers, or at least to let no one see them. . . . . . And I confess that if it [the theory of the earth's motion] is false, all the principles of my philosophy are also false, for

* *Discours*. pt. v. *Œuvres*, t. i, p. 168.

it is clearly demonstrated by them, and it is so bound up with every part of my treatise that I could not detach it from them without making the rest defective. But as I would not for all the world there should go forth from me an essay wherein there should be found the least word which would be disapproved by the Church, I prefer to suppress it rather than let it appear in a mutilated condition." * Probably only a fragment of the whole work ever saw the light. This was published by Clerselier in correct form, in 1677, entitled, *Le Monde, ou Traité de la Lumière.*

But our philosopher was not destined to end his days in Holland. The latter part of his life there was greatly embittered by controversy, particularly with a Protestant theologian, Voët, who had become rector of the University of Utrecht, and who had accused Descartes of atheism. In a letter to his friend Chanut, November 1, 1646, he complains : "A father (Bourdin) thought he had sufficient ground for accusing me of being a skeptic, because I have refuted the skeptics, and a clergyman (Voëtius) has undertaken to make out that I am an atheist, alleging no other reason except that I have tried to prove the existence of God." † After four years of persistent attack upon the new philosophy, Voët secured a judgment of condemnation on the part of the University, and finally, the matter going the length of libel, the magistrates of Utrecht took it up and settled it by prohibiting publications for or against Descartes. In the University of Leyden, also, a kind of interdict was placed on the writings of the philosopher. Annoyed

* *Œuvres*, t. vi, p. 238.
† *Œuvres*, t. ix, p. 416.

and disturbed by frequent and unreasonable opposition, he thought Holland no longer safe, and made up his mind to return to his own country. Not long after he received from the Queen of Sweden an invitation to visit Stockholm. Queen Christina had become interested in the philosophy of Descartes, through his personal friend Chanut, who was then French ambassador at the court of Sweden. The queen desired to meet the philosopher and to hear from his own lips an exposition of his system. Accordingly, though greatly dreading the long journey, the strange country, and the severe winter, he set out for Stockholm, where he arrived early in October, 1649, and took up his lodgings under the friendly roof of Chanut, and in November began to instruct the queen in philosophy. But the requirements of royalty did not suit the habits of the philosopher. Since the early days at the college of La Flèche, Descartes had been accustomed to lie in bed until the middle of the forenoon. The practice, at first permitted to favor a feeble child, was kept up in after years, because conducive to undisturbed reflection. It was most convenient, however, to his royal pupil to meet her instructor when her mind was freshest and when no cares of state would interrupt her lesson. Accordingly Descartes was obliged to go to the palace every morning at five o'clock. The winter was unusually severe, and the frail constitution of the philosopher succumbed to it. He died of inflammation of the lungs, February 11, 1650, before he had completed his fifty-fourth year. The queen, in her grief, would have buried him among kings and raised a mausoleum for him. But Chanut prevailed on her to allow the remains to be placed in the Catholic cemetery with simple rites. "A priest, some torches, and four persons of distinction who stood at the head and foot of the coffin—such was the funeral of Descartes. M. de Chanut, in honor of the memory of his friend and of a great man, raised over his grave a square pyramid with inscriptions. Holland, where he had been persecuted during his life, caused a medal to be struck in his honor when he was dead. Sixteen years after— that is to say in 1666—his remains were transported to France, and deposited in the church of Ste. Geneviève. On the 24th of June, 1667, a solemn service was performed for him with the greatest magnificence. After the service a funeral oration was to have been delivered, but there came an express order from the court forbidding it."* His name had stood for some years upon the Index.

* Thomas, *Notes sur l'Éloge. Œuvres*, t. i, p. 116.

THE PHILOSOPHY OF DESCARTES AND ITS INFLUENCE.

THE thinking of Descartes, by general consent, marks the beginning of modern speculative philosophy. If originality be a test of intellectual greatness, there are but few thinkers in ancient or modern times who can be placed alongside of this remarkable man. The seclusion in which Descartes sought steadfastly to spend his days was merely intended to promote the deeper seclusion of his intellectual life. He desired a first free look at the world, without and within, uninfluenced by the present, untrammeled by the past. Of course it was a vain desire. From the past came down to him the problems which still awaited solution, and the particular form in which they presented themselves was determined by the times in which he lived. The very discipline in the course of which he became aware of them, and by which his mind was prepared to deal with them, precluded a purely individual result, nor would such a result, if attainable, have been of great value. Pure, absolute originality in thought is no more possible than abstract individuality of existence. What Descartes says of himself was therefore not quite true, that had his father given him no education, he should have written the same works, only he should have written all in French. It is safe to say that, but for that scholastic training, he would have written nothing of account, and his name would not have survived the century in which he lived. For the studies which absorbed his eager mind at the college of La Flèche brought to his attention the deepest problems of existence and determined him to that lonely career the single object of which was to solve them. And with such originality and independence as is compatible with that organic connection with other minds, whereby the thought of all becomes the thought of each, the solitary thinker addressed himself to his task, and the sustained effort of more than twenty years, with scarcely a break, marks the strength of the original impulse. Much of his thinking, after two centuries and a half of scientific progress, has now become obsolete; much still remains an imperishable addition to the sum of human philosophy.

Let us attempt a somewhat free reproduction of his thought. In the endeavor to arrive at a true conception of the philosophical system of Descartes, the fact of his early predilection for mathematics must not be overlooked. The influence of those youthful studies, in a branch of knowledge to which he was himself destined to make a very important addition, survived through all, and determined his whole intellectual scheme. "Chiefly I loved the mathematics; I was surprised that upon foundations so solid and stable no loftier structure had been raised." The necessary sequence of intuitions in the demonstrations of geometry, wherein the mind, starting from the simplest truths, arrives by such successive intuitions at the knowledge of all that can be known of the relations of figures in space, presented itself to the mind of Descartes as the type of all human knowledge whatever. He looked upon knowledge as one interconnected whole, each special science being a member of it, so related to all the rest that it is easier to learn all than to learn any one detached from the whole. Hence is suggested a sort of universal mathematics, or *mathesis*, which is Descartes' Novum Organum. This view of the nature of the object and the process of human cognition is fully unfolded in the early and little known " Rules for the Direction of the Mind," a treatise of much greater importance than the Discourse on Method for the right comprehension of Descartes' theory of knowledge.* The mathematical sciences furnished also a universal rule of certainty. The mind of Descartes sought clearness as the first requisite in all satisfactory thinking. Geometry affords clear conceptions. Indeed that only which can be clearly and distinctly conceived is to be admitted as true in the mathematics generally.

This principle seemed to Descartes worthy to be made the universal rule for thought. " Only that— not in mathematics alone, but everywhere—which can be clearly and distinctly conceived, is true." (Absence of contradiction is the negative test of clearness, hence the logical law of non-contradiction as the reverse side of the principle.) But the principle itself, like the science of mathematics, from whence by generalization it was derived, belongs only to the sphere of abstract thought. It affords a criterion of the true, but stands for no concrete reality. Philosophy is the science of being ; Descartes, with his mathematical rule of certainty, becomes interested in philosophy. What he finds existing as such does not satisfy him. He cannot "clearly and distinctly conceive" it. He therefore rejects it all. He goes further ; on reflection he finds that he has from child-

* See extract from Rule II, below, p. 63.

hood received into his mind innumerable beliefs which will not stand the proposed test. They are worthless to the thinker, who desires only absolute truths perceived to be such. He will make a clean sweep of them. He will begin his thinking all over again, in the light of the new principle. He will make a clear space and wait to see what will appear. But the space is not clear, nor can it be, for he is himself there in the middle of it awaiting the disclosure; but that is precisely what the disclosure is: *Je pense, donc je suis.* Myself the thinker am a reality. My own existence in the act of thinking is as clearly and distinctly known to me as any truth of mathematics can be. This truth is itself a type of certainty. Whatever hereafter, and only that which, is as certainly and distinctly conceived by me as my own being is, shall be admitted as real. Descartes' thinking begins with abstract thought, mathematics; thence he derives his fundamental rule of certainty; but in the application of it he arrives at a concrete truth, the being of the individual thinker. He reaches thus a new starting-point, and one of cardinal importance for all succeeding philosophy. Philosophical speculation thereafter must turn on the *ego*, which Descartes thus made the pivot of his own thinking concerning real existence. But the self thus discovered and inexpugnable, undeniably existent, is only *myself*. Are there possibly other selves, finite like me, an infinite Self also above all? Descartes soon satisfies himself of the necessary existence of the latter, the original Self. But there is a little preliminary parade of skeptical skill. How do I know, after all, that in my clearest thought I am not deceived; might not some powerful being so control my mental process as to make me take the false for true ; well, even then, I should still be thinking, though thinking I was deceived ; and if I was thinking no matter what, I should be existing. But among my thoughts there is one which cannot have come from myself—the thought of infinite perfection. I am consciously finite, imperfect, yet this thought of infinite perfection is undeniably within me ; according to the principle *De nihilo nihil* it must have a cause. There is no adequate cause for this thought but the Being who is actually infinite in perfection—such a Being then must have put this thought within me. Such a Being must as certainly exist as I myself do, from whom other and finite thoughts proceed. Moreover, as Augustine and Anselm have argued, the idea of the Infinite Being is proof of the existence of such a Being, for this idea contains existence as a necessary predicate. Descartes makes use of the common ontological arguments to support his own, while at the same time he contends that his own is entirely distinct. And indeed it is, in one form of it, that where he employs the principle of causality, as above indicated. The effect cannot transcend the cause ; but if God did not exist, the presence of the idea of infinite perfection within a finite consciousness would be inexplicable ; the effect would transcend the cause. But such a Being cannot deceive. To imagine that he could do so would be to suppose something contradictory. Now the discovery of the divine existence is one of the highest philosophical importance, for it makes indubitable the rule of certainty assumed at the outset, " whatever I clearly and distinctly conceive is true." It cannot be that He who is absolute truth and the source of my being should have made me so that in obeying the laws of my mind I should go astray.

Descartes has, as appears, three distinct principles of certainty; viz., 1. Whatever is clearly and distinctly conceived is true, the type of which is mathematical intuition; 2. Whatever is known as clearly and distinctly as my own being is real; 3. The Divine veracity. Which of these is fundamental to the other two? It is difficult to say. Apparently he regards the last as the basis of all.*

In addition, it is to be observed, he employs the logical principle of non-contradiction in connection with his first rule, and the real principle of causality, in establishing the being of God.

Assured of the existence of God as creator and preserver (and preservation, for him, is continued creation) of his own finite existence, Descartes now inquires whether there may not reasonably be supposed to exist other finite beings like himself, as well as what in general he has hitherto assumed to be an external world. In regard to these he speedily assures himself that he has not been deceived. The way is thus open to determine the inner reality and the laws of the world of nature and of spirit. The objects of our knowledge are things, and their affections, and eternal truths, which latter exist for thought only. Among the eternal verities are to be reckoned the law of causality (*ex nihilo nihil*), of non-contradiction, and the necessary existence of the thinking self. Of things there are two classes, minds and bodies; more strictly, thinking substances and extended substances, since thought is the essence of mind, extension, of body. Substance is that which so exists that it needs nothing else for its

---

* See close of Fifth Meditation.

existence. Only one such substance can be conceived, *i. e.*, God. But in a modified sense we may speak of things created as substances, requiring the aid of God (*concursus Dei*) for their existence. Each form of substance has its preëminent attribute from which all others, its modes, derive ; viz., from thought, which is the essence of mind, imagination, sensation, will ; from extension, which is the essence of body, figure and motion. Extension and thought, body and mind, are mutually opposed and exclusive, each being substance, or essential attribute of different substances. Thought is purely internal, extension is wholly external. There is no community or analogy between them. In man, composed of body and mind, the two opposed substances are united as closely as possible, yet are wholly distinct. The whole material world consists only of extension and its modes, figure and motion. No atoms exist, nor has the world limits. Matter, as extension, has only the capacity of being formed and moved ; actual form and motion must come from another source, viz., from the Being who is the ultimate ground of extension. In the beginning God divided matter into innumerable parts of various sizes and forms, and set them moving in all directions, whence at last arose the world. God had his own ends in view in the formation of the world, but it is presumptuous for the human mind to try to discover them. Final causes are excluded from philosophy.* The whole explanation of the material world is mechanical and mathematical. Matter in motion brings about everything. The universe is absolutely full : there is no vacuum ; hence, when once set in motion, the particles move

---

* Descartes, however, in his explanation of the body, makes use of the principle of design.

in a circular manner, each pressing into the place left by another. The vortices thus arising explain the revolution of the planets and the gravitation of bodies to their centers. Light and heat are explained by the vibratory movement of the most subtle form of matter—the first element; besides which are the second, the element of air, and the third, the element of earth, of which the planets are formed. In the organic world, the mechanical explanation is still retained. Plants and animals are mere machines. The animal soul is the blood, the circulation of which constitutes life. The blood, filtered by the brain, becomes the animal spirits. In man, who is undeniably at once body and soul, the two opposed substances, spirit and matter, thought and extension, are intimately conjoined. An explanation of such union is found in the pineal gland, or the *conarium*, which, being the only part of the brain which is single and the spot where the animal spirits meet, may be assumed to be the seat of the soul* and its organ of communication with the body. But as thought and extension are mutually exclusive in their nature, their connection in the brain must be regarded as supernatural, willed by God. Sensations from impressions on the sense organs there exist as perceptions, and thence volitions are transmitted through the nerves to the muscles, whence bodily movements arise. The passions are explained as due to ideas strengthened by the action of the animal spirits forcing their way to the heart through the pores of the brain and the rest of the body, the result being a confused but vivid state of feeling. The passions, like the ideas, are theoretical and practical. All are to be deduced from six primary ones, viz., wonder, love, hate, desire,

* See below, *Treatise on Man*, and *Passions*.

joy, and sadness, the most important of which is the first, wonder, which is purely theoretical ; the remaining five are practical, being accompanied by a tendency to bodily motions. The most perfect of all the passions is intellectual love of God. All moral action consists in mastery of the passions, and this is the secret of a happy life. The passions partake of the body, ideas are of the mind only—pure thought. Mind, as such, always thinks. In the human mind ideas differ as respects clearness and origin. As respects clearness, they are adequate or inadequate ; in origin, they are formed by the action of the individual mind, or borrowed, adventitious, or innate. The innate ideas are simply thought itself, the ultimate ideas of things derived from the nature of the human mind ; thus, also, the idea of God and of ourselves is innate. Of the adventitious ideas, to which belong sensuous perceptions, must be distinguished those which correspond with modes of external things and those which are simply modes of thought, belonging only to the subject mind, such as time and color, sound, taste. Of ideas fashioned by ourselves, such as the siren, the centaur, these are pure inventions, having no external objects corresponding to them. In any idea regarded simply as a representation, there is neither truth nor error. Truth and error arise with judgments, and judgments are a combination of intellect and will. Error comes from not withholding the judgment till clear and distinct intuition is gained, for the Divine veracity is pledged that every clear and distinct perception shall be true. The Divine mind is free from error because it has no inadequate ideas. God's will is not like man's, conditioned on intelligence ; rather the reverse is true. The Divine will establishes even the eternal verities and the nature of good itself. The will of God must be conceived of as absolutely free from the control of necessity. The human will is most free when most subject to the determination of the intellect. The highest freedom is not indifference, but perfection in truth and character.

Such, in brief statement, are the main features of Descartes' philosophy.

Like every epoch-making system, that of Descartes contained within itself the germs of others, and of systems opposed to it and to each other. Descartes' own system was an unresolved dualism. It contained the principles of materialism, of subjective idealism, and of pantheism. There can even be seen, in one or two passages, a fugitive fore-gleam of the critical philosophy of Kant.

We must notice briefly the influence of this system on succeeding thought. Descartes, like all great original thinkers, had disciples whose simple aim was to communicate and expound the system unchanged. The new philosophy found acceptance at the universities in the Netherlands. It was taught at Leyden, at Utrecht, at Gröningen, and at Franeker. At the same time the system was violently attacked. It was found to be in conflict with the Bible, and theological controversy waxed warm. The motion of the earth and the infinity of the universe did not accord with ecclesiastical opinion, nor with the prevailing interpretation of the Scriptures. Cartesian theologians in defense advocated an allegorical explanation of biblical language. The doctrine had already been condemned by the Synod of Dort (1656), and in the following year by that of Delft. It aroused the opposition of the Roman Church also, and the "Meditations" were

placed upon the "*Index librorum prohibitorum*"—
"*donec corrigantur.*" And, in consequence, in after
years even the dead body of the philosopher was at
first refused interment in a church in Paris, and although this was finally allowed, funeral ceremonies
and the erection of a monument were forbidden. The
reigning monarch, Louis XIV., in league with the Jesuits, interdicted the teaching of the Cartesian doctrine
in the universities, and indeed throughout France.
This opposition was perhaps mainly due to the fact
that the Jansenists had adopted Cartesianism. But it
was occasioned also by the conflict between the metaphysical theory of Descartes, that the essence of body
is extension, and the church doctrine of the real presence of Christ in the sacrament. The same body
cannot exist in different spaces at once; transubstantiation cannot therefore be true. Both the Jansenist
Arnauld* and the Jesuit Mesland† had urged this
conflict with the Eucharistic doctrine of the philosopher's teaching concerning body and its extension,
and Descartes had replied to their objections. But
while the system had to encounter the hostility of the
theologians of the day, both Catholic and Protestant,
it found ready acceptance with those who cultivated
literature in that most brilliant age. The new and
striking views, the beautiful method, the charming
lucidity of presentation, made a profound impression
upon the French mind; they took powerful hold of the
foremost writers in prose and poetry, and thus contributed greatly to the formation of the classic style.
Cartesianism became the literary fashion. It was cul-

* *Œuvres*, t. ii, p. 35, Arnauld's objection; t. ii, p. 78, Descartes' reply.

† *Œuvres*, t. ix, pp. 172 and 192, replies to Mesland.

tivated by ladies and adopted by society. Accordingly it soon was made a target for the wits of the day, as the "Femmes Savantes" of Molière bears witness, and later the Jesuit Daniel's "Voyage du monde de Descartes." *

The first important step in the development of the Cartesian doctrine was taken in the theory of occasionalism by Arnold Geulincx (1625-1669), professor of philosophy at Leyden. He assumed as an axiom that an efficient cause must be conscious not only of the effect but of the mode of its production.† *Impossibile est ut is faciat qui nescit quomodo fiat.* Extension and motion have no relation to thought or sensation in the way of causation. Body cannot act upon mind, volition cannot originate motion, because he who wills knows not how his volition acts on his brain, nerves, and muscles. Hence there can be no reciprocal action of soul and body, and God alone is the efficient cause of all that happens. God has so connected these most opposed things, the motion of matter and the volition of the will, that when a volition arises the appropriate motion occurs, and *vice versa*, there being no causal connection between the two; but God himself, *on occasion* of the one, produces the other. Philaretus ‡ (pseudonym), the editor of the Ethics of Geulincx, to make this correspondence intelligible, employs the illustration of the two clocks, which Leib-

---

* See Bouillier, "*Histoire de la Philosophie Cartésienne*," t. i, p. 425.

A Latin version of Daniel's book exists, "*Iter per Mundum Cartesii.*" Amsterdam, 1694.

† Bouillier, t. i, p. 286.

‡ Bontekoe. See Erdmann, *Hist. of Philos. Modern*, pp. 29, 30, trans.

nitz afterward uses in the explanation of his own theory.

Père Nicholas Malebranche (1638–1715), of the Oratory of Jesus in Paris, a profound theologian of the Augustinian type, and an enthusiastic disciple of Descartes, applied the principles of the latter to the solution of the problem of knowledge. He accepted the doctrine of the two mutually opposed substances, body and mind, *i. e.*, extension and thought, between which there can be no reciprocal influence (*influxus physicus*), and adopted Occasionalism, whether as influenced by Geulincx, or as the necessary consequence of dualism. The special problem was to show the possibility of a knowledge of matter by mind, there being no natural community, but, on the contrary, the most complete opposition, between the two. Like Geulincx in explaining action, Malebranche, in explaining knowledge, is obliged to have recourse to the third, and indeed, strictly speaking, *i. e.*, according to the definition, only true substance, God. Accordingly, Malebranche says God is the place of spirits; we see things in God. "God is through his presence so closely united with our souls that we can say that he is the place of minds, exactly as space is the place of bodies."* Bodies, which are modifications of extension, are knowable only through ideas; they exist, therefore, in the only form in which we can know them, in God alone, who is the universal reason, the intelligible world, the intelligible, that is *to us* the only real, extension. That which we see in God, then, is not external things themselves, but the *ideas* of things, the intelligible world. Not only these *ideas*, but our sensations and our volitions, are produced in

* *Recherche*, liv. iii, pt. ii, ch. vi. Kuno Fischer, *Descartes and his School*, p. 578, trans.

us by God alone. Hence not only the idealism but the *pantheistic* tendency of the system of Malebranche.

Baruch (Benedictus) de Spinoza (born in Amsterdam, 1632, died at The Hague, 1677), made the philosophy of Descartes his starting-point and completely transformed its dualism into a monism, in which God is declared to be the one sole substance (*Substantia una et unica*). Spinoza adopted from Descartes the mathematical way of looking at things. Philosophical and mathematical certainty are identical with him. Like Descartes, therefore, he totally excludes final causes, but with more emphatic protest, and not only from physics but from ethics. Efficient causation he also denies. Mathematics (philosophy, therefore) knows nothing of causes, but only of reasons, nothing of effects, but only of consequents.* The method of presentation is mathematical. Of this, also, an example had been given in Descartes, who, in what he calls his synthetic demonstration of the being of God † had presented the proof *in more geometrico*. The earliest published work of Spinoza was an exposition, in the mathematical form, of the principles of Descartes' philosophy, and the same form is employed in the Ethics, which is the chief exponent of his own philosophical views. The fundamental notions in Spinoza's system are those of substance, attribute, and mode. The whole system turns on the definition of substance, adopted from Descartes.‡ "By substance I understand that which is in itself and is conceived

---

* Cf. Erdmann, *Hist. of Philos. Modern*, p. 52, trans., for the true meaning of the term *causa* in Spinoza's writings.

† *Réponses aux Secondes Objections. Œuvres*, t. i, pp. 451-465.

‡ *Principes*, pte. i, § 51.

through itself; that is, that the conception of which does not require the conception of anything else from which it must be formed."* There necessarily can exist, then, but one substance; all else is attribute or mode. The absolute substance is not ground of all being, but rather *is* all being. To this one unconditioned, all-inclusive being, Spinoza assigns the name *God*, but the name *nature* is equally appropriate, hence he says, *Deus sive natura*. But nature may be *natura naturans*, that which is in itself, the absolute substance, the unconditioned ; or *natura naturata*, the *modes* of this absolute substance, the world as a whole, or the sum total of conditions of existence, which are both but two aspects of the one reality. Attributes appear in Spinoza's scheme to differ from modes only in this, that they pertain to substance, not in *reality*, like modes, but rather only *in intellectu*, in the view of finite mind, which is itself (however contradictorily), for Spinoza, but a mode of infinite substance. Herein Spinoza differs from Descartes, who taught that attribute constitutes the essence of substance ; apparently, the difference is between an objective and a subjective conception of attribute.† The one substance must then be *conceived* under the two attributes, thought and extension, as thinking substance and extended substance, while in reality there is but one sole substance (*Deus sive natura*). This distinction between what *is* and what must be *thought* is suggestive of Transcendentalism, but Spinoza's position is not that of Kant, but that of the dogmatist ; he held, with Descartes, that what is clearly thought does not differ from what is. It is difficult at this point to repel the

* *Ethics*, Def. 3.
† Cf. Erdmann, *Hist. of Philos. Modern.* p. 67.

charge of inconsistency, and the difficulty is greatly increased when we find these attributes, which are affirmed to exist, not in reality, but only for the human understanding as necessary notions, treated as independent and mutually opposed substances. No less than Descartes, Spinoza strenuously insists that neither spirit can act on matter, nor matter on spirit; but he insists further that each *is* the other, different forms of one and the same substance, just as "the idea of the circle and the actual circle are the same thing, now under the attribute of thought, and again under that of extension." Again, when explaining the possibility of particular or individual existence in a system which posits one sole substance and affirms *omnis determinatio est negatio*, Spinoza refers them to the infinite *modes* of the one substance of which, like waves of the sea,* they are the transient expression, having in themselves apart no reality, and constituting, all taken together, a realm of conditioned existence, each member dependent on the rest, and all bound together by the chain of necessity, a realm of appearance, fugitive, and, for pure thought, appearance only. Hence Spinoza's acosmism.† The dualism of Descartes is thus transformed by Spinoza into an abstract monism, but the system was implicitly contained in Descartes' definition of substance, which Spinoza takes for his starting-point.

In precisely the opposite direction, the first great German philosopher, Gottfried Wilhelm Leibnitz (1646–1716), starting also from the notion of substance, which he defines, however, as living activity, develops the doctrine of the plurality of substances. As with

* Erdmann's comparison, see *Hist. of Philos. Modern*, p. 61.
† Hegel thus designates the system.

Spinoza, thought not extension, mind not matter, is the essential form of being ; but in opposition to him, individuality—and, therefore, plurality—of mind-substances is asserted. The universe, physical and spiritual, is an aggregate—or, rather hierarchy—of such individual minds, which Leibnitz calls *monads*. While rejecting the position of Descartes that thought, as such, is necessarily conscious, Leibnitz retains, and develops into an essential element of his own theory, a distinction which Descartes had pointed out in the nature of perceptions between clear and obscure, distinct and confused. All monads are souls, all have perceptions, but not all have consciousness. Hence the gradation ; inorganic nature moves, plants sleep, animals dream, spirits think; God, the supreme monad, whence all radiate, is absolute creative Intelligence, who, being the source of all, knows all completely.

Leibnitz, who, with Descartes, denied (as, indeed, his own theory of the monads required) any influence reciprocally between body and mind, rejected also the theory of Occasionalism, and substituted for it the doctrine of the Preëstablished Harmony, in illustration of which he uses the comparison of two clocks, originally so perfect in construction that each, although entirely independent of the other, keeps exact time with it.*

The philosophy of Leibnitz is idealism, or *spiritism*, Descartes had made the essence of matter to consist in extension ; Leibnitz conceives the essence of substance to be activity, life, mind. The monads are perceptive in all degrees, from complete unconscious-

* Descartes had already employed the illustration of a single clock in explaining the human body as a machine.

ness in the inorganic world, to full self-consciousness of spirit in man and deity. Individualism has replaced monism. Each monad is isolated and independent of the rest. Each is living substance, or soul, and the monads are innumerable. In place of the one substance of Spinoza (and virtually of Malebranche), instead of the two opposed substances of Descartes, we have, then, in Leibnitz, an indefinitely great number of substances, alike in being souls, but unlike in the degree of participation in psychical life. In place of occasionalism we have the eternally preëstablished harmony, through which, out of isolated monads, a universe becomes possible.*

The theory of knowledge connects Leibnitz with Locke, whose doctrine of empiricism he opposed. John Locke (1632–1704) interested himself as a philosopher in the problem of knowledge. Innate ideas, adventitious ideas, and fictitious ideas was the classification Descartes had made of the ideas of the mind ; teaching, at the same time, that to have an idea the mind must be conscious of having it. Locke easily made it appear that, *with this condition*, there could be no innate ideas, and that the human mind was in possession only of the adventitious ideas, or those derived from other sources than the thinking faculty itself, which sources Locke found to be two, sensation and reflection, *i. e.*, outer and inner sense. The thinking faculty is, prior to experience, a *tabula rasa*. Hence the theory of knowledge is that of pure empiricism.

The further development of Locke's empiricism into the philosophical skepticism of Hume, the sub-

---

* In his *Théodicée* Leibnitz carries out the thought of Descartes [Med. IV] that the perfection of the universe as a whole requires the imperfection of its parts. Cf. Bishop Butler, *Analogy*, ch. vii.

jective idealism of Berkeley, the materialism of the French Encyclopedists and the *Système de la Nature*, it is not necessary here to trace. It may be remarked, however, that the skepticism of Hume recalls, *by contrast*, the provisional doubting of all things by Descartes, that the idealism of Berkeley was already suggested in the *Je pense, donc je suis;* and that the French materialistic movement renews the first great French philosopher's attempt to resolve all bodily life into mechanism and motion. Leibnitz, by his doctrine of unconscious mental activity, in opposition to Descartes' limitation of mind to consciousness, was able to give its true significance to the theory of the innate ideas (the ἔννοιαι ἰδέαι of the Greeks), and thus, by giving emphasis to the intellectual principles, as Locke to the empirical element, opened the path to a reconstruction of philosophy at the hands of Kant, who, partly in opposition to, partly in agreement with, dogmatism on the one hand, and empiricism on the other, but mainly by introducing the new method and principle of criticism, brought in a new epoch and changed thereafter the whole aspect of philosophy.

It would be entirely incorrect to say that Descartes had forestalled Kant, or that the principles of the critical philosophy are contained in the *Meditations*, or the *Principles*, of the great French thinker, yet there are interesting passages in the *Rules for the Direction of the Mind*, and in the *Principles* also, which show that he was fully aware of the fundamental importance of the problem of the nature of cognition itself, and states that problem almost in the very language of Kant,* while in his doctrine of space and time, but particularly of the latter, which he regards as nothing more than a *modus cogitandi*, he reminds the reader of the famous exposition in the Transcendental Æsthetic of the Critique of Pure Reason.

* See Kuno Fischer, *Descartes and his School*, p. 495, trans.

THE SELECTIONS.

THE DISCOURSE UPON METHOD,

PARTS I, II, III.

THE DISCOURSE UPON METHOD.*

PART FIRST.

. . . . My design is not to point out the method which everyone must follow for the right direction of his understanding, but merely to show how I have attempted to conduct my own. Those who take it upon themselves to give precepts to others must assume that they are themselves better instructed than those to whom they give them, and if they make the least error, they are answerable for it. But as I offer this production merely as a piece of personal history, or of fiction, if you please, in which, among some examples which may well be imitated, there will be found, perhaps, many others also which one might reasonably decline to follow, I hope that it may prove useful to some and harmful to none, and that all will take my frankness kindly.

I was brought up to letters from my childhood, and because I was led to believe that by means of them clear and certain knowledge of all that was useful in life might be acquired, I had an extreme desire for learning. But no sooner had I completed the whole course of studies at the end of which it is customary for one to be received into the circle of the learned, than I changed my opinion entirely. For I found myself involved in so many doubts and errors, that it seemed to me that I had derived no other advantage

* *Œuvres*, t. i, p. 124.

from my endeavors to instruct myself but only to find out more and more how ignorant I was. And yet I was in one of the most celebrated schools in Europe, where I thought there must be learned men if there were any such in the world. I had acquired all that others learned there, and more than that, not being content with the sciences which were taught us, I ran through all the books I could get hold of which treated of matters considered most curious and rare. Moreover, I knew what others thought about me, and I did not perceive that they considered me inferior to my fellow-students, albeit there were among them some who were destined to fill the places of our masters. And finally, our time appeared to me to be as flourishing and as prolific of good minds as any preceding time had been. Such considerations emboldened me to judge all others by myself, and served to convince me that there did not exist in the world any such wisdom as I had been led to hope for. However, I did not cease to think well of scholastic pursuits. I knew that the languages taught in the schools were indispensable for the understanding of the ancient books; that light and graceful stories stimulate the mind; that the memorable deeds of history exalt it, and that when read with discretion they help to form the judgment; that the reading of all good books is like conversation with the noble men of bygone times—a studied conversation, even, in which only their best thoughts are disclosed. . . . . But I thought I had already given time enough to languages and to the literature of the ancients, to their histories and to their fables. To talk with men of other times is like traveling. It is well to know something of the manners of foreign peoples, in order that we may judge our own more wisely, and that we may not suppose that what is different from our own habits is ridiculous and contrary to reason, as those do who have not seen the world. But if one spends too much time in traveling in foreign countries, he becomes at last a stranger in his own ; and when one is too curious to know what has been done in past ages, he is liable to remain ignorant of what is going on in his own time. Moreover, fiction represents many events as possible which are not so ; and even the most faithful histories, if they do not deviate from truth nor dignify events to make them more impressive, at least they almost always omit the meaner and the less illustrious incidents, so that it comes about that the rest is not what it really was, and those who govern their conduct by the examples there furnished are liable to fall into the extravagances of the paladins of our romances, and to conceive designs which surpass their ability.

Eloquence I held in high esteem, and I was in love with poetry ; but I regarded both as the gifts of genius rather than the fruit of study. Those who have the strongest reasoning powers and who best digest their thoughts in order to make them clear and intelligible, are always the best able to speak persuasively, although they may talk the dialect of Lower Brittany and have never learned rhetoric ; and those who have the most delightful fancies, and who can express them with sweetness and grace, are the best poets, although the art of poetry is unknown to them.

Above all I was delighted with the mathematics, on account of the certainty and evidence of their demonstrations, but I had not as yet found out their true use, and although I supposed that they were of service only in the mechanic arts, I was surprised that upon foundations so solid and stable no loftier structure had been raised : while, on the other hand, I compared the writings of the ancient moralists to palaces very proud and very magnificent, but which are built on nothing but sand or mud. .... I revered our theology, and, as much as anyone, I strove to gain heaven ; but when I learned, as an assured fact, that the way is open no less to the most ignorant than to the most learned, and that the revealed truths which conduct us thither lie beyond the reach of our intelligence, I did not presume to submit them to the feebleness of my reasonings, and I thought that, to undertake the examination of them and succeed in the attempt, required extraordinary divine assistance and more than human gifts. I had nothing to say of philosophy, save that, seeing it had been cultivated by the best minds for many ages, and still there was nothing in it which might not be brought into dispute, and which was, therefore, not free from doubt, I had not the presumption to hope for better success therein than others ; and considering how many diverse opinions may be held upon the same subject and defended by the learned, while not more than one of them can be true, I regarded as pretty nearly false all that was merely probable. Then, as to the other sciences which derive their principles from philosophy, I judged that nothing solid could be built upon foundations so unstable ; and neither the fame nor the emolument they promised me were sufficient to induce me to acquire them ; for, thanks to a kind Providence, I did not find myself in a condition of life which required me to make science a profession for the bettering of my estate ; and although I did not profess to despise fame, like a cynic, still I thought very little of that which I could not hope to acquire except on false pretenses. And finally, as for the pseudo-sciences, I thought I was already sufficiently acquainted with their value to be proof against the promises of the alchemist, the predictions of the astrologer, the impostures of the magician, the artifices and vain boasting of those who profess to know more than they actually do know.*

For these reasons, so soon as I was old enough to be no longer subject to the control of my teachers, I abandoned literary pursuits altogether, and, being resolved to seek no other knowledge than that which I was able to find within myself or in the great book of the world, I spent the remainder of my youth in traveling, in seeing courts and armies, in mingling with people of various dispositions and conditions in life, in collecting a variety of experiences, putting myself to the proof in the crises of fortune, and reflecting on all occasions on whatever might present itself, so as to derive from it what profit I might. For it appeared to me that I might find a great deal more of truth in reasonings such as everyone carries on with reference to the affairs which immediately concern himself, and where the issue will bring speedy punishment if he make a mistake, than in those which a man of letters conducts in his private study with regard to speculations, which have no other effect and are of no further consequence to him than to tickle his vanity the less they are understood by common people, and the more they require wit and skill to make them seem probable. And I always had an extreme desire to learn how to

* Lewes in his *Biographical History of Philosophy*, p. 363, finds "a remarkable resemblance" between Descartes' *Discourse* and the Arabian Philosopher Algazzali's *Revivification of the Sciences of Religion*.

distinguish the true from the false, so that I might see clearly and proceed with assurance in the affairs of this present life.

It is true that while I was employed only in observing the manners of foreigners, I found very little to establish my mind, and saw as much diversity here as I had seen before in the opinions of philosophers. So that the principal benefit I derived from it was that, observing many things which, although they appear to us to be very extravagant and ridiculous, are yet commonly received and approved by other great peoples, I gradually became emancipated from many errors which tend to obscure the natural light within us, and make us less capable of listening to reason. But after I had spent some years thus in studying in the book of the world, and trying to gain some experience, I formed one day the resolution to study within myself, and to devote all the powers of my mind to choosing the paths which I must thereafter follow; a project attended with much greater success, as I think, than it would have been had I never left my country nor my books.

PART SECOND.

I was then in Germany, whither the wars, which were not yet ended there, had summoned me; and when I was returning to the army, from the coronation of the emperor, the coming on of the winter detained me in a quarter where, finding no one I wished to talk with, and fortunately having no cares nor passions to trouble me, I spent the whole day shut up in a room heated by a stove, where I had all the leisure I desired to hold converse with my own thoughts. One of the first thoughts to occur to me was that there is often less completeness in works made up of many parts and by the hands of different masters than in those upon which only one has labored. Thus we see that buildings which a single architect has undertaken and erected are usually much more beautiful and symmetrical than those which many have tried to reconstruct, using old walls which were built for other purposes.

So those old cities which, at the beginning being nothing but straggling villages, have in course of time become great towns, are generally so badly arranged, compared with the regularly laid out towns which an engineer plots according to his fancy on a level plain, that although, when you look at single buildings by themselves, you find often as much or even more art than in those of other cities, and yet to see how they are placed, a great building here, a little one there, and how crooked and irregular the streets are, you would say that chance rather than the will of men in the use of their reason had so disposed them. .... And so I thought that the sciences contained in books, at least those in which the proofs were merely probable and not demonstrations, being the gradual accumulation of opinions of many different persons, by no means come so near the truth as the plain reasoning of a man of good sense in regard to the matters which present themselves to him.

And I thought still further that, because we all have been children before we were men, and for a long time of necessity were under the control of our inclinations and our tutors, who were often of different minds, and none of whom perhaps gave us the best of counsels, it is almost impossible that our judgments should be as free from error and as solid as they would have been if we had had the entire use of our reason from the moment of our birth, and had always been guided by that alone. . . . .

As for all the opinions which I had accepted up to that time, I was persuaded that I could do no better than get rid of them at once, in order to replace them afterward with better ones, or perhaps with the same, if I should succeed in making them square with reason. And I firmly believed that in this way I should have much greater success in the conduct of my life than if I should build only on the old foundations, and should rely only on the principles which I had allowed myself to be persuaded of in my youth, without ever having examined whether they were true. . . . .

My design has never reached further than the attempt to reform my own opinions, and to build upon a foundation altogether my own. But although I am well enough pleased with my work to present you here a sketch of it, I would not on that account advise anyone to imitate me. . . . . The simple resolution to strip one's self of all that he has hitherto believed is not an example for everyone to follow. . . . .

But having discovered while at college that there is nothing whatever so strange or incredible that has not been said by some philosopher; and afterward, in my travels, having observed that not all those who cherish opinions quite contrary to our own are therefore barbarians or savages, but that many of these peoples use their reason as well or better than we do; and having considered how differently the same man, with the same mind, would turn out, if he were brought up from infancy among the French or the Germans, from what he would if he always lived among the Chinese or with cannibals; and observing how, even in fashions of dress, the same thing which pleased us ten years ago, and, it may be, will please us again ten years hence, appears to us now extravagant and ridiculous; so that it is rather custom and example than certain knowledge which persuades us; and yet a plurality of votes is no proof that a thing is true, especially where truths are difficult of discovery, in which case it is much more likely that a man left to himself will find them out sooner than people in general —taking all these things into consideration, and not being able to select anyone whose opinions seemed to me to be preferable to those of others, I found myself, as it were, compelled to take myself as my guide. But like a man who walks alone and in the dark, I resolved to go so slowly and to use so much caution in everything, that, even if I did not get on very far, I should at least keep from falling. Likewise I was unwilling at the start to reject summarily any opinion which might have insinuated itself into my belief without having been introduced there by reason, but I would first spend time enough to draw up a plan of the work I was undertaking and to discover the true method for arriving at the knowledge of whatever my mind was capable of.

I had studied, in earlier years, of the branches of philosophy, logic, and in mathematics, geometrical analysis and algebra, three arts or sciences which seemed likely to afford some assistance to my design. But on examination of them I observed, in respect to logic, that its syllogism and the greater part of its processes are of service principally in explaining to another what one already knows himself, or, like the art of Lully, they enable him to talk without judgment on matters in which he is ignorant, rather than help him to acquire knowledge of them; and while it contains in reality many very true and very excellent precepts, there are nevertheless mixed with these many others which are either harmful or superfluous, and which are almost as difficult to separate from the rest as to draw forth a Diana or a Minerva from a block of marble which is not yet rough-hewn. Moreover, as regards the analysis of the ancients and the algebra of the moderns, besides that they relate only to very abstract matters, and of no practical use, the first is always so restricted to the consideration of figures that it cannot employ the understanding without fatiguing the imagination, and in the second one is so confined to certain rules and symbols that, in place of a science which cultivates the mind, we have only a confused and obscure art productive of mental embarrassment. For this reason I thought that some other method should be sought out which, comprising the advantages of these three, should be exempt from their defects. And as a multiplicity of laws often furnishes excuses for vices, so that a state is best governed which has but few and those strictly obeyed; in like manner, in place of the multitude of precepts of which logic is composed, I believed I should find the four following rules quite sufficient, provided I should firmly and steadfastly resolve not to fail of observing them in a single instance.*

The first rule was never to receive anything as a truth which I did not clearly know to be such; that is, to avoid haste and prejudice, and not to comprehend anything more in my judgments than that which should present itself so clearly and so distinctly to my

---

* Compare Rules for the Direction of the Mind, below, p. 61, *et seq.*

mind that I should have no occasion to entertain a doubt of it.

The second rule was to divide every difficulty which I should examine into as many parts as possible, or as might be required for resolving it.

The third rule was to conduct my thoughts in an orderly manner, beginning with objects the most simple and the easiest to understand, in order to ascend as it were by steps to the knowledge of the most composite, assuming some order to exist even in things which did not appear to be naturally connected.

The last rule was to make enumerations so complete, and reviews so comprehensive, that I should be certain of omitting nothing.

Those long chains of reasoning, quite simple and easy, which geometers are wont to employ in the accomplishment of their most difficult demonstrations, led me to think that everything which might fall under the cognizance of the human mind might be connected together in a similar manner, and that, provided only one should take care not to receive anything as true which was not so, and if one were always careful to preserve the order necessary for deducing one truth from another, there would be none so remote at which he might not at last arrive, nor so concealed which he might not discover. And I had no great difficulty in finding those with which to make a beginning, for I knew already that these must be the simplest and easiest to apprehend ; and considering that, among all those who had up to this time made discoveries in the sciences, it was the mathematicians alone who had been able to arrive at demonstrations—that is to say, at proofs certain and evident—I did not doubt that I should begin with the same truths which they have investigated, although I had looked for no other advantage from them than to accustom my mind to nourish itself upon truths and not to be satisfied with false reasons. But I had no intention to attempt to learn all the sciences which pass under the name of mathematics; and perceiving that, while their subjects were different, they all agreed in this, that they considered nothing else but the various relations and proportions existing therein, I thought that it would be of advantage to examine solely proportions in general, considering them only in subjects which would serve to render my knowledge of them more easy, at the same time not restricting them in any wise thereto, in order so much the better afterward to apply them to all others to which they might be suited. Next, having observed that, in order to comprehend them, it was necessary for me sometimes to consider each of them in particular, and sometimes merely to remember them, or to combine many of them together, I thought that for the better consideration of them in particular I ought to conceive them in lines, because I could find nothing more simple, and nothing that I could represent more distinctly to my imagination and my senses; but that, to retain them or to comprehend many of them together, it would be necessary for me to represent them by certain symbols as concise as possible, and for this purpose I might employ with the greatest advantage geometrical analysis and algebra, and that I might correct all the defects of the one by the other.

And I am free to say that the exact observance of these few rules which I had laid down gave me such facility in solving all the questions to which these two sciences apply, that in the two or three months which I spent in examining them, having begun with the simplest and most general, and each truth that I discovered being a rule which was of service to me afterward in the discovery of others, not only did I arrive at many which formerly I had considered very difficult, but it seemed to me, toward the end, that I was able to determine even in those matters where I was ignorant by what means and how far it would be possible to resolve them. In this I shall not appear to you to be very vain, perhaps, if you will only consider that there is, in respect to each case, but one truth, and that he who finds it knows as much about it as anyone can know; as, for example, a child, who has learned arithmetic, when he has made an addition according to the rules, can be assured that he has found out, in respect to the sum that he has computed, all that it is possible for the human mind to discover. Because, in a word, the method which shows one how to follow the true order, and to take account exactly of all the circumstances of the subject under investigation, contains all that which gives certitude to the rules of arithmetic. But that which pleased me most in this method was the fact that by means of it I was using my reason in everything, if not perfectly, yet in a manner the very best in my power; besides, I noticed that in following it my mind was accustoming itself by degrees to conceive its object more clearly and distinctly; and, without restricting it to any particular subject, I hoped to apply it as successfully to the difficulties of other sciences as I had done to those of algebra. Not that I had dared to undertake at once to examine all that presented themselves, for that would have been contrary to the order which the method had prescribed, but observing that their principles must in every case be derived from philosophy, in which I had not yet found any that were certain, I thought it to be necessary first of all to attempt to establish them there, and that, this being of all things of the greatest importance, and an inquiry where, above all, haste and prejudice were to be feared, I ought not to undertake the task until I had reached a riper age than that of twenty-three years, which was then my age, and until I had spent a considerable time in eradicating from my mind all those false ideas which I had received previously, as well as in accumulating a stock of experiences to form the matter of my reasonings, and in exercising myself constantly in the method which I had prescribed for myself, in order to strengthen myself therein more and more.

PART THIRD.

AND finally, since before one begins to rebuild the house in which he is living, it is not enough that he should tear it down, and provide materials and architects, or study architecture for himself, and then make a careful design, but it is also necessary that he should be provided with some other house, in which he may comfortably lodge while the new one is building; in like manner, in order that I might not lead an irresolute life during the time in which reason required me to remain undecided in my opinions, and in order that I might not thenceforward fail of living as happily as possible, I formed for myself a provisional moral code consisting of only three or four maxims which I desire to lay before you.

The first was to obey the laws and customs of my native land, holding steadfastly to the religion in which, by the grace of God, I had been brought up from infancy, and to govern myself in every other concern in accordance with opinions the most moderate and furthest from excess, such as were commonly put in practice by the most sensible people among those with whom I had to live. Because, beginning from that time onward to count for nothing my own opinions, for the reason that I wished to submit them all to examination, I was convinced that I could not do better than to follow those of the most sensible. And although there might be just as sensible people among the Persians or the Chinese as among ourselves, it appeared to me to be more to my advantage to regulate my conduct by those with whom I had to live; and, in order to know what their opinions really were, I ought rather to observe what they practiced than what they said, not only because that, in the corruption of our manners, very few people are willing to say all that they think, but also because most persons are ignorant of their own thoughts; for the act of thought in which one thinks anything being distinct from that in which he perceives that he thinks it, the one may often be without the other. And among many opinions equally acceptable, I chose only the most moderate, not only because those are always the most suitable to put in practice, and probably the best, all excess being usually bad, but also in order that I might find myself less astray from the true path than I should if, having chosen one of the extremes, it should turn out that it was the other which should have been followed. And, in particular, I set down as excess all pledges whereby one restricts his liberty; not that I disapproved of laws, which, to remedy the inconstancy of feeble minds, allow, when one has a good end in view, or even, for security in business transactions, when the end is quite indifferent, that vows or contracts should be made which bind a person to his engagements; but because I did not see anything anywhere which remained always in the same state, and for myself in particular, who had engaged to improve my opinions more and more, and not to make them worse, I thought it would be committing a great sin against good sense if, because I approved something then, I should oblige myself to approve it ever afterward, when perhaps it had ceased to be good or I had ceased to consider it so.

My second maxim was to be as firm and resolute in my conduct as I could, and to follow the most doubtful opinions, when I had once made up my mind to do so, with no less constancy than if they were very well grounded; imitating in this respect travelers, who, on finding out that they are lost in a forest, should not wander about, turning now to this side and now to that, still less stay in one spot, but always move on as nearly as possible in the same direction, and not change it except for sufficient reasons, although, perhaps, at the beginning, it was nothing but chance which led them to choose it, because, in this way, although they may not come out precisely where they may have wished, they will in the end at least arrive somewhere, where they will probably be better off than in the middle of a forest. In a similar manner, in the conduct of life, where actions often do not admit of delay, it is a truth very certain that when it is not in our power to discern the truest opinion, we ought to follow the most probable; and even although we may not see more probability in some than in others, we ought nevertheless to commit ourselves to some opinions, and thereafter consider them in their relation to conduct as being no longer doubtful, but perfectly true and certain, because the reason is so which made them choose it. This rule observed has delivered me from all the repentings and regrets which vex the consciences of those weak and wavering souls who allow themselves inconsiderately to put in practice, as if they were good, things which they afterward judge to be bad.

My third maxim was to try always to conquer myself rather than fortune, and to change my desires rather than the order of the world, and, in general, to accustom myself to believe that there is nothing whatever so entirely within our power as our thoughts are, so that after we have done our best in respect to things external to us, whatever there is lacking to success is, as regards ourselves, absolutely impossible. And this of itself seemed to me enough to prevent me from desiring for the future anything which I could not obtain, and thus to make me contented; for, inasmuch as our will is naturally inclined to desire only those things which our understanding represents to us as being somehow attainable, it is certain that, if we consider all the good things which are external to us as equally removed from our power, we shall feel no more regret at the loss of those which seem to be due to our birth, when we shall be deprived of them through no fault of our own, than we should feel at not possessing the kingdoms of China or Mexico; and making a virtue of necessity, as they say, we shall no more desire to be well when ill, nor to be at liberty while in prison, than we should now desire to have bodies made of some matter as incorruptible as diamonds, or wings to fly with like birds. But I own that long practice is needed, and often repeated reflection, to accustom one's self to look on all things from this point of view ; and I believe that chiefly in this consisted the secret of those philosophers who in former times were able to deliver themselves from the sway of fortune, and, despite suffering and poverty, to vie with their gods in felicity. For, steadfastly considering the limits assigned to them by nature, they so fully persuaded themselves that nothing whatever was in their power but their thoughts, that, by itself alone, this was enough to keep them from having any yearning for other things ; and over their thoughts they held a sway so absolute that they had therein good reason to look upon themselves as being richer, more powerful, more free, and more happy than any of their fellow-men, who, without this philosophy, favored, as they might be, by nature and by fortune, could never thus control all that they desired.

Finally, to make a conclusion of my code of morals, I was minded to pass in review the various occupations of men in this life, with a view of choosing the best ; and, without wishing to pronounce upon those of others, I thought that I could do no better than to keep on in the same pursuit in which I was engaged, that is to say, spending all my life in the cultivation of my reason, and in making as much progress as I could in the knowledge of truth, following out the method I had laid down for myself. I have found, since I began to make use of this method, satisfactions so great as I do not believe more sweet or more innocent can be known in this life : and discovering every day, by means of it, important truths, as it seemed to me, and of which most men were ignorant, the gratification I had from it so filled my mind that nothing else affected me at all. Besides, the three preceding maxims were founded simply on the design I had of carrying on my work of self-instruction. For inasmuch as God has given to each one of us some light for discerning the true from the false, I could not believe I should be content with the opinions of others for a single moment, if I had not proposed to use my own judgment in examining them when the proper time should arrive; and I could not have followed them without scruple had I not been confident that in doing so I should lose no opportunity of finding out better ones, if such should exist; and finally, I should not have been able to limit my desires nor be content, had I not followed a path by which I felt sure of attaining all the knowledge I should be capable of, and as well all the real good which should ever be within my power. Inasmuch as our will is never inclined to pursue or to avoid anything except as our understanding represents it as good or bad, all that is needed for one to act rightly is that he judge correctly; and the best judgment he can form is all that is necessary to secure his best action, that is to say, the acquisition of all the virtues, together with all other goods within one's power: and when all that is assured, contentment must follow.

After I had thus become satisfied of the worth of these maxims and had given them a place by themselves alongside the verities of the Faith, which have always stood first in my belief, I judged that as for all the rest of my opinions I might freely begin to rid myself of them. And inasmuch as I hoped to be able the better to bring this about by mingling with my fellow-men than by staying any longer shut up in the room where I had all these thoughts, the winter was hardly well over before I set out on my travels again. And in all the nine years that followed I did nothing but roam from place to place, as a spectator rather than an actor in the drama of life ; and while I gave particular attention in each case to that in it which afforded occasion for doubt, and wherein one might be mistaken, at the same time I was rooting out from my own mind the errors which had already insinuated themselves. Not, however, that in so doing I imitated the skeptics, who doubt only for doubt's sake, and desire permanent uncertainty ; for, on the contrary, my whole design tended only to assurance and to the rejection of the shifting soil or sand, to find solid foundation on the rock or the hard clay.

In this I was quite successful, as I thought, inasmuch as, in my endeavor to detect the falsity or uncertainty of the propositions I was examining, not by feeble conjecture, but by clear and sure reasoning, I met with none so doubtful that I could not draw from it some quite certain conclusion, even if it were only this, that the proposition contained nothing certain. And as in pulling down an old house we generally save what is good of the ruins to use in building up the new one, so, while destroying all those among my opinions which I decided to be ill-founded, I made various observations and acquired many experiences which since have been of use to me in establishing more certain ones. And, in addition, I kept on practicing the method I had prescribed for myself ; for besides taking care in general to conduct all my thinking according to the rules, I reserved from time to time certain hours which I spent in the particular applications of it to the difficulties of mathematics, as well as to some others which I was able to render quasi-mathematical, by detaching them from all the principles of other sciences which I did not find to be well established, as you shall see I have done in many cases which are explained in this volume.* And thus, without appearing to live differently from those who, having no occupation but to live an agreeable and innocent life, devote themselves to the dissevering of pleasures from vices, and who, to enjoy their leisure without *ennui*, engage in all forms of recreation which are honorable, I was still carrying out my design, and making more progress in the knowledge of truth than perhaps I should have done by reading books or mingling with men of letters.

Nevertheless these nine years rolled away before I had reached any decision on the questions commonly in dispute among the learned, or had begun to seek foundations for a philosophy more certain than that in vogue. And the example of many men of excellent minds, who formerly had the same design, but who seemed to me not to have succeeded in it, led me to imagine it a work of so much difficulty that perhaps I should not so soon have dared to undertake it, if I had not learned that certain persons were already spreading the rumor abroad that I had accomplished it. I cannot say upon what they based their opinion; and if I contributed anything thereto in my conversation, it must have been by my confessing my ignorance more openly than those are wont to do who have studied a little, and perhaps also by making known the reasons I had for doubting of many things which others held for certain, rather than of boasting

* The *Dioptrics*, the *Meteors*, and the *Geometry* originally appeared in the same volume with the *Discourse on Method*.

of any new doctrine. But as I had too honest a soul to wish to be taken for other than I was, I thought I ought by all means to try to make myself worthy of the reputation they had given me; and this desire, just eight years ago, made me resolve to abandon all places where I might make acquaintances, and to retire to this spot, in a country * where the long duration of the war has led to the establishment of such order that the troops maintained here serve only to make the people enjoy with the greater security the blessings of peace, and where amid a great crowd of people, very active and more interested in their own affairs than curious in regard to those of others, without lacking any of the conveniences to be found in the most populous towns, I have been able to live as solitary and retired as in the most remote deserts.†

* Holland, where he lived in many different villages from 1629 to 1649. See Kuno Fischer, *Descartes*, p. 207, trans.

† The remaining three parts of the *Méthode*, which discuss topics treated in other writings, may be found translated in the work of Professor Veitch, which contains the Discourse entire.

RULES FOR THE DIRECTION OF THE MIND.

RULES FOR THE DIRECTION OF THE MIND.

RULE I.—*The end of studies should be the discipline of the mind, such as shall enable it to pass true and solid judgments upon any subject which may present itself.*

Whenever men perceive a resemblance between two things, they are wont to apply to both, even in respects in which they differ, what they have found to be true of either. In this way they compare, improperly, the sciences, which consist solely of the work of the mind, with the arts, which require definite practice and a certain bodily aptitude. And as they see that one man is not able to learn all arts at once, but that he only becomes skillful in any who cultivates that alone, since the same hands cannot successfully work the soil and touch the lyre (and devote themselves at the same time to employments so different), they think that the same is true of the sciences, and, distinguishing them by the subjects of which they treat, they believe it to be necessary to study each by itself, apart from the rest. But this is a great mistake; for as the sciences all together are nothing but the human intelligence, which always remains one and the same, no matter what be the variety of the subjects to which it applies itself, inasmuch as this variety changes its nature no more than the diversity of objects upon which it shines changes the nature of the sun, there is no need of confining the human mind within any limit. Indeed it is not the same with the knowledge of a truth and the practice of an art; one truth discovered, far from being a hindrance to us, aids us in discovering another. And certainly it seems to me surprising that the greater part of men study with diligence plants and their virtues, the courses of the stars, the transformations of metals, and a thousand similar objects, while hardly anyone occupies himself with intelligence or this universal science of which we are speaking; and yet, if other studies have any value, it is less on their own account than for the aid which they afford to this. Accordingly it is not without purpose that we place this rule at the head of the whole list, for nothing diverts us from the truth more than the directing of our efforts toward particular ends, instead of turning them upon this single universal end. . . . .

It must be understood, at the outset, that the sciences are so bound together that it is easier to learn them all than to detach any one of them from the rest. If, then, one wishes seriously to search for truth, he need not devote himself to a single science; they all lie close together and depend one upon another. . . . .

RULE II.—*We should occupy ourselves only with those subjects in reference to which the mind is capable of acquiring certain and indubitable knowledge.* . . . . But if we rigidly adhere to our rule there will remain but few things to the study of which we can devote ourselves. There exists in the sciences hardly a single question upon which men of intellectual ability have not held different opinions. But whenever two men pass contrary judgments on the same thing, it is certain that one of the two is in the wrong. More than that, neither of them has the truth ; for if one of them had a clear and precise insight into it, he could so exhibit it to his opponent as to end the discussion by compelling his conviction. We cannot, then, hope to attain complete knowledge of all those things upon which only probable opinions exist, because we cannot without presumption expect from ourselves more than others have been able to accomplish. It follows from this, if we reckon rightly, that among existing sciences there remain only geometry and arithmetic, to which the observance of our rule would bring us. . . . .

Arithmetic and geometry are much more certain than the other sciences, because the objects of them are in themselves so simple and so clear that they need not suppose anything which experience can call in question, and both proceed by a chain of consequences which reason deduces one from another. They are also the easiest and the clearest of all the sciences, and their object is such as we desire; for, except from want of attention, it is hardly supposable that a man should go astray in them. We must not be surprised, however, that many minds apply themselves by preference to other studies, or to philosophy. Indeed everyone allows himself more freely the right to make his guess if the matter be dark than if it be clear, and it is much easier to have on any question some vague ideas than to arrive at the truth itself on the simplest of all. From all this it must be concluded, not that arithmetic and geometry are the only sciences to be learned, but that he who seeks the path of truth must not occupy himself with any subject upon which he cannot have a knowledge equal in certainty to the demonstrations of arithmetic and geometry.

RULE III.—*In regard to the subject of our studies we should seek, not what others may have thought about it, not what we ourselves may suspect to be true, but what we can see clearly and with evidence, or deduce with certainty.* This is the only way of arriving at scientific truth. We never shall be mathematicians, although we have learned by heart all the demonstrations of others, if we are not able by ourselves to solve every kind of problem. In like manner, though we have read all the arguments of Plato and Aristotle, we shall not be philosophers, if we are not able to pass a solid judgment on any question whatever. In reality we should have learned, not a science, but so much history. . . . . Let us now declare the means whereby our understanding can rise to knowledge without fear of error. There are two such means : intuition and deduction. By intuition I mean not the varying testimony of the senses, nor the delusive judgment of imagination naturally extravagant, but the conception of an attentive mind so distinct and so clear that no doubt remains to it with regard to that which it comprehends ; or, what amounts to the same thing, the self-evidencing conception of a sound and attentive mind, a conception which springs from the light of reason alone, and is more certain, because more simple, than deduction itself, which, nevertheless, as I have said already, can be performed by any man. Thus anyone can see intuitively that he exists; that he thinks; that a triangle is bounded by three sides, neither more nor less ; that a globe has but one surface ; and so of many other things, which are more numerous than one commonly thinks, because he does not deign to attend to matters so simple. . . . . It may perhaps be asked why to intuition we add this other mode of knowing, by deduction, that is to say, the process which, from something of which we have certain knowledge, draws consequences which necessarily follow therefrom. But we are obliged to admit this second step; for there are a great many things which, without being evident of themselves, nevertheless bear the mark of certainty if only they are deduced from true and incontestable principles by a continuous and uninterrupted movement of thought, with distinct intuition of each thing; just as we know that the last link of a long chain holds to the first, although we cannot take in with one glance of the eye the intermediate links, provided that, after having run over them in succession, we can recall them all, each as being joined to its fellows, from the first up to the last. Thus we distinguish intuition from deduction, inasmuch as in the latter case there is conceived a certain progress or succession, while it is not so in the former ; and besides, deduction does not require present evidence, like intuition, but borrows in some sort all its certainty from memory ; whence it follows that primary propositions, derived immediately from principles, may be said to be known, according to the way we view them, now by intuition, now by deduction ; although the principles themselves can be known only by intuition, the remote consequences only by deduction.

These are the two surest paths to knowledge ; the mind ought not to follow any more than these ; it ought to abandon all others as doubtful and liable to lead to error : which, however, is not saying that the truths of revelation are not the most certain of all our knowledge ; for faith, which establishes them, is, as in everything which is obscure, an act, not of the intellect, but of the will, and if it have any foundation whatever in human intelligence it is through one of these two ways of which I have just spoken that it can and should be discovered, as I shall some day point out with more detail.

Rule IV.—*Necessity of method in the search for truth.*—The minds of men are urged on by curiosity so blind that they frequently enter upon paths unknown to them, with no well-grounded expectation, but merely to see whether what they are seeking for may not be there, very much as those do who in the insane desire to find a treasure run about continually from place to place, to see whether some traveler may not have left one there : in such a spirit as this almost all chemists, the majority of geometers, and a good number of philosophers, pursue their studies. And, indeed, I do not deny that they have not sometimes the good fortune to hit upon some truth ; but I do not on that account admit that they are the more skillful, but only the more fortunate. It is better even never to dream of seeking truth, than to try to find it without method ; for it is certain that studies without order and confused meditations obscure the natural lights and blind the mind. Those who accustom themselves thus to walk in the dark so enfeeble the mental vision that they cannot bear the light of day ; a truth confirmed by experience, since we see men who never have occupied themselves with letters judge more soundly and more correctly on what presents itself to their attention than those do who have passed their lives in the schools. But by method I mean sure and simple rules, which, rigidly observed, will prevent our ever supposing what is false to be true, and will cause the mind, without ever consuming its energies to no purpose, and by gradually increasing its knowledge, to raise itself to exact knowledge of all that it is capable of attaining.

These two points must be well noted, *not to take the false for the true*, and *to attempt to arrive at the knowledge of all things*. Indeed, if we are ignorant of anything of all that we are able to know, it is because we have never discovered any means which can conduct us to such knowledge, or because we have fallen into the opposite error. But if the method shows clearly how intuition must be employed to avoid taking the false for the true, and how deduction necessarily operates to conduct us to the knowledge of all things, it will be complete in my opinion, and nothing will be wanting to it, since there is no science save by intuition and deduction, as I have said above. Nevertheless, it cannot go the length of teaching how to perform these operations, because they are the simplest and first of all; so that, if our mind does not know in advance how to perform them, it cannot understand any of the rules of method, however simple they may be. As for other mental operations which logic attempts to lay down rules for in aid of these two first means, they are here of no utility whatever; more than that, they must be classed as obstacles; for nothing can be added to the pure light of reason which does not in a manner obscure it.

As the usefulness of this method is such that to devote one's self to the study of letters without it is harmful rather than useful, I am fond of thinking that for a long time superior minds, left to their natural bent, have had some glimpse of it. In truth the human mind possesses a certain divine element, wherein are lodged the first germs of useful knowledge, which in spite of neglect and the constraint of ill-conducted studies bear their spontaneous fruits. Of this we have proof in the easiest of all the sciences, arithmetic and geometry. Indeed it has been observed that the ancient geometers made use of a kind of analysis, which they employed in the solution of problems, although they begrudged to posterity the knowledge of it. And do we not see flourishing a certain species of arithmetic, namely algebra, which has for its object to operate upon numbers as the ancients operated upon forms? But these two modes of analysis are nothing else than spontaneous fruits of the principles of this natural method, and I am not surprised that, when applied to objects so simple, they should have proved more successful than in other sciences, where greater obstacles arrested their development; still, even in those sciences, had they been cultivated with diligence, they might have attained a full maturity.

This is the design that I propose in this treatise. Indeed, I should not attach very much importance to these rules, if their only use was to solve certain problems with which calculators and geometers amuse themselves in their leisure moments. If this were the case, what else should I be doing but to occupy myself with trifles with, perhaps, more subtlety than others? Again, although in this treatise I speak often of forms and numbers, because there is no other science from which can be taken examples more evident and more certain, he who attentively follows my thought will see that I do not in the least consider herein the ordinary mathematics, but that I am revealing another method, of which they are rather the veil than the inner reality. Indeed it is to contain the first elements of human reason, and to aid us in causing the truths confined in any subject to come forth; and, to speak freely, I am convinced that it is superior to every other human means of knowledge, because it is the origin and the source of all truths. But I say that the mathematics are the veil of this method, not that I wish to hide it and wrap it up, to keep it from the vulgar; on the contrary, I wish to clothe and adorn it in such a manner that it shall be brought more within the grasp of the mind.

When I began to devote myself to mathematics, I had read most of the works of those who had cultivated those sciences, and by preference I studied arithmetic and geometry, because they were said to be the most simple and, as it were, the key to all the other sciences; but neither in the one nor in the other did I meet with an author who completely satisfied me. I saw therein divers propositions respecting numbers, the truth of which, after the calculation was performed, I recognized; as to geometrical figures, many truths were obvious at sight, and others were inferred by analogy; but it did not appear to me to be said with sufficient clearness to the mind why things were as they were shown to be, and by what means the discovery of them was reached. Accordingly, I was not more surprised that able and learned men should abandon these sciences, when they had hardly blossomed out, as being puerile and useless forms of knowledge, than that they should be reluctant to devote themselves to them as being difficult and embarrassing studies. Indeed there is nothing more idle than to occupy one's self with numbers and imaginary forms, if one means to stop with the knowledge of such trifles; and it is idle to apply one's self to the superficial demonstrations of them which chance more frequently than art has brought to light—to apply one's self thereto, I mean, with so much diligence that one comes to dislike, in a manner, to make use of his own reason; to say nothing of the extreme difficulty of disentangling, by that method, from the confusion of the numbers in which they are involved, new complications which may present themselves.

But when, on the other hand, I asked myself why was it then that the earliest philosophers would admit to the study of wisdom only those who had studied mathematics, as if this science were the easiest of all and the one most necessary for preparing and disciplining the mind to comprehend the more advanced, I suspected that they had knowledge of a certain mathematical science different from that of our times. Not that I believe that they had a perfect knowledge of it ; their insensate transports and their religious sacrifices on occasion of the most trivial discoveries show how much in their infancy these studies then were. I am not more impressed by the eulogies which historians lavished on some of their inventions, because, in spite of their simplicity, it is well understood that the ignorant and easily astonished multitude had praised them as prodigies. But I am persuaded that certain primitive germs of truth which nature has implanted in the human intellect, which we smother in ourselves by much reading, and by receiving into our minds errors so many and various, had, in that simple, naïve antiquity, so much vigor and vitality that men enlightened by that light of reason, which made them prefer virtue to pleasures, the honorable to the useful, although they might not know the reason of this preference, formed true ideas both of philosophy and of mathematics, although they could not at that time advance those sciences to perfection.

I believe I find some traces of these true mathematics in Pappus and Diophantes, who, although they are not of extreme antiquity, lived nevertheless in times long preceding ours. But I willingly believe that these writers themselves, by a culpable ruse, suppressed the knowledge of them; like some artisans who conceal their secret, they feared, perhaps, that the ease and simplicity of their method, if become popular, would diminish its importance, and they preferred to make themselves admired by leaving to us, as the product of their art, certain barren truths deduced with subtlety, rather than to teach us that art itself, the knowledge of which would end our admiration. Indeed, certain men of great intellect in this age have attempted to disclose this method; for it appears to be nothing else than what is called by the barbarous name of *algebra*, which needs only to be disengaged from that crowd of signs and those unintelligible figures which overwhelm it, to have imparted to it that clearness and supreme facility which, in our view, ought to characterize it as a branch of true mathematics.

When these reflections had withdrawn me from the special study of arithmetic and geometry, with a view to summon myself to the search for a science of mathematics in general, I asked myself, in the first place, what precisely was the meaning of this word *mathematics*, and why arithmetic and geometry only, and not also astronomy, music, optics, mechanics, and so many other sciences, should be considered as forming a part of it; for it is not enough here to know the etymology of the word. In reality the word *mathematics* meaning nothing but *science*, those which I have just named have as much right as geometry to be called *mathematics;* and nevertheless there is no one, however little instructed, who cannot distinguish at once what belongs to mathematics, properly so called, from what belongs to the other sciences. But on reflecting attentively upon these things, I discovered that all the sciences which have for their end investigations concerning order and measure, are related to mathematics, it being of small importance whether this measure be sought in numbers, forms, stars, sounds, or any other object; that, accordingly, there ought to exist a general science which should explain all that can be known about order and measure, considered independently of any application to a particular subject, and that, indeed, this science has its own proper name, consecrated by long usage, to wit, *mathematics;* since it contains that in consideration of which the other sciences are said to form a part of mathematics. And a proof that it far surpasses in facility and importance the sciences which depend upon it is that it embraces at once all the objects to which these are devoted and a great many others besides; and consequently, if it contain any difficulties, these exist in the rest, which have themselves the peculiar ones arising from their particular subject-matter, and which do not exist for the general science.

Now, since everybody knows the name of this science, since the object of it is conceived without even thinking much upon it, how comes it about that the knowledge of other sciences, which depend upon this, is painfully sought, and that no one puts himself to the trouble of studying this science itself? I should certainly be surprised, if I did not know that everybody regarded it as being very easy, and if I had not long ago observed that the human mind, neglecting what it believes to be easy, is always in haste to run after what is novel and advanced. As for me, who am conscious of my weakness, I resolved, in the pursuit of knowledge, constantly to observe such an order that, beginning always with the simplest and the easiest branches, I should never take a step in advance to pass on to others, so long as I thought anything was still to be desired in respect to the first. That is why I have cultivated, up to this day, as well as I was able, this universal mathematical science, so that I believe I am able to devote myself in the future to sciences more advanced, with no fear of my efforts being premature. . . . .

RULE V.—The whole method consists in the order and arrangement of the subjects upon which the mind is to exert itself with the view to attain truth. To follow it, *it is necessary to reduce, by degrees, complicated and obscure propositions to the most simple, and to proceed again from the intuition of these last, in order to arrive, in the same gradual manner, at the knowledge of others.* The perfection of method consists in this alone, and this rule must be observed as faithfully by him who would enter into science as the thread of Theseus must be held by one who would penetrate the labyrinth. But many do not reflect on what method directs them to do, or else ignore it completely, or take it for granted that they have no need of it ; and they often discuss the most difficult subjects with so little order that they may be likened to one who would spring to the top of a high building at a bound, paying no attention to the stairway which leads up to it, or not perceiving that there is any. In this way the astrologers proceed who, without knowing the nature of the stars, without even having carefully observed their motions, hope to be able to determine their influences. In the same way proceed many who study mechanics without understanding physics, and undertake in a haphazard way to make new machines ; and most philosophers do the same thing who, neglecting the study of facts, imagine that truth will spring out of their brains, like Minerva from the head of Jupiter. . . . .

RULE VI.—*To distinguish the simpler things from those which are more complex, it is necessary, in every series of objects, or in every case where we have deduced some truths from others, to take note of the simplest of all, and to observe how all the rest stand removed from this, whether more or less or equally.*

Although this rule may appear to teach nothing new, it nevertheless contains the whole secret of the method, and there is none more useful in this entire treatise. It teaches us that all things may be arranged in different series, not in so far as they belong to some kind of existence (a division which finds place in the categories of philosophers), but in so far as they can be understood one by means of another, so that, when we encounter a difficulty, we can tell whether it concerns things in which it is for our advantage to examine those preceding, up to the first, and in what order this must be done. But in order to do this rightly, it must be observed at once that in view of the application of our rule,—which does not consider things in isolation, but compares them one with another, in order to understand one by means of another,—they may be called either absolute or relative. I call absolute whatever is a simple, indecomposable element of the subject under consideration ; as, for example, all that is viewed as being independent, viz., cause, simple, universal, one, equal, similar, right, etc.; and I say that whatever is more simple is whatever is more easy to comprehend, and what we might make use of in the solution of problems. I call relative whatever is of the same nature, or at least by one side is joined to the absolute, so that it can be traced to it and deduced from it. But this term includes also certain other things which I call relations, such as all that is embraced under the terms dependent, viz., effect, composite, particular, multiple, unequal, dissimilar, oblique, etc. These relations are removed from the absolute in proportion as they contain the greater number of relations subordinate to them—relations which our rule recommends that we distinguish one from another, and take note of, in their connections and mutual order, so that by proceeding step by step through all we may be able to arrive in due succession at that which is most absolute.

But the whole art consists in seeking always for the most absolute. In reality, certain things seen from one point of view are more absolute than as seen from another ; and looked at in another way, they are more relative. Thus the universal is more absolute than the particular, because its nature is more simple ; but at the same time it can be said to be more relative, because it requires individuals for its existence. Moreover, certain things are indeed more absolute than others, but not the most absolute of all. If we regard individuals, the species is absolute ; if we regard the genus, it is relative. In mensurable bodies, extension is the absolute ; but, in extension, it is length, etc. Indeed, to make it more apparent that we are considering things here, not in respect to their individual nature, but in respect to the series in which we place them in order to understand one by means of another, we have designedly put in the number of things absolute, cause and equality, although by their nature they are relatives; for, in the language of philosophers, cause and effect are two correlative terms. Nevertheless, if we wish to know what effect is, we must first know what cause is, and not effect before cause. So things equal correspond to one another; but to know the unequal, it must be compared with the equal.

It is to be observed, in the second place, that there are a few simple necessary elements that we can perceive by themselves, independently of all others, I do not say at first, but by the aid of experience and the light which is in us. Also I say that it is necessary to observe these with care; for it is these which we call the most simple of each series. All the rest can be perceived only by deducing them from these, whether immediately and proximately, or after one or two conclusions or a greater number,—conclusions the number of which it is necessary still to note, in order to know whether they are removed by more or fewer steps from the first and simplest proposition; such throughout must be the concatenation, which is to produce that orderly succession of problems to which every inquiry methodically conducted must be reduced. But inasmuch as it is not easy to recall all these steps, and it is less important to retain them in memory than to be able by a certain penetration of mind to discern them, it is necessary to train the mind so that it shall be able to retrace them when there is need. But I have discovered that the best way to succeed in this is to accustom ourselves to reflect with attention on the least things which we have previously ascertained.

Let us observe, in the third place, that it is not necessary to begin our investigation by an inquiry into difficult matters ; but before undertaking a problem, to take at random and without deliberation the first truths which present themselves, to see whether from these others may not be deduced, and from these latter others still, and so on. This done, we must reflect attentively on the truths already found, and carefully observe why we were able to discover some before the rest, and more easily, and note what they are. Thus, when we approach any question whatever, we shall know with what inquiry it will be necessary to begin. For example, I see that the number 6 is the double of 3 ; I seek the double of 6, that is to say 12 ; I seek next the double of this, that is to say 24, and of that, or 48 ; and thence I deduce, which is not difficult, that there is the same proportion between 3 and 6 as between 6 and 12, and between 12 and 24, etc., and thus the numbers 3, 6, 12, 24, 48, are in a continuous proportion. Although all these things are so simple that they seem almost puerile, they explain to me, when I reflect upon them attentively, how complicated are all questions having to do with proportions, and with the relations of things, and in what order their solution is to be sought, which contains the whole science of the pure mathematics. . . . .

RULE VII.—*In order to make knowledge complete, it is necessary the mind should run over, in a movement uninterrupted and orderly, all matters pertaining to the end in view, and then sum them up in a methodical and sufficient enumeration.*

The observance of this rule is necessary to enable one to place among certainties those truths which, as we have said above, are not immediately deduced from self-evident principles. They are reached, indeed, by means of a train of consequences so long that it is not easy to retrace the path we have followed. Accordingly we say that the faculty of memory must be aided by a constant effort of thought. If, for example, after various operations, I discover the relation between the quantities A and B, then between B and C, next between C and D, finally between D and E, I do not thereby perceive the relation between A and E, and I cannot with certainty infer it from the relations known, unless my memory represents them all to me. So I run through the series in such a way that imagination at the same time sees one and passes on to the next, until I can go from first to last with such rapidity that, almost without the aid of memory, I can seize the whole at one glance. This method, while relieving the memory, corrects the sluggishness of the mind and enlarges its range. I add that the movement of the mind must not be interrupted ; often those who try to draw conclusions too rapidly from remote principles are unable to follow the chain of intermediate deductions with sufficient care to prevent some escaping them. And yet, if one consequence, though it be the least important of all, has been forgotten, the chain is broken, and the certainty of the conclusion is shaken.

I say further that knowledge needs enumeration to complete it. Indeed, the other precepts are of use in solving an infinity of problems ; but enumeration alone can enable us to pass, upon any subject which may engage our attention, a safe and well-founded judgment, in consequence of its allowing absolutely nothing to escape, and having certain evidence in respect to everything. But enumeration, or induction, here means careful and exact scrutiny of all that relates to the question proposed. But this scrutiny must be such that we can conclude with certainty that we have omitted nothing by oversight. When, then, we have employed it, and still the difficulty is not cleared up, we shall be at least so much the wiser that we shall know that the solution cannot be reached by any of the ways known to us; and if perchance—what may often enough happen—we have been able to traverse all the paths open to man for arriving at truth, we shall be able to say with assurance that the solution surpasses the range of human intelligence. It must be observed further that by sufficient enumeration or induction we understand the means which conduct us to truth more surely than any other, except intuition pure and simple. Indeed, if the case is such that we cannot take it back to intuition, we must not rely upon syllogistic forms, but upon induction alone. For in all cases when we have deduced propositions immediately one from another, if the deduction has been evident, they will be traceable to a true intuition. But if we deduce a proposition from numerous other propositions, disconnected and multiform, it frequently happens that our intellectual capacity is not such that it can take in the whole at one view; in this case we must be satisfied with the certainty of the induction. Just as when we are unable at one glance to take in all the links of a long chain, yet if we have seen that each is linked to the next, this warrants us in saying that the first is joined to the last. . . . .

But in some cases this enumeration must be complete, in others distinct; in others it need have neither of these two characters, but, as I have said, it must be sufficient. For example, if I wish to prove how many corporeal or sensible existences there are, I shall not say that there is such a number, neither more nor less, until I certainly know that I have taken every one into account and distinguished each from the others. But if I wish, by the same method, to prove that the rational soul is not corporeal, it will not be necessary for the enumeration to be complete; but it will be sufficient if I collect all bodies under certain classes, and show that the soul cannot belong to any one of them. If, finally, I wish to demonstrate by enumeration that the superficies of a circle is greater than that of any other figure of equal perimeter, I shall not pass in review all the figures, but I shall content myself with the proof of what I lay down concerning certain figures, and conclude the same by induction for all the rest. I said further that the enumeration should be methodical, because there is no better way of avoiding the defects of which we have spoken than to introduce order into our inquiries, and because, if we had to seek by itself each thing related to the principal object of our inquiry, it would frequently happen that a whole lifetime would be insufficient for it, whether on account of the number of the objects or the frequent recurrence of the same objects. But if we arrange all things in the best order, they will be seen most frequently to form fixed and determinate classes, of which it will be sufficient to know one only, or to know this rather than that, or simply something of one of them; and at least we shall not have to retrace our steps to no purpose. This method is so good that by means of it one may in the end attain without difficulty, and in a short time, a knowledge which at the start might have seemed immense.

Finally our last three propositions must not be separated, but must be kept all together before the mind, because they contribute equally to the perfection of the method. It matters little which we place first; and if we do not here develop them further, it is because that in the remainder of this treatise we have scarcely anything else to do than to explain them, by showing the particular application of the general principles we have just laid down.

RULE VIII.—*If in the course of our investigations anything presents itself which the mind cannot perfectly comprehend, we must stop at that point and not examine what comes next, but spare ourselves fruitless labor.*

This rule follows necessarily from reasons which support the second. Yet it must not be regarded as containing nothing new for the advancement of knowledge, although it might seem merely to dissuade us from the pursuit of certain things; nor that it teaches no truth whatever, because it appears merely to warn students not to lose their time, by almost the same motive as the second. But those who perfectly comprehend the seven preceding rules can by this learn how in every science it is possible for them to reach a point beyond which there remains nothing further to be desired. He, in fact, who in the solution of a difficulty has followed exactly the preceding rules, warned by this to stop somewhere, will understand that there is no means of attaining what he is seeking; and that not through any defect of his mind, but on account of the nature of the difficulty, or of our human limitations. But the recognition of this fact is no less a part of true knowledge than whatever throws light on the nature of things, and surely it is no proof of a good mind to urge its curiosity beyond this point.

Let us illustrate all this by one or two examples. If a man versed only in mathematics is investigating the line called in dioptrics *the anaclastic*, in which parallel rays are refracted in such a manner that after refraction they all meet in one point, he will easily see, according to the fifth and sixth rules, that the determination of this line depends on the relation of the angles of refraction to the angles of incidence. But when he finds himself unable to make this investigation, which does not come within the jurisdiction of mathematics, but of physics, he ought to stop there, where it would be of no avail to seek the solution of the difficulty from philosophers and from experience. In accepting the opinions of others he would violate the third rule. Besides, the case is composite and relative; whereas it is only in things simple and absolute that we ought to accept experience (as authority), a position we shall make good in its proper place. Further, it will be to no purpose for him to suppose among these various angles a relation which he shall suspect to be the true one; that would not be seeking the anaclastic, but merely a line which might tally with his supposition.

But if a man knowing something besides mathematics, desiring to know the truth, according to the first rule, about everything which may present itself to him, has met with the same difficulty, he will go on further, and will find out that the relation between the angles of incidence and the angles of refraction depends upon their variation occasioned by the varying of the media; that this variation in its turn depends on the medium, because the ray of light penetrates through the whole of the transparent body; he will see that this property of thus penetrating a body requires the nature of light to be understood; that finally, to understand the nature of light, it is necessary to know what in general a natural power is, the last and most absolute term of this whole series of inquiries. After he has seen all these propositions clearly, by the aid of intuition, he will go back over the same steps again, according to the fifth rule; and if at the second step he cannot at once comprehend the nature of light, he will enumerate, according to the seventh rule, all the other natural powers, in order that through the knowledge of one of them he may be able at least to deduce by analogy the knowledge of the one of which he is ignorant. This done, he will inquire how the ray of light traverses a perfectly transparent medium, and, thus following the order of the propositions, he will at last arrive at the anaclastic itself, which many philosophers, it is true, have hitherto sought in vain, but which, in our opinion, presents no difficulty to him who will avail himself of our method.

But let us give the noblest example of all. Let a man propose to himself, as a problem, the investigation of all the truths of the knowledge of which the human mind is capable, a problem which, in my opinion, all those who are in earnest in their desire to attain wisdom, ought, at least once in their lives, to propose to themselves; he will find, by the help of the rules I have given, that the first thing to be known is intelligence itself, since upon this depends the knowledge of all other things, and not reciprocally. Next investigating what immediately follows the knowledge of pure intellect, he will pass in review all the other means of knowing which we possess, intellect excepted; he will find that there are only two, imagination and the senses. He will then give his whole attention to the examination and distinction of these three means of knowing; and perceiving that, properly speaking, truth and error can exist only in the intellectual activity by itself, and that the other two modes of knowing furnish only the occasions for its exercise, he will carefully avoid all that can lead him astray, and he will consider all the ways open to man for arriving at truth, in order to follow the right one. But these are not so numerous that he cannot easily discover them all by a sufficient enumeration. . . . .

But there is here no question more important to be settled than to know what human knowledge is, and how far it extends,* two things which we combine in one and the same question, which must be considered before anything else, according to the rules given above. There is here a question which a man must examine once in his life, if he love the truth, though but little, because this inquiry contains the whole method and, as it were, the true instrument of science. Nothing appears to me more absurd than boldly to argue concerning the mysteries of nature, the influence of the stars, the secrets of the future, without once having raised the question whether the human mind is competent to these things. And it should not seem to us a difficult and arduous task thus to fix the limits of our mind of which we have consciousness, when we are deliberating about passing a judgment upon things external to us, and which are completely foreign to us. It is not a labor any greater than to seek to embrace in thought the objects which

---

*Cf. Kuno Fischer, *Descartes and his School*, p. 495 trans.; Locke's *Essay Upon the Human Understanding*, *Epistle to the Reader;* Kant's *Critique of Pure Reason, Introduction.*

this world includes, in order to understand how each of them may be comprehended by our mind. In reality there is nothing so multiform and so scattered which cannot be brought within certain limits, and reduced to a certain number of main divisions, by means of the enumeration we have described. To make trial of it, in the question above proposed, we shall divide into two parts all that relates thereto ; it is relative, in fact, either to us, who have the capacity of knowing ; or to things, which may be known : these two points shall be treated separately. And at the outset we observe that in us intellect alone is capable of knowledge, but that it may be hindered or helped by three other faculties ; to wit, imagination, the senses, and memory. It is necessary then to see successively, wherein these faculties can harm us, in order to avoid it, and wherein they can serve us, in order to profit by it. This first point shall be completely treated by a sufficient enumeration, according as the following rule shall make it appear.

It is then necessary to pass to objects themselves, and to consider them only in so far as our intelligence can deal with them. Under this relation we divide them into things simple and things complex or composite. The simple can be only spiritual or corporeal, or spiritual and corporeal at the same time. The composite are of two sorts; the one the mind discovers before it is able to say anything positive of them ; it constructs the other itself, a process which shall be set forth more at length in the twelfth rule, where it will be shown that error can be found only in things which the intellect has put together. Let us also divide these last into two species, those which are deduced from things the most simple, which are known by themselves; to which we devote the next book*: and those which presuppose others, which experience teaches us are essentially composite; the third book shall be entirely devoted to them. But in this entire treatise we shall attempt to follow with exactness and make plain the paths which can conduct man to the discovery of truth, so that the most ordinary mind, provided it shall be profoundly penetrated with this method, shall see that truth is interdicted to him no more than to anybody else, and that if he is ignorant of anything it is not the fault of his mind or of his capacity.† But whenever he shall desire to know anything, either he will discover it at once, or, perhaps, he will find that his knowledge depends on an experiment which it is not within his power to make; and then he will not blame his mind because it is forced to arrest its activity so soon; or, finally, he will perceive that the thing sought lies beyond the range of human intellect, and, in that case, he will not think himself more ignorant, because to have arrived at this result is in itself a piece of knowledge worth as much as another.

RULE IX.—*It is necessary to direct the whole energy of the mind upon things which are easiest and least important, and to hold it there for a long time until the habit is acquired of seeing truth clearly and distinctly.*

* The second and third books probably were never written.

† Cf. Lord Bacon's estimate of the value of his own method. "Our method of discovering the sciences is such as to leave little to the acuteness and strength of wit, and indeed rather to level wit and intellect. For as in the drawing of a straight line or accurate circle by the hand, much depends upon its steadiness and practice, but if a ruler or compass be employed there is little occasion for either; so it is with our method."—*Novum Organum,* bk. i, 61.

Having set forth the two mental operations, intuition and deduction, the only ones which can conduct us to knowledge, we shall continue to explain, in this rule and the next, the means by which we can become skillful in the performance of these processes, and at the same time cultivate the two principal talents of the mind, viz., perspicacity, through the distinct envisaging of each thing, and sagacity, through the skillful deducing of one thing from another. The way in which we use our eyes is sufficient to make us understand how to employ intuition. He who is bent on taking in many things at one look sees nothing distinctly; in the same way, he who, in one act of thought, would attend to many objects at once, confuses his mind. On the other hand, workmen who are employed on delicate operations, and who are accustomed to look attentively at each point in particular, acquire, by practice, the ability to see the smallest and finest objects. Likewise those who do not expend their thought upon a thousand different things, but who employ its whole energy in the consideration of the simplest and easiest, acquire great quickness of apprehension. . . . .

RULE X.—*In order that the mind may acquire facility, it must be exercised in finding out things which others have already discovered, and in practicing in a methodical way even the commonest arts, especially those which exhibit order or require it.*

I confess that I was born with such a mental disposition that my greatest happiness in studies consisted not in following the arguments of others, but in finding them out for myself. This disposition of itself, while I was still young, interested me in scientific studies; and whenever any book promised me by its title a new discovery, before going on to read it I tried whether my own natural sagacity might not be able to conduct me to something similar, and I took great care that too much reading should not beguile me of this innocent pleasure. I succeeded in this so many times that I was conscious at last of reaching truth no longer as other men do, after blind and uncertain efforts, rather by a stroke of good luck than by art, but long experience taught me certain fixed rules, which aid me wonderfully, and of which I have reaped the advantage in finding out many truths. Accordingly I have practiced this method with diligence, persuaded that from the beginning I have followed the most useful course.

But inasmuch as all minds are not equally qualified to discover truth by themselves alone, this rule teaches us that one must not occupy himself at the start with the most difficult and arduous subjects, but begin with arts the least important and the most simple,—those, above all, where order reigns, such as the trades of the maker of tapestry, of the weaver, of the women who embroider or make lace; such as, also, combinations of numbers, and everything which relates to arithmetic: as many other similar arts, which as wonderfully exercise the mind, provided we are not indebted to others for the knowledge of them, but discover them for ourselves. Indeed, while they contain nothing obscure, and are perfectly within the range of human intelligence, they make distinctly manifest to us innumerable methods, diverse from each other, and nevertheless regular. But it is in the rigorous observance of sequence that almost all human sagacity consists. Accordingly we have enjoined the necessity of examining these things methodically; but method, in these subordinate arts, is nothing else than the constant observance of the order which exists in them, or which a happy invention has put there. . . . .

It is necessary, then, to make a beginning with easy things, but with method, in order to accustom ourselves to penetrate by means of open and familiar paths, as if in sport, to the innermost truth of these things. By this means we shall, insensibly and in a shorter time than we might expect, become capable of deducing with equal facility from self-evident principles a great number of propositions which might seem to us very difficult and very complicated. Many persons, perhaps, are surprised that, while we are considering the means whereby we are enabled to deduce truths one from another, we omit to speak of the rules of the logicians, who think to direct human reason by prescribing to it certain formulas of reasoning so conclusive that the mind which trusts to their guidance, although it may dispense with giving close attention to the deduction itself, is yet enabled by the form alone to reach a certain conclusion. We observe however that truth often escapes the confining forms, while those who employ them remain bound by them. This does not happen so often to those who do not make use of them, and our experience proves that the most subtle sophisms deceive only the sophists, almost never those who use their simple reason.

Accordingly, fearing that reason may give us the slip when we are on the search for truth in some matter, we reject all these formulas as opposed to our design, and collect together only what will help us in keeping our thought attentive, as we shall show in the sequel. But to produce the more complete conviction that this syllogistic art is of no use in the discovery of truth, it needs only to be observed that logicians cannot form a syllogism yielding a truth in its conclusion without having the matter of it beforehand, that is to say, without having known in advance the truth which the syllogism develops. Whence it follows that this form can yield them nothing new ; and, therefore, that the common logic is entirely useless to him who wishes to discover truth, but is of advantage only in setting forth more readily to others truths already known, and, therefore, it should be transferred from philosophy to rhetoric.

RULE XI.—*When by intuition we have assured ourselves of the truth of certain simple propositions, if we are to proceed to draw conclusions therefrom, it is of no use to go on without arresting for a moment the progress of our thought, in order to reflect upon the mutual relations of these truths, and to bring as many as possible of these relations before the mind in one view : by this means we give to our knowledge more certainty and to our thought greater breadth.*

Here is the place to explain more clearly what we have said of intuition in the third and seventh rules. In the one we opposed it to deduction, in the other merely to enumeration, which we defined the collecting together of many distinct things, while the simple operation of deducing of one thing from another was accomplished by intuition. This must be the case ; for we require two conditions for intuition, to wit, that the proposition should appear clear and distinct, next that it be comprehended as a whole at once and not part by part. Deduction, on the contrary, if we are considering its formation, as in the third rule, does not appear to operate instantaneously, but it implies a certain movement of the mind inferring one thing from another; accordingly in that rule we were right in distinguishing it from intuition. But if we consider it as accomplished, in accordance with what we said in the seventh rule, then it no longer designates a movement, but the limit of a movement. Accordingly, let us suppose that it [the deduction] is perceived by intuition when it is simple and clear, but not when it is manifold and involved. Then we gave it the name enumeration and induction, because it cannot be comprehended in one whole at a glance of the mind, but its certainty depends in some measure on the memory, whose function is to hold in the mind the judgments passed on each of the parts in order that a single judgment may be concluded from them.

All these distinctions are necessary for the understanding of this rule. The ninth having treated of intuition, and the tenth of enumeration, the present rule shows how these two rules aid and complete each other, so that they seem to make but one, by virtue of a movement of thought which considers attentively each object and at the same time passes on to others. We find in this the double advantage, on the one hand, of knowing with more certainty the conclusion with which we are concerned, and, on the other, of rendering the mind more skillful in the discovery of others. Indeed the memory upon which we said depends the certainty of conclusions too complex for intuition to take in at a single view; the memory, feeble and wandering by nature, needs to be renewed and reënforced by this continual and repeated movement of thought. Thus when, after many operations,

I have come to recognize the relation between a first and a second quantity, between a second and a third, between a third and a fourth, finally between a fourth and a fifth, I do not thereby foresee the relation of the first to the fifth, and I cannot deduce it from the relations already known without recalling them all. It is therefore necessary that my thought run over them anew, until at last I am able to pass from the first to the last so quickly as to seem, almost without the aid of memory, to embrace the whole in a single intuition. This method, as everyone knows, corrects the sluggishness of the mind, and also increases its grasp. But it must be noticed further that the usefulness of this rule consists principally in this, that by accustoming ourselves to reflect upon the mutual dependence of simple propositions, we acquire facility in distinguishing at a glance the more or the less relative and perceiving the steps by which they are to be brought back to the absolute. . . . .

RULE XII.—*Finally, all the resources of intellect, of imagination, of the senses, of memory, must be employed, in order to have a distinct intuition of simple propositions, to compare suitably what is sought with what is known, and to find out the things which are thus to be compared together; in a word, no one of the means of knowledge with which the human mind is provided, is to be neglected.*

This rule includes all that has been said above, and shows in a general way what is to be particularly explained. For the attainment of knowledge, only two things are to be taken into account: we who know, and the objects which are to be known. There are within us four faculties which we can employ in knowing; the intellect, the imagination, the senses, and the memory. The intellect alone is capable of conceiving truth. It must, nevertheless, avail itself of the imagination, the senses, and the memory, in order not to leave unemployed any of our means of knowledge. So far as concerns the objects themselves, three things only are to be considered: first, we must see what presents itself to us spontaneously; then how one thing is known by means of another; finally, what things are deduced from others, and from what they are deduced. This enumeration seems to me to be complete. It embraces all that the faculties of man can attain. . . .

It is to be conceived, first of all, that the external senses, in so far as they form part of the body, although we direct them to objects by our own action—that is to say, by means of local movement—never perceive except passively; that is to say, in the same way as wax receives the impression of a seal. And it must not be supposed that this comparison is to be taken merely in the way of analogy, but it is to be conceived that the external form of the body, in perceiving, is really modified by the object in the same way that the surface of the wax is modified by the seal. This is true not only when we touch a body in respect to its figure, hardness, roughness, etc., but also when through contact we perceive heat and cold. The same is true of the other senses. . . . .

In the second place, it is to be conceived that at the instant when the external sense is set in motion by the object, the form which it receives is borne to another part of the body which is called the *common sense;* and that instantaneously, and without their being a real passing of anything from one point to another; just as, while I am writing, I know that at the instant when each letter is traced upon the paper, not only the point of the pen is in motion, but also that it cannot receive the least motion which is not simultaneously communicated to the entire pen, the upper part of which describes in the air the same figures, although nothing real passes from one end to the other. But who can suppose the connection of the parts of the human body less complete than that of the pen, and where shall we find an image more simple to represent it?

It is to be conceived, in the third place, that the common sense plays the part of the seal, which imprints on the imagination, as upon wax, those forms or *ideas* which the external senses convey to it pure and incorporeal; that this imagination is a true part of the body, and of such extent that its different parts can take on many forms distinct one from another, and even retain the impression of them for a long time; in this case it is called memory.

In the fourth place it is to be conceived that the moving force, or the nerves themselves, have their origin in the brain, which contains the imagination which moves them in a thousand ways, as the common sense is moved by the external sense, or the entire pen by its lower end; an example which shows how imagination can be the cause of a great number of movements in the nerves without its being necessary that it should have the impression of them in itself, provided that it have other impressions from which these movements may result; in fact, the entire pen is not moved just as the point is. Rather, it appears, through the main part of it, to follow an exactly opposite inverted movement. This explains the origin of all movements of all animals, although we ascribe to them no knowledge of things, but simply imagination purely corporeal, and also the production in ourselves of all those operations which do not require the aid of reason.

Finally, in the fifth place, it is to be conceived that this energy, whereby, in the proper sense, we know objects, is purely spiritual, and is no less distinct from the entire body than is the blood from the bones and the hand from the eye; that it is one and identical, whether with the imagination it receives the forms which the common sense conveys to it, or applies itself to those which the memory keeps in store, or fashions new ones which seize upon the imagination so powerfully that it cannot at the same time receive the ideas which the common sense is bringing to it, or transmit them to the active powers, according to the mode of disposing of them which is proper to it. In all these cases the energy which knows is sometimes passive and sometimes active; now it resembles the seal and again the wax—a comparison, however, which must be regarded as merely an analogy, because among material objects there is nothing which resembles it. It is always one and the same energy which, when applying itself, together with imagination, to the common sense, is called seeing, touching, etc.; to the imagination, in so far as it revives the various forms [of sense], is called remembering; to the imagination which creates new forms, is called imagining or conceiving; which, lastly, when it acts alone, is called comprehending, which we shall explain more at length in its proper place.

Also, by reason of these different faculties, it receives the different names of pure intellect, imagination, memory, sensibility. It is properly called mind when it forms in the imagination new ideas, or when it applies itself to those already formed there, and we consider it as the cause of these different operations. It will be necessary further on to note the distinction in these terms. All these things being once well understood, the attentive reader will have no trouble as to deciding what assistance each one of these faculties can afford us, and up to what point art can supply the natural defects of the mind. For, as the intellect can be moved by the imagination, and act upon it, as this latter in its turn can act upon the senses aiding the will in applying them to objects, and as the senses, on the other hand, act upon it by painting images of bodily objects there; as memory, moreover, at least that which is corporeal and which resembles the memory of brutes, is identical with imagination; it follows therefrom that when intellect is occupied with things which have no corporeal nature, nor anything analogous thereto, it will look in vain for help from these faculties. More than that, in order that its action be not hindered, it is necessary to banish the senses, and to deprive the imagination, so far as possible, of every distinct impression.

If, on the contrary, the intellect propose to itself to examine something which can be referred to a body, it must form in the imagination the most distinct idea possible of it. To succeed in this more easily, it must exhibit to the external senses the same object which this idea represents. A plurality of objects will not facilitate distinct intuition of an individual object; but if from this plurality it is desired to separate an individual, as is often necessary, the imagination must be relieved of all that which would divide the attention, in order that what remains may be the more deeply graven on the memory. In the case of memory itself, it will not be necessary to present the objects themselves to the external senses, but only to afford it abstracted images of them, which, provided they do not lead us into error, are all the better in proportion as they are brief and comprehensive. These are the precepts to be observed, if nothing is to be omitted as regards the first part of our rule.

Let us come to the second part and distinguish carefully the notions of simple things from those of composite things; let us see in which falsity may exist, in order to be on our guard with reference to these; those in which certainty can be found, in order to apply ourselves exclusively to the study of them. Here, as in our preceding inquiry, certain propositions must be admitted, which perhaps will not receive universal assent; but it matters little if they are no more believed to be true than are those imaginary circles employed by astronomers to include the phenomena of their science, provided they assist us in distinguishing the objects in reference to which our knowledge can be true or false.

We say, then, in the first place, that things must be considered under another point of view when we examine them in relation to our intelligence which knows them, than when we are speaking of them in reference to their real existence. For instance, suppose a body having extension and figure: in itself, we affirm that it is something one and simple; in reality it cannot be said to be composite because it has corporeality, extension, and figure, since these elements never exist independently of one another. But in relation to our intelligence, it is a compound of these three elements, because each of them presents itself separately to our mind before we have time to consider that they are all found united in one and the same subject. Thus considering here things merely in their relation to our intelligence, we shall call simple those only the notion of which is so clear and so distinct that the mind cannot divide it into other notions still more simple; such are figure, extension, movement, etc. We conceive all others as being, in some manner, composed of these; which is to be taken in the widest meaning, not excepting even things which it is possible for us to abstract from these simple notions, as when it is said that figure is the limit of extension, meaning there by limit something more general than figure, since we can speak of the limit of duration, of movement, etc.

In this case, although the notion of limit is abstracted from that of figure, it is not for that reason to be regarded as being more simple than the latter. On the contrary, when we attribute it to other things essentially different from figure, such as duration and movement, it is necessary to abstract it even from these notions, and, consequently, it is a compound of quite diverse elements, to each one of which it can be applied only equivocally. We say, in the second place, that things called simple in relation to our intelligence are either purely intellectual, or purely material, or intellectual and material at the same time. The purely intellectual are the things which intelligence knows by the aid of a certain natural light, and without the help of any corporeal image. But there is a great number of this kind; and, for example, it is impossible to form a material image of doubt, of ignorance, of the action of the will, which it may be permitted me to call volition, and of so many other things, which, nevertheless, we really know, and so easily that all that is necessary is that we be endowed with reason. The purely material are the things which are known only in bodies, as figure, extension, movement, etc. Finally, those must be called common which are indifferently attributed to bodies and to minds, such as existence, unity, duration, and others similar. To this class are to be referred those common notions which are, as it were, the bonds which unite together different simple natures, and upon the evidence of which rest the conclusions of reasoning; for example, the proposition, two things equal to a third are equal to each other, and again, two things which cannot be related in the same way to a third are mutually different. But these ideas may be known, either by pure intelligence, or by intelligence considering the images of material objects.

Among the number of simple things must be placed their negation and their privation, in so far as these fall under our intelligence, because the idea of nonentity, of the instant, of rest, is no less a true idea than that of existence, of duration, of movement. This way of looking at the matter will allow us to say, consequently, that all the other things that we know are composed of these simple elements: thus, when I judge that a figure is not in motion, I can say that my idea is composed, in a sort, of figure and of rest, and so of others.

We say, in the third place, that these simple elements are all known by themselves, and contain nothing false; which will readily appear, if we distinguish the faculty of intelligence which sees* and knows these things from that which judges,† affirming and

---

* Reason intuitive. Cf. Erdmann, *Hist. of Philos. Modern*, pp. 12, 13.

† Reason discursive, understanding.

denying. It is possible, indeed, that we may think ourselves to be ignorant of things which we really know; for example, if we suppose that beyond what we can see, and what we can reach by thought, things still contain something unknown to us, and that this supposition may be false. This being so, it is plain that we deceive ourselves, if we think we do not know absolutely any one of these simple natures, for if our intelligence puts itself in the least degree in relation to them, which is necessary, since we are supposed to pass some judgment upon them, it must be concluded from this that we know it absolutely. Otherwise we cannot say that it is simple, but rather, composed, first, of that which we know of it, then, of that of which we believe ourselves to be ignorant.

We say, in the fourth place, that the connection of these simple things among themselves is either necessary or contingent. It is necessary, when the idea of one is so combined with the idea of the other that, when we wish to judge them separately, it is impossible to conceive one of the two distinctly. In this manner figure is combined with extension, movement with duration or time, because it is impossible to conceive figure without extension, and movement without duration. In the same way, when I say that four and three make seven, this connection is necessary, because the number seven cannot be conceived distinctly without including in it in a confused manner the number four and the number three. Likewise, further, all that is proved of figures and numbers is necessarily connected with the thing regarding which affirmation is made. This necessity exists not only with respect to sensible objects. For example, if Socrates says he doubts everything, this consequence necessarily follows, that he knows at least that he doubts; and this, that he knows that something may be true or false; for these are notions which necessarily accompany doubt. The connection is contingent, when things are not inseparably bound together; for example, when we say the body is living, the man is clothed. There are also many propositions which are necessarily connected together, and which the majority class with the contingent, because the relation between them is not observed; for example, I am, therefore God is; I know, therefore, I have a mind distinct from my body. Finally, it is to be observed that there is a great number of necessary propositions, of which the reciprocal is contingent: thus, although, from the fact that I exist, I conclude with certainty that God exists, I cannot reciprocally affirm, from the fact that God exists, that I exist.

We say, in the fifth place, that we can know nothing beyond these simple natures and the compounds formed from them; and, also, that it is often much easier to examine several of them joined together than to abstract one from the rest. Thus I can know a triangle without ever having noticed that this knowledge contains that of the angle, the line, the number three, figure, extension, etc.; which does not prevent our saying that the nature of the triangle is a compound of all these natures, and that they are better known than the triangle, since they are what are comprised in it. Moreover, there are in this same notion of the triangle many others which exist there and escape our notice, such as the size of the angles, which are equal to two right angles, and the innumerable relations of the sides to the angles, or to the capacity of the area.

We say, in the sixth place, that the natures called compound are known by us, either because we find by experience that they are composite, or because we combine them ourselves. We know, for example, all that we perceive by the senses, all that we hear said by others, and, in general, all that reaches our understanding, whether from elsewhere or from the reflections of the understanding itself. It is to be noted here that the understanding cannot be deceived by any experience, if it limit itself to a precise intuition of the object, such as it possesses in the idea of it or its image. Let it not be supposed from this that the imagination faithfully represents to us the objects of the senses; the senses themselves do not reflect the true form of things; and finally, external objects are not always such as they appear to us; we are in all these respects liable to error, just as if we should accept a tale as true history. A man afflicted with the jaundice thinks that everything is yellow, because his eye is of that color; a mind diseased and melancholy may take for realities the vain phantoms of its imagination. But these same things will not lead into error the intelligence of the wise man, because, while he knows that all that comes to him from imagination was really imprinted there, he will never affirm that the notion has come unaltered from the external objects to the senses, from the senses to the imagination, at least not until he has some other means of assuring himself of the fact. On the other hand, it is we who ourselves combine the objects of our knowledge whenever we think that they contain something which our mind perceives immediately without any experience. Thus, when the man who is ill with the jaundice persuades himself that what he sees is yellow, his knowledge is composed both of that which his imagination represents to him, and of that which he derives from himself, to wit, that the yellow color comes not from a defect of his eye, but from the fact that the things which he sees are really yellow. It follows from all this that we can deceive ourselves only when we ourselves combine the notions which we receive.

We say, in the seventh place, that this combination may be made in three ways, by impulse, by conjecture, or by deduction. Those make up their judgments on things by impulse who allow themselves to believe anything without being persuaded by any reason, but are determined, simply, either by some superior authority, or by their own free will, or by the influence of their imagination. The first never deceives; the second rarely ; the third almost always : but the first does not belong to this treatise, because it does not fall under the rules of the method. Combination is made by conjecture when, for example, from the fact that water, being far distant from the center of the earth, it is [assumed to be] of a thinner substance ; from the fact that air being placed above the earth, is also much lighter than it, we conclude that above the air there is nothing but an etherial substance, very pure, and much thinner than the air itself. The notions which we combine in this way do not deceive us, provided we accept them only as probabilities, never as truths : but they do not make us any wiser. There remains deduction only, whereby we may combine notions of the accuracy of which we may be sure; and, nevertheless, a great many errors may be committed in it. For example, when from the fact that there is nothing in the air which sight, touch, or any other sense can perceive, we conclude that the space which contains it is empty, we improperly connect the nature of the void with that of space ; but this always happens whenever we think we can deduce from a particular and contingent thing something general and necessary. But it is in our power to avoid this error, by never making any combinations in our thought except those which we recognize to be necessary ; as, for example, when we conclude that nothing can be figured which is not extended, since figure has a necessary relation to extension.

From all this it follows, . . . that we have set forth clearly, and, as it seems to me, by a sufficient enumeration, what we could show at the beginning only confusedly and without method ; to wit, that there are only two ways open to man for attaining a certain knowledge of truth : clear intuition and necessary deduction. . . .

MEDITATIONS
UPON THE FIRST PHILOSOPHY, IN WHICH ARE CLEARLY PROVED THE EXISTENCE OF GOD AND THE REAL DISTINCTION BETWEEN THE SOUL AND THE BODY OF MAN.

MEDITATIONS

UPON THE FIRST PHILOSOPHY, IN WHICH ARE CLEARLY PROVED THE EXISTENCE OF GOD AND THE REAL DISTINCTION BETWEEN THE SOUL AND THE BODY OF MAN.

FIRST MEDITATION.*

Of the things which may be doubted.

NOT to-day, for the first time, have I become aware that, from my earliest years, I have accepted a multitude of false opinions as true, and that what I have based on principles so ill-assured cannot be otherwise than extremely doubtful. Ever since I became convinced of this, I have considered that I ought for once in my life seriously to undertake to rid myself of all the false opinions which I have hitherto received, and to begin entirely anew from the foundations, if I wished to establish anything in the sciences that should be solid and stable. But, because it seemed to me to be a great undertaking, I have waited till I should attain an age so ripe that I could not hope for another after it at which I should be more fit to accomplish the task. I have, in consequence, delayed so long that I believe I should be at fault if I should

* *Œuvres*, t. i, p. 235. The Meditations may be found translated entire in Veitch's *Descartes*.

hereafter spend in deliberating the time which remains for action. To-day, then, in accordance with my design, having freed my mind from every kind of care, by good fortune being disturbed by no passions, and having secured to myself a peaceful and solitary retreat, I shall devote myself, in sober earnest and with entire freedom, to the business of destroying all my former opinions.* But, in order to do this, it will not be necessary for me to prove that every one of them is false, in doing which I might never reach the end. But inasmuch as reason convinces me that I ought to restrain myself from admitting as true things which are not entirely certain and indubitable, not less carefully than those which appear to me to be manifestly false, there will be sufficient reason for me to reject all of them if I can find in any one of them any grounds for doubt. However, it will not be necessary that I examine each one in particular, which would be infinite labor; but, inasmuch as the destruction of the foundations necessarily involves the ruin of the whole edifice, I will apply myself at once to the principles upon which all my old opinions rest.

All that I have hitherto received as most true and assured I have learned from the senses or by means of the senses. But I have sometimes found that these senses were deceivers, and it is the part of prudence never to trust entirely those who have once deceived us.†

---

* Cf. *Principles of Philosophy*, part I, 1, 2.
 1. The seeker after truth once in his life, so far as it is possible, should doubt all things.
 2. What is doubtful should be considered false.
 Œuvres, t. iii, pp. 63, 64. Veitch's *Descartes*, p. 193.

† Cf. *Princ.* I, 4. Why we may doubt of sensible things.

But although the senses may deceive us sometimes in regard to things which are scarcely perceptible and very distant, yet there are many other things of which we cannot entertain a reasonable doubt, although we know them by means of the senses; for example, that I am here, seated by the fire, in my dressing-gown, holding this paper in my hands, and other things of such a nature. And how can I deny that these hands and this body are mine? Only by imitating those crazy people, whose brains are so disturbed and confused by the black vapors of the bile that they constantly affirm that they are kings, while in fact they are very poor; that they are clothed in gold and purple, while they are quite naked; or who imagine themselves to be pitchers, or to have glass bodies. But what! These are fools, and I should be no less extravagant if I should follow their example. Nevertheless, I have to consider that I am a man, and that I fall asleep and in my dreams imagine the same things or even sometimes things less probable than these crazy people do while they are awake. How often have I dreamed in the night that I was in this place, that I was dressed, that I was before the fire, although I was quite naked in my bed. It seems to me indeed at present that I am looking on this paper not with eyes asleep, that this head which I shake is not in a drowse, that it is with deliberate purpose I stretch out my hand, and that I perceive it. What happens in sleep does not appear so clear and distinct as all this.

But when I consider it carefully, I remember that I have often been deceived, while asleep, by similar illusions, and, pondering on the matter, I see so plainly that there are no certain marks by which the waking is distinguished from the sleeping state that I am quite astonished, and my astonishment is so great as almost to persuade me that I am asleep.*

Let us, then, suppose that we are asleep, and that all these particular events—that we open our eyes, shake our heads, stretch out our hands, and such like things—are only false illusions, and let us think that perhaps neither our hands nor our entire bodies are such as we perceive them. Nevertheless, we must at least admit that the things which we imagine in sleep are like pictures and paintings, which can only be formed after the likeness of something real and veritable. Accordingly, these things in general—namely, eyes, head, hands, body—are not imaginary, but real and existent. For truly, painters, even when they strive with the utmost art to represent sirens and satyrs by extravagant and fantastical figures, cannot, nevertheless, give them forms and natures entirely novel, but only make a certain mixture and combination of divers creatures, or, even if their imagination is extravagant enough to invent something so new the like whereof has never been seen, and their work represents something purely fictitious and absolutely false, certainly, at the very least, the colors of which they are composed must be real.

By the same reason, granting that these things in general, namely, body, eyes, head, hands, and other like things, may be imaginary, nevertheless it must be admitted that there are at least some other things still

---

* Épistémon.—Have you never heard in the old comedies that stock-phrase for expressing astonishment: *Am I, then, asleep?* How can you be certain that your life is not a continuous dream, and that all that you perceive by the senses is not as false as when you are asleep?—Recherche de la Vérité. (*Œuvres*, t. xi, p. 350.)

more simple and universal, which are true and existent, of the combination of which, no more nor less than that formed from certain real colors, all these images of things which dwell in the mind, be they true and real, or fictitious and fantastic, are formed. Of this nature is corporeal being in general and its extension, together with the figure of things extended, their quantity or size, and their number, as also the place where they are, the time which measures their duration, and other similar things. Accordingly, perhaps, we shall not from this conclude incorrectly, if we say that physics, astronomy, medicine, and all the other sciences which are occupied with the consideration of things composite, are very doubtful and uncertain, but that arithmetic, geometry, and the other sciences of that nature, which treat only of things quite simple and quite general, without being much concerned whether they exist in reality or not, contain something certain and indubitable, because, whether I am awake or asleep, two and three taken together always make five, and a square never has more than four sides, and it does not seem possible that truths so clear and so evident can be suspected of any falsity or uncertainty.

Nevertheless, for a long time I have cherished the belief that there is a God who can do everything and by whom I was made and created such as I am. But how do I know that he has not caused that there should be no earth, no heavens, no extended body, no figure, no size, no place, and that, nevertheless, I should have perceptions of all these things, and that everything should seem to me to exist not otherwise than as I perceive it? And even in like manner as I judge that others deceive themselves in matters that they know best, how do I know that he has not caused that I deceive myself every time that I add two to three, or number the sides of a square, or judge of anything still more simple, if anything more simple can be imagined?* But it may be that God has not willed that I should be deceived in this manner, since he is called supremely good. Nevertheless, if it is repugnant to his goodness to create me such that I should deceive myself constantly, it would appear also to be contrary to it to permit me to deceive myself sometimes, and yet I cannot doubt that he does permit it. . . . .

I shall suppose, then, not that God, who is very good and the sovereign source of truth, but that a certain evil genius, no less wily and deceitful than powerful, has employed all his ingenuity to deceive me. I shall think that the heavens, the air, the earth, colors, figures, sounds, and all other external things, are nothing but illusions and idle fancies which he employs to impose upon my credulity. I shall consider myself as having no hands, no eyes, no flesh, no blood, as having no senses, but, as believing falsely that I possess all these things. I shall obstinately adhere to this opinion ; and if by this means it will not be in my power to arrive at the knowledge of any truth, at all events it is in my power to suspend my judgment. Therefore I shall take diligent care not to receive into my faith any falsehood, and I shall prepare my mind so well against all the wiles of this great deceiver, that, powerful and crafty as he may be, he will never be able to impose upon me. . . . .

---

*Cf. *Princ.*, I, 5. Why we may doubt even of mathematical demonstrations.

SECOND MEDITATION.

Of the nature of the human mind; and that it is more easily known than the body.

YESTERDAY'S meditation has filled my mind with so many doubts that it is henceforth impossible for me to forget them, and yet I do not see how I can resolve them. .... I shall nevertheless make an effort and follow on once more in the way on which I entered yesterday; withdrawing myself from everything in which I can imagine the least doubt, just as if I knew it to be absolutely false; and I shall keep steadily on in this path until I have found something certain, or at least, if I can do nothing else, until I have found out certainly that there is nothing in the world that is certain.* Archimedes, in order to move the terrestrial globe from its place and transport it into another, required only a point which should be firm and immovable, and even so may I entertain high hopes if only I am fortunate enough to find barely one thing which is certain and indubitable. †

---

* *Eudoxe.*—But for fear you will refuse to follow me further, I assure you that these doubts, which at the outset make you afraid, are like the phantoms and the shadowy forms which appear in the night-time in the uncertain glimmer of a feeble light. Fear pursues you if you flee from them; but march up to them, lay your hands upon them, and you will find them nothing but air, nothing but shadow, and your fears will vanish forever.—Recherche de la Vérité. (*Œuvres*, t. xi, p. 352.)

† *Eudoxe.*—Only give me your attention. I am going to lead you further than you think. Indeed, from this universal doubt,

I make the supposition, then, that all things which I see are false; I persuade myself that nothing has ever existed of all that my memory, filled with illusions, has represented to me; I consider that I have no senses; I assume that body, figure, extension, motion, and place are only fictions of my mind. What is there, then, which can be held to be true? Perhaps nothing at all, except the statement that there is nothing at all that is true. But how do I know that there is not something different from those things which I have just pronounced uncertain, concerning which there cannot be entertained the least doubt? Is there not some God, or some other power, who puts these thoughts into my mind? That is not necessary, for perhaps I am capable of producing them of myself. Myself then! at the very least am I not something?

But I have already denied that I have any senses or any body; nevertheless I hesitate, for what follows from that? Am I so dependent upon the body and the senses that I cannot exist without them? But I have persuaded myself that there is nothing at all in the world, that there are no heavens, no earth, no minds, no bodies; am I then also persuaded that I am not? Far from it! Without doubt I exist, if I am persuaded, or solely if I have thought anything whatever. But there is I know not what deceiver, very powerful, very crafty, who employs all his cunning continually to delude me. There is still no doubt that I exist, if he deceives me; and let him deceive me as he may, he will never bring it about that I shall be nothing, so long as I shall think some-

as from a fixed and immovable point, I am resolved to derive the knowledge of God, of yourself, and of the whole universe.—Recherche de la Vérité. (*Œuvres*, t. xi, p. 353).

thing exists. Accordingly, having considered it well, and carefully examined everything, I am obliged to conclude and to hold for certain that this proposition, *I am, I exist*, is necessarily true, every time that I pronounce it or conceive it in my mind.

NOTE.—Compare the following passages illustrative of the proposition *I think, therefore I exist:*

And observing that this truth, *I think, therefore I am*, was so firm and so certain that no suggestions of skeptics, however extravagant, could ever shake it, I concluded that I might accept it without scruple as the first principle of the philosophy I was in search of.—*Discourse on Method, Part IV.* (*Œuvres*, t. i, p. 158.)
Principles, I, 7, and 9.

7. For it is contradictory [*repugnat*] to suppose that anything which thinks, at the same time in which it thinks, does not exist. And hence this knowledge, *ego cogito, ergo sum*, is the first and most certain of any which presents itself to one who philosophizes in an orderly manner.

9. What thought is.

By the word thought [*cogitatio*] I mean all that which, when we are conscious, takes place in us, in so far as there is in us a consciousness of these things. And accordingly, not only to understand, to will, to imagine, but even to feel, is the same here as to think. For if I say, *I see*, or *I walk, therefore I am;* and have in mind the seeing or the walking which is performed by the body, the conclusion is not absolutely certain; because, as often happens in sleep, I can think that I see, or that I walk, although I do not open my eyes, or stir from my place, and even, possibly, although I have no body; but if I have in mind the sense itself, or consciousness, of seeing or walking, which in that case is referred to the mind, which alone perceives, or thinks, itself to see or to walk, it is manifestly certain. [Lat.]

By the term *thought* I understand all that is within us in such manner that we are immediately conscious of it by ourselves and have of it an inner knowledge ; thus all the operations of the will, the understanding, the imagination, the senses, are thoughts. But I add *immediately* to exclude the things which follow and depend upon our thoughts ; for example, voluntary movement, which has in truth the will for its source (*principe*), but still is not itself a thought. Thus, to walk is not a thought, but rather the feeling or the knowledge that one has that he is walking.—Reply to Second Objection. (Geom. proof, Def. 1, *Œuvres*, t. i, p. 145.)

Cogito, ergo sum, not a conclusion of a syllogism.

When anyone says, *I think, therefore I am*, or *I exist*, he does not conclude his existence from his thought by force of any syllogism, but as a thing known by itself ; he sees it by a simple inspection of the mind, as appears from this, that if he should deduce it by syllogism, he must first know this major to be true, *Whatever thinks is*, or *exists :* but on the contrary he learns it from his perceiving within himself that it would be impossible that he should think if he did not exist. For it is the property of our mind to form general propositions from the knowledge of particular ones.—Reply to Second Objection. (*Œuvres*, t. i, p. 427.) See Bouillier, t. i, p. 63.

In criticism of the Second Meditation your friends bring forward six things. The first is that in saying *I think, therefore I am*, the author of the Instances* will have it that I presuppose this major, *he who thinks is ;* and accordingly that I have at the start adopted a presupposition (*préjuge*). Wherein he misuses again the term *presupposition ;* for although the name might be applied to this proposition when uttered unreflectingly, and it might be believed to be true solely because of its being remembered as a judgment previously passed, yet it cannot be said to be a presupposition when one gives his mind to it, because it appears so evident to the understanding that a man cannot help believing it, even though it be the first time in his life that he has thought about it, and consequently there is no presupposition whatever in the case. But the more considerable error here

* Gassendi.

is that this author supposes that the knowledge of particular propositions is always to be deduced from universals, according to the order of syllogisms in logic; wherein he shows that he knows very little how truth is to be sought; for it is certain that, in order to find it, we must always begin with the particular notions, in order thence to arrive at the general notions, although we can reciprocally, also, having reached the general, deduce therefrom other particular truths. Thus, when one is teaching a child the elements of geometry, he will not make him understand the general truth, *when from two equal quantities equal parts are taken, the remainders are equal*, or that *the whole is greater than any of its parts*, unless he shows him examples of it in particular cases.—Letter to Clerselier, on the objections of Gassendi. (*Œuvres*, t. ii. pp. 305-6.)

These interpretations by Descartes of his own thought must be borne in mind when in the *Principles* we find him placing among the common notions, or axioms, this universal: *He who thinks cannot be non-existent while he thinks.*

It is manifest that Descartes believed that, in reaching this innermost point of personal self-consciousness, he had reached the point of coincidence of thought and reality. From this vantage-ground he will now look out to see what further revelations await him. But the *cogito, ergo sum*, is the primary datum and starting-point. In the apprehension of this existential truth he finds himself no longer in the realm of abstract thought, but face to face with reality. Is this basis of his system a fact, then, or a principle? A fact, surely, but the supersensible and spiritual fact of personal existence.

> Descartes' *I think, therefore I am*, not identical with something similar in the writings of St. Augustine: "Quid, si falleris? Si enim fallor, sum. Nam qui non est, utique nec falli potest, ac per hoc sum, si fallor. Quia ergo sum, qui fallor, quomodo esse me fallor, quando certum est me esse si fallor."—*Augustine, De Civitate Dei*, l. xi, c. 26. *
>
> I am obliged to you for calling my attention to the passage of St. Augustine to which my *I think, therefore I*

---

* See Hamilton's Reid, Note A., p. 744.

am, bears some resemblance; I read the passage to-day in the town library, and I find, indeed, that he makes use of it to prove the certainty of our own being, and then to show that there is within us a certain image of the Trinity, in that we are, we know that we are, and we love this being and this knowledge within us; whereas I employ it to show that this *I* which thinks is *an immaterial substance*, and has nothing corporeal in it, which are two very different things, and it is so simple and natural an inference, from the fact of one's doubting to conclude that he exists, that it might have fallen from anybody's pen; however, I am none the less pleased to meet with it in St. Augustine, if only to close the mouths of those small wits who have tried to raise difficulties about this principle.—Letter to M. (de Zuytlichem) (Huyghens?). (*Œuvres*, t. viii, p. 421.)

But I do not yet know with sufficient clearness what I am, I who am certain that I am; wherefore I must be on my guard henceforth not unadvisedly to take something else for myself, and so fall into a mistake in this knowledge, which I maintain to be more certain and more evident than all that I have gained before it. Accordingly, I shall now consider anew that which I believed to be before I entered into these last reflections; and of my old opinions I shall cut off everyone which is in the least oppugned by the arguments which I have just stated, so that there shall remain only that precisely which is entirely certain and indubitable. What is it, then, which I have believed myself to be hitherto? Undoubtedly, I have thought that I was a man. But what, then, is a man? Shall I say that a man is a reasonable animal? No, surely, for then it would be necessary for me to find out what *animal* is and what *reasonable* is, and thus from a single question I should fall by degrees into an infinitude of others more difficult and more embarrassing;

and I am not willing to squander the little time and leisure that remain to me in solving difficulties of that sort.* But I pause rather to consider here the thoughts which arose before of themselves in my mind, and which were inspired in me by my own nature simply, whenever I addressed myself to the consideration of my being. I considered myself, in the first place, as having a face, hands, arms, and all this mechanism composed of bone and flesh, such as it appears in a corpse, which I designated by the name *body*. I considered, moreover, that I took food, that I walked, that I felt and that I thought, and I referred all these actions to the mind; but I did not stop to think what this mind was, or, indeed, if I did stop to think, I imagined that it was something extremely rare and subtile, like breath, a flame, or a very thin vapor, which was instilled and spread through my grosser parts. As to the nature of the body, I had no doubt whatever; but I thought I knew it very distinctly; and had I desired to explain

---

* *Eudoxe.*—For example, if I should ask Épistémon what a man is, and he should answer, as they do in the schools, that a man is a rational animal; and then, to explain these two terms, which are no less obscure than the first, he should conduct us through all the steps which they call metaphysical, we should be involved in a labyrinth from which it would be impossible to escape. In fact, from this question there arise two others; first, what is an animal? second, what is rational? And further, if, to explain animal, he should tell us it is something living, and that something living is an animated body, that body is corporeal substance, you see that the questions, like the branches of a genealogical tree, would go on increasing and multiplying; and at last all these fine questions would end in mere tautology, which would make nothing clearer, and would leave us in our former ignorance.—Recherche de la Vérité. (*Œuvres*, t. xi. p. 355.)

it according to the notions I then had of it, I should have described it in this manner.

By the term body I understand all that can be bounded by some figure; which can be contained within some place, and fill a space in such a manner that every other body is excluded therefrom; which can have sensations either by touch, or by sight, or by hearing, or by taste, or by smell, which can be moved in various ways,—not, in truth, by itself, but by some outward thing by which it may be touched, and the impression of which it may receive; for to have the power of being moved by itself, as also of feeling and of thinking, I did not believe at all that this belonged to the nature of body; on the contrary, I was astonished rather to find such powers occurring in any bodies. But as for me, what am I, now that I am supposing that there is a certain genius extremely powerful, and, if I dare say it, malicious and crafty, who employs all his energies and all his cunning to deceive me? Can I assure myself that I have the least of all those things which I have just now said belong to the nature of body? I pause to think attentively; I go over and over all these things in my mind, and I do not meet with any one which I can say is in me. It is not necessary to stop to enumerate them. Let us, then, pass on to the attributes of the soul, and see whether any one of them is in me.

The first are my taking food and walking; but if it be true that I have no body, it is also true that I cannot walk or feed myself. Another is perceiving; but perception is impossible without the body, although I have thought before that I perceived many things during sleep which, on awaking, I have recognized as not being really perceived. Another is thinking; and I find here an attribute which belongs to me; thought alone cannot be detached from me. I am, I exist that is certain; but how long? As long as I think; because it might happen that if I should cease entirely from thinking I might in the same moment cease utterly from being.* I am admitting nothing now which is not necessarily true; I am, then, to speak with precision, a thing which thinks, that is to say, a mind, an understanding, or a reason; † terms the significance of which was unknown to me before.

But I am a truly existing thing; but what thing? I have said; a thing which thinks; and what more? I stir up my imagination to see whether I am not still something in addition. I am not this collection of members which is called the human body; I am not a thin and penetrating vapor diffused throughout these members; I am not a wind, a breath, a vapor; nor anything at all of all that I am able to picture or imagine myself to be, since I have assumed that all that is nothing at all, and that without changing this assumption I find that I do not cease to be certain that I am something.

But what is it, then, that I am? A thing which thinks. What is a thing which thinks? It is a thing which doubts, which understands, which conceives, which affirms, which denies, which wills, which wills not, which imagines also, and which perceives. Surely, it is no small matter if all these things belong to my nature. But why do they not belong to it? Am I not that even which now doubts almost everything;

* See reply to Hyperaspistes, cited below, p. 128.
† For Hobbes's objection and Descartes' reply see *Obj. et Rép.*, *Œuvres*, t. i, p. 468 et seq.

which nevertheless understands and conceives certain things; which is assured and affirms these only to be true, and denies the rest; which wills and desires to know more; which wills not to be deceived; which imagines many things, even sometimes in spite of myself; and which also perceives many, as if by the interposition of bodily organs. Is there nothing of all that which is as true as it is certain that I am and that I exist, even although I were always sleeping, and he who gave me my being were using all his skill to deceive me? Is there also any of these attributes which can be distinguished from my thought, or which can be said to be separate from myself? For it is so evident of itself that it is I who doubt, who understand, and who desire, that there is no need here of adding anything to explain it. And I also certainly have the power of imagining; for although it might happen (as I have already supposed) that the things which I have imagined were not true, nevertheless this power of imagining does not cease really to exist in me, and to form part of my thought.

Finally, I am the same being which perceives; that is, which has knowledge of certain things as if by the organs of sense, since in reality I see light, I hear noise, I feel warmth. But I have been told that these appearances are false, and that I am asleep. Granted; nevertheless, at least, it is very certain that it appears to me that I see light, that I hear noise, and that I feel warmth; that cannot be false; and it is just that which in me I call perceiving; and that, precisely, is nothing else than thinking. From this point I begin to know what I am with more clearness and distinctness than heretofore.

But nevertheless it still appears to me, and I cannot

help believing, that corporeal things, the images of which are formed by thought, which fall under the senses, and which the senses themselves observe, are not much more distinctly known than that—I know not what—part of myself which does not fall under the imagination : although, indeed, it would be very strange to say that I know and comprehend more distinctly things whose existence appears to me doubtful, which are unknown to me, and which do not belong to me, than those of the truth of which I am persuaded, which are known to me, which belong to my proper nature—in a word, than myself. But I see well enough how it is ; my mind is a vagabond, which takes delight in leading me astray, and will not suffer itself to be kept within the strict bounds of truth.

Let us then give it free rein for once, and, granting every sort of liberty, let us allow it to dwell upon the objects which appear to it externally, in order that hereafter, when we shall proceed to withdraw it gently and at the right time, and detain it upon the consideration of its own being and the things which it finds within itself, thenceforward it shall be more easily regulated and guided. Let us then consider the things which are commonly thought to be the easiest of all to know, and that are believed to be most distinctly known,—that is to say, bodies that we touch and see ; not, indeed, such bodies in general,—for these general notions are usually a little more confused ; but let us consider a particular body. Let us take, for instance, this piece of wax. . . . .

What then ! I who appear to conceive of this piece of wax with so much clearness and distinctness, do I not know myself not only with much more truth and certainty, but even with much more distinctness and clearness! For if I judge that the wax is or exists, from the fact that I see it, certainly it follows much more evidently that I am or that I exist myself, from the fact that I see it, for it may be that what I see is not in reality wax; it may also be that I have not eyes even to see anything; but it cannot be that while I see, or—what I do not distinguish therefrom—while I think I see, I who think am not something. Likewise, if I judge that the wax exists from the fact that I touch it, the same thing will follow, to wit: that I am; and if I judge so because my imagination—or something else, whatever it may be—persuades me thus, I shall always draw the same conclusion. And what I have said here of the wax is applicable to all other things external to me, and which are to be met with outside of me. And, moreover, if the notion or perception of the wax appeared to me more clear and distinct after not only the seeing it and the touching it, but after many other causes had rendered it most manifest to me, with how much greater evidence, distinctness, and clearness, must it be admitted that I know at present myself, since all the reasons which contribute to the knowing and the conceiving of the nature of the wax prove much better the nature of my mind; and, besides, there are so many other things in the mind itself which can contribute to the revelation of its nature, that those which depend upon the body, as these do, hardly deserve to be taken into the account.

But at last, by degrees almost imperceptible to myself, I have reached the point I desired, because, since there is one thing at present manifest to me, that bodies themselves are not really known by the senses or by the faculty of imagination, and that they are not known from the fact that they are seen or touched, but solely from the fact that they are understood, or at least comprehended by thought,—I see clearly that there is nothing which is more easy for me to know than my mind.* But because it is difficult to rid one's self so promptly of an opinion to which one has been accustomed for a long time, it will be well for me to stop a while at this point, in order that by longer meditation I may impress more deeply upon my memory this new knowledge.

* Cf. *Princ.* I, 8, 11. (*Œuvres*, t. iii, pp. 67-69.) Veitch's *Descartes*, pp. 195-197.

THIRD MEDITATION.

Of God: that he exists.

.... I am certain then that I am a thing that thinks; but do I not then also know that which is necessary to make me certain of anything? Certainly, in this primary knowledge there is nothing which assures me of its truth but the clear and distinct perception of what I affirm, which test of truth would not be sufficient to assure me that what I affirm is true, if it could ever happen that a thing which I conceive thus clearly and distinctly should prove false: and, accordingly, it appears to me that I can now lay down this as a general rule, that all things which we conceive very clearly and very distinctly are true.*

And, certainly, since I have no reason to believe that there is a God who can deceive, and as I have not yet even considered the arguments which prove that there is a God, the reason for doubt which depends solely on that opinion is very frivolous, and, so to speak, metaphysical. But in order to be able to remove it entirely I must examine whether there is a God, so soon as the occasion shall present itself; and if I find that there is one, I must also examine whether he can be a deceiver: for without the knowledge of these two truths I do not see that I can ever be certain of anything. And in order that I may have occasion to

---

* Cf. *Discourse*, pt. iv. (*Œuvres*, t. i, p. 159.) Veitch's *Descartes*, p. 35. Also, *Princ.* I, 45–50. See below.

examine into this matter without interrupting the order of meditation which I have proposed to myself, which is to pass by degrees from notions which I shall find first in my mind to those which I shall be able to discover afterward, it is necessary here that I divide all my thoughts into certain classes, and that I consider in which of these classes truth and error properly exist.

Among my thoughts, some are, as it were, the images of things, and it is to these alone that the term *idea** properly belongs; as when I represent to myself a man, or a chimera, or the heavens, or an angel, or God even. Moreover, besides that, there are certain other forms; as when I desire and fear, when I affirm or deny, I do then, indeed, conceive something as the subject of the action of my mind, but I add also something else by this action to the idea that I have of this thing and of this class of thoughts; some are called volitions or affections, and others judgments.

Now, so far as ideas are concerned, if they are considered simply in themselves, and as having no relation to anything else, they cannot, properly speaking, be false; because, whether I imagine a goat or a chimera, it is no less true that I imagine the one than the other. There can be no fear, also, of encountering falsity in affections or volitions; for although I may desire things evil, or even things which never have existed, nevertheless, for all that, it is no less true that I desire them.

Thus there remain judgments alone, in which I must be diligently on guard against being deceived. But the principal error, and the one of most common

---

* Geom. proof, Def. II. (*Œuvres*, t. i, p. 452.) Veitch's *Descartes*, Note XI, p. 276.

occurrence, consists in my judging that the ideas which are in me are like or are conformed to things which are outside of me; for certainly, if I consider simply the ideas as certain modes or forms of my thought, without desiring to refer them to anything external, they can hardly afford any occasion of error. But, among my ideas, some appear to me to be born with me,* others to be strangers and to come

---

* It is not without reason that I am assured that the human soul, wherever it may be, always thinks, even in the mother's womb. What reason more certain or more evident could be desired than that which I employ, since I have proved that its nature or its essence consists in its being a thing which thinks, just as the essence of the body consists in being a thing extended; for it is not possible to deprive anything of its own essence; and therefore it seems to me that no more account should be made of him who denies that his soul was thinking at a time when he does not remember to have perceived that it was thinking, than if he should deny that his body was extended at a time when he did not perceive that there was any extension. I do not say that I am persuaded that the mind of the babe in its mother's womb thinks on metaphysical subjects; on the contrary,—if I may be permitted to form a conjecture upon a matter concerning which so little can be known,—since we find every day that our mind is so closely united to the body that it almost constantly suffers from it, and although a mind acting in a body sound and strong enjoys some freedom to think on other things besides those which the senses present to it, nevertheless experience teaches us only too often that there is no such freedom in the case of sick people, nor for those who are asleep, nor for infants, and that there is generally less as age is less advanced; there is nothing more reasonable than to believe that the mind newly joined to the infant body is occupied only with feeling or being obscurely conscious of the ideas of pain, of pleasure, of cold, of warmth, or such like, which spring from the union or—so to speak—the mixture of the mind with the body. And nevertheless, in this state even, the mind has not less in itself the ideas of God, of itself, and of all those truths which are self-evident, than adult persons do when they are not thinking of

from without, and others to be made and invented by myself.

As regards the faculty to conceive what in general is called a thing, or a truth, or a thought, it appears to me that I have that [power] from no other source than my own nature; but if I now hear some noise, if I see the sun, if I feel warmth, up to this moment I have judged that these sensations proceeded from things which coexist outside of me; and, finally, it appears to me that sirens, hippogriffs, and all other similar chimeras are fictions and inventions of my mind. But also, on the other hand, perhaps I may persuade myself that all these ideas are of the kind that I have called foreign, and which come from without, or, indeed, that they are all born with me, or, perhaps, that they have all been made by me; for I have not yet clearly discovered their true source. And what I have principally to do at this point is to consider with respect to those which appear to me to come from objects outside of me, what are the reasons which oblige me to think that they resemble those objects.

The first of these reasons is that I am so taught by nature; and the second, that I discover in myself that these ideas do not depend upon my will; for frequently they present themselves to me in spite of myself, as, at this time, whether I will or no, I feel warmth, and therefore I am persuaded that this feeling—or, if you please, this idea—of warmth is produced

them; for it does not acquire them afterward with increasing age. And I do not doubt that at that time, if it were freed from the bondage of the body, it would find these ideas within itself. —Reply to Hyperaspistes. Lettres (*Œuvres* t. viii, p. 268). Cf. Veitch's *Descartes*, Note VI, p. 287.

in me by something different from myself, to wit, by the heat of the fire before which I am seated. And I see nothing which appears to me more reasonable than to judge that this foreign thing emits and impresses upon me its likeness rather than something else. Now I must see whether these reasons are sufficiently strong and convincing. When I say that it seems to me that this is taught me by nature, I understand, by this word nature, simply a certain inclination which impels me to believe it, and not a natural light which makes me know that it is true.* But these two expressions are very different. For I can call in question nothing which the natural light has made me see to be true, as, for instance, it has so often made me see that from the fact that I doubt I can conclude that I exist; inasmuch as I have in me no other faculty or power for distinguishing the true from the false, which can teach me that what this light shows me to be true is not so, and in which I can put so much confidence as I can in this.

But as concerns those inclinations which also appear to be natural to me, I have often observed that when there was a choice to be made between virtues and vices, that they have carried me not less toward the evil than toward the good ; and therefore it is that I have no more reason to follow them in matters where the true and the false are concerned. And as for the other reason, that these ideas must come from some other source than myself, since they do not depend upon my will, I do not find it any more convincing. For in quite the same way as those inclinations of which I am just now speaking are found in me notwithstanding that they do not always agree

* Cf. Hobbes' objection and Descartes' reply cited below.

with my will, so, perhaps, there may be in me some faculty or power adequate to produce these ideas, without the aid of any external things, although it may not be known to me; as, indeed, it has always appeared to me up to the present that they are formed within me thus when I was asleep, without the aid of the objects which they represent. And even if I should admit that they are formed by these objects it would not necessarily follow that they must resemble them.

On the other hand, I have observed in many instances that there is a great difference between the object and its idea. As, for example, I find in myself two ideas of the sun quite different: the one has its origin in the senses, and is to be put in the class of those which I have said above come from without; by which it appears to me extremely small; the other is drawn from astronomical considerations, that is to say, from certain notions born with me, or at least formed by myself, in whatever way that may be; by which it appears to me many times greater than the whole earth. Certainly these two ideas which I conceive of the sun cannot both be like the same sun; and reason makes me believe that that which comes immediately from its appearance is the one which least resembles it.

All this makes me sufficiently aware that, up to this hour, it has not been by a judgment certain and premeditated, but solely by a blind and forward impulse, that I have believed that there were things external to myself, and different from my own being, which, by the organs of my senses, or by some other means, whatever it may be, send into me their ideas or images, and imprint there their resemblances.

But there presents itself still another way of finding out whether, among the things the ideas of which I have in me, there are any which exist externally to me. To wit: if these ideas are considered only in so far as they are certain modes of thought, I do not discover among them any difference or inequality, and all appear to proceed from me in the same way; but considering them as images, of which some represent one thing and others another, it is evident that they are very different from one another. For, in reality, those which represent to me substances are without doubt something more, and contain in themselves, so to speak, more objective reality,* that is to say, participate by representation in more degrees of being, or perfection, than those which represent to me simply modes or accidents. Moreover, that by which I conceive a God, sovereign, eternal, infinite, immutable, all-knowing, all-powerful, and creator universal of all things external to himself, this, I say, has certainly in itself more objective reality than those by which finite substances are represented to me.

Now it is a thing manifest by the natural light that there must be at least as much reality in the efficient and total cause as in its effect, for whence can the effect draw its reality save from its cause, and how could this cause communicate it to it, if it did not have it in itself? And from this it follows not only that nothing cannot produce anything, but also, that that which is more perfect, that is to say, which contains in itself more reality, cannot be a result of or be dependent upon the less perfect. And this truth is not

---

* Cf. Reply to Second Objections, Geom. proof, Def. III (Œuvres, t. i, 452); Veitch, *Descartes*, p.267 and Note III, p. 285.

only clear and evident in the effects which have that reality which philosophers call actual or formal, but also in the ideas wherein is considered simply that reality which they call objective : for example, the stone which has not yet existed not only cannot now begin to be, unless it is produced by something which has in itself formally or eminently* all that which enters into the composition of the stone, that is to say, which contains in itself the same things, or others more excellent than those which are in the stone; and heat cannot be produced in a subject which was before devoid of it unless it be by something which is of an order, a degree, or a kind at least as perfect as heat; and so of other things.

But still, besides that, the idea of heat, or of the stone, cannot be in me, unless it has been put there by some cause which contains in itself as much reality as I conceive to be in the heat or in the stone ; for although this cause may not transmit to my idea anything of its own actual or formal reality, it must not on that account be imagined that this cause is less real ; but it must be understood that every idea being a work of the mind, its nature is such that there is not to be demanded of it any other formal reality than that which it receives and borrows from thought, or the mind, of which it is simply a mode, that is to say, a manner or way of thinking. But in order that an idea contain one such objective reality rather than another, it must derive this, without doubt, from some cause, in which there exists at least as much of formal reality as this idea contains of objective reality ; for if we suppose that there is found anything in an idea

* Cf. Reply to Second Objections, Geom. proof, Def. IV (*Œuvres*, t. i, p. 452); Veitch, *Descartes*, p. 268 and Note VII, p. 289.

which is not met with in its cause, it must then be that it has this from nothing. But imperfect as may be this mode of existence by which a thing exists objectively, or by representation in the understanding through its idea, certainly it cannot, nevertheless, be said that this mode and manner of being is nothing, nor, consequently, that this idea derives its origin from nothing. Nor ought I, moreover, to imagine that, because the reality which I consider in my ideas is only objective, it is not necessary that the same reality should be formally or actually in the causes of these ideas, but that it is enough that it be also objective in them; because, just as this mode of existing objectively belongs to ideas from their own natures, likewise the manner or mode of existing formally belongs to the causes of these ideas (at least to the first and principal) from their own nature. And although it might happen that one idea should give birth to another idea, this, nevertheless, cannot go on to infinity; but an end must be reached in a first idea, the cause of which may be the model (*patron*) or original in which is contained, formally and actually, all the reality or perfection which is found simply objectively, or by representation, in those ideas.

Consequently, the natural light makes it clearly evident to me that ideas exist in me as pictures or images which may easily fall short of the perfection of the things from which they are derived, but which never can contain anything greater or more perfect. The longer and more carefully I consider all these things the more clearly and distinctly I recognize that they are true.

But what, finally, shall I conclude from all this?

This: namely, that if the reality or objective perfection of any one of my ideas is such that I know clearly that this same reality or perfection is not in me, neither formally nor eminently, and that, consequently, I cannot be the cause of it myself, it follows thence, necessarily, that I am not alone in the world, but that there is also something else which exists and which is the cause of this idea ; whereas, if there were not found in me such an idea, I should have no argument which could convince me and make certain to me the existence of any other thing than myself, for I have examined them all carefully, and I have not been able to find any other up to the present time.

But among all these ideas which are within me, besides those which represent myself to me, in respect to which there cannot be here any difficulty, there is another which represents a God to me ; others, things corporeal and inanimate ; others, angels ; others, animals ; and others, finally, which represent to me men like myself. But, so far as concerns the ideas which represent to me other men, or animals, or angels, I easily conceive that they may be formed by the mixture and composition of ideas that I have of things corporeal and of God, even although besides myself there were no other men in the world, nor any animals, nor any angels. And so far as concerns the ideas of corporeal things, I do not recognize in them anything so great or so excellent as might not possibly have come from myself ; for when I consider them more closely, and examine them in the same way in which I examined yesterday the idea of the wax, I find that there is but a very little in them that I can conceive clearly and distinctly ; to wit, magnitude, or, rather, extension in length, breadth, and depth ; figure, which results from the termination of this extension; position, which bodies differently shaped hold severally in respect to each other ; and motion, or change of this position, to which there may be added substance, duration, and number.

As for other things, such as light, colors, sounds, odors, flavors, heat, cold, and other qualities which fall under the sense of touch, they occur in my thought in so much obscurity and confusion that I do not know even whether they are true or false ; that is to say, whether the ideas which I conceive of these qualities are indeed ideas of any real things, or whether they represent to me mere chimeras, which cannot exist. . . . .

But to speak truly, it is not necessary that I attribute to them any other author than myself ; for if they be false, that is to say, if they represent things which are not, the natural light makes me understand that they proceed from nothing ; that is to say that they are in me only because there is wanting something to my nature, and that it is not wholly perfect ; and if these ideas be true, nevertheless, since they manifest so little reality to me that I cannot distinguish the thing represented from non-being, I do not see why I may not be the author of them. As for the clear and distinct ideas which I have of corporeal things, there are some of them which it seems to me I might have drawn from the idea that I have of myself ; for instance, those I have of substance, of duration, of number, and of other similar things. For when I think that a stone is a substance, or a thing which is capable of existing of itself, and that I am also myself a substance ; although I conceive indeed that I am a thing which thinks and is not extended, and that the stone, on the contrary, is a thing extended and which does not think, and that thus between these two conceptions there is a notable difference, nevertheless they seem to agree in this respect, that they both represent substances. Likewise, when I think that I am now existing, and remember besides having existed before, and when I conceive many diverse thoughts, the number of which I know, I then acquire the ideas within me of duration and number, which, thereafter, I can transfer to all other things as I please. As for the other qualities of which the ideas of corporeal things are composed, to wit, extension, figure, situation, and motion, it is true that they are not formally within me, since I am only a thing which thinks; but because these are only certain modes of substance, and I myself am a substance, it seems as if they might be contained within me eminently.

There remains, therefore, the idea of God only, in which it must be considered whether there be anything which could not have come from myself.

By the name God I understand a substance infinite, eternal, immutable, independent, omniscient, omnipotent, and by which myself and all other things which are (if it be true that any of these exist) have been created and produced. But these prerogatives are so great and so exalted that the more attentively I consider them, the less am I persuaded that the idea which I have of them can derive its origin from myself alone. And consequently it must necessarily be inferred from all that I have said before that God exists: for although the idea of substance may be in me from the fact that I am a substance; nevertheless I, who am a finite being, should not have the idea of an infinite substance, if it had not been put into me by some substance which was in reality infinite.

And I ought not to imagine that I do not conceive the infinite by a true idea, but solely by the negation of what is finite, just as I comprehend rest and darkness by the negation of motion and of light; since on the contrary I see clearly that there is more reality in infinite substance than in finite substance, and, accordingly, that I have in me, in a certain sense, rather the notion of the infinite than of the finite; for how could it be that I should know that I doubt and that I desire, that is to say, that anything is wanting to me, and that I am not in every respect perfect, unless I had in me some idea of an existence more perfect than my own, by comparison with which I should recognize the defects of my own nature.

And it cannot be said that perhaps this idea is materially false, and consequently that I may derive it from nothing, that is to say, that it may exist in me because I have some defect, as I have already said of the ideas of heat and cold, and other similar things; for, on the contrary, this idea being clear and very distinct, and containing in itself more objective reality than any other, there is none which is in itself more true, or which can less be suspected of error and falsity.

This idea, I say, of a being supremely perfect and infinite, is very true; for although one may feign that such a being does not exist, one, nevertheless, cannot feign that the idea of it does not represent anything real to me, as I said above of the idea of cold. It is also very clear and very distinct, since all that my mind conceives clearly and distinctly of reality and truth, and which contains in itself any perfection, is contained and summed up in this idea. And this still remains true, although I do not comprehend the infinite, and there exists in God an infinitude of things which I cannot comprehend, nor perhaps even attain to any conception of them whatever, because it is of the nature of the infinite that I, who am finite and limited, cannot comprehend it ; and it is enough that I well understand this, and that I judge that all things that I conceive clearly, and in which I know there is any perfection, and perhaps also an infinitude of other things of which I am ignorant, are in God formally or eminently, to render the idea which I have of him the most true, the most clear, and the most distinct of all that are in my mind.*

But it may be also that I am something more than I imagine, and that all the perfections which I attribute to the nature of a God are in some manner in me potentially, though they have not yet presented themselves and become manifest by their activity. Indeed, I am aware already that my knowledge increases and grows more perfect little by little, and I do not see anything to prevent its increasing thus more and more even to infinity ; nor even why, when it has thus increased and grown perfect, I should not be able to acquire by means of it all the other perfections of the Divine nature; nor, finally, why the capacity which I have for the acquisition of these perfections— if it be true that it now exists within me—should not be sufficient to produce the ideas of them.

Nevertheless, on looking a little more closely at it, I perceive that this cannot be ; for, in the first place, although it may be true that my knowledge acquires every day new degrees of perfection, and that there

* Cf. Kuno Fischer's *Descartes* (trans.), p. 358.

may be in my nature many things potentially which are not yet there in actuality, nevertheless, none of these endowments pertain, nor do they in any degree approximate, to the idea which I have of Divinity, in whom nothing is found merely in potentiality, but all is there in actuality and reality. And, indeed, is it not an infallible and very evident proof of imperfection in my knowledge, that it increases little by little and by degrees is enlarged? Moreover, although my knowledge might become enlarged more and more, still I do not fail to perceive that it could not become actually infinite, since it will never arrive at so high a point of perfection that it would not still be capable of making further progress.

But I conceive God as actually infinite in so high a degree that there can be nothing added to the supreme perfection which he possesses. And, finally, I very well understand that the objective existence of an idea cannot be caused by a being which exists barely potentially, but solely by one which exists formally or actually. And certainly, in all that I have just said, I do not see anything which may not be very easily comprehended by natural light on the part of those who are willing to think upon it carefully; but, when I relax my attention a little, my mind becomes obscured, and, as it were, blinded by the images of sensible objects, so that it does not readily recall the reason why the idea which I have of a being more perfect than my own must necessarily have been put in me by a being who is in reality more perfect.

It is for this reason that I wish to go on further and to consider whether I, who have this idea of God, could exist in case there were no God. And I ask, from whom have I my existence? Perhaps from myself, or from my parents, or from other causes less perfect than God; for nothing can be imagined more perfect nor even equal to him. But if I were independent of every other, and if I had been myself the author of my being, I should not have any doubts, I should not be conscious of desires, and, in fine, there would not be wanting to me any perfection; for I should have endowed myself with all those of which I have in myself any idea, and accordingly I should be God. And I ought not to imagine that the things which are wanting to me are, perhaps, more difficult to acquire than those which I already possess; for, on the contrary, it is very certain that it had been much more difficult that I—that is to say, a thing or substance which thinks—should proceed from nothing, than that I should acquire light and knowledge of many things of which I am ignorant, and which are only accidents of this substance. . . . .

And although I might suppose that I had always been as I am now, I cannot in that case escape the force of this reasoning and fail to perceive that it is necessary that God should be the author of my existence. For the whole duration of my life might be divided into an infinitude of parts, each one of them being dependent in no manner on the rest; and so, from the fact that I have existed just before, it does not follow that I must now exist, except as some cause at this moment produces me and creates me, so to say, anew; that is to say, preserves me. In reality, it is a thing very clear and very evident to all those who will consider with attention the nature of time, that a substance, for its preservation during all the moments of its duration, requires the same power and the same act which would be necessary to produce it and to create it *de novo* if it did not already exist ; so that it is something which the natural light makes us see clearly, that conservation and creation differ only in respect to our thought, and not in reality.

I have, then, at this point only to ask myself and make appeal to myself, to see whether I have in me any power and any virtue, by means of which I could cause that I who now exist should exist a moment afterward ; because, since I am nothing but a thing which thinks (or at least, since up to this time nothing further has been considered than precisely this part of myself), if such a power did reside in me, surely I ought at least to conceive it and to have knowledge of it ; but I am not aware of any such thing in me, and from that I know evidently that I depend upon some being other than myself.

But it may be that this being on whom I depend is not God, and that I was produced either by my parents or by some other causes less perfect than he is. But this cannot be true ; for, as I have already said, it is a thing very evident that there must be at least as much reality in the cause as in its effect ; and consequently, since I am a thing which thinks and I have in me some idea of a God, whatever may be the ultimate cause of my being, it must necessarily be admitted that it is also a thing which thinks, and that it has in itself the idea of all the perfections which I attribute to God. Then must the inquiry be renewed, whether this cause derives its origin and its existence from itself, or from something else. Because, if it derive it from itself, it follows, from reasons which I have already advanced, that this cause is God ; since, having the power to be and to exist of itself, it must have also without doubt the power to possess in actuality all the perfections of which it has in itself the ideas, that is to say, all those which I conceive to be in God. But if it derive its existence from some other cause than itself, it must be inquired anew, for the same reason, of this second cause, whether it exists of itself or through another, until, step by step, at last an ultimate cause is reached, which will prove to be God. And it is very manifest that in this there can be no infinite regression, seeing that the question here is not so much as to the cause which at some other time brought me into being, as concerning that which at the present moment keeps me in being.

It cannot be supposed, further, that possibly many causes together have concurred in producing me, and that from one I have received the idea of one of the perfections which I attribute to God, from another the idea of some other, consequently that all these perfections are to be found, indeed, somewhere in the universe, but are not to be met with united and collected in one sole being, which is God; because, on the contrary, the unity, the simplicity, or the inseparability of all things which are in God is one of the principal perfections which I conceive to exist in him; and surely the idea of this unity of all the perfections of God could not have been put into me by any cause from which I did not also receive the ideas of all the other perfections; because it could not have brought it about that I should comprehend all these joined together and inseparable, without having caused, consequently, at the same time, that I should know what they were, and that I should become acquainted with all of them in some degree.

Finally, so far as concerns my parents, to whom it

appears that I owe my birth, although all that I ever could believe of them were true, it nevertheless could not be true that it is they who keep me in existence, nor even who made me and brought me forth in so far as I am a thing which thinks; there being no relation between the corporeal action by which I am accustomed to believe that they engendered me, and the production of such a substance; but what they at the most contributed to my birth is that they put certain dispositions into this matter in which I have judged up to this time that I—that is to say, my mind, which alone I now take to be myself—is inclosed; and accordingly there cannot be here any difficulty in regard to them, but it must necessarily be concluded, from the fact alone that I exist, and that the idea of a being supremely perfect—that is to say, of God—is in me, the existence of God is very evidently demonstrated.*

There remains only to inquire how I have come by this idea, for I did not receive it through the senses, and it never presented itself contrary to my expectations, as the idea of sensible things commonly do, when these things present themselves, or seem to do so, to the exterior organs of sense; it is not, moreover, a

* For other statements of the argument for the being of God, see *Discours de la Méthode*, pt. IV, *Œuvres*, t. i, pp. 159-163; Veitch's trans., pp. 34-37; *Principes*, i, 18-22, *Œuvres*, t. iii, pp. 74-78; Veitch's trans., pp. 201-203; Obj. et Rép., Props. I-III, *Œuvres*, t. i, pp. 460-462; Veitch's trans., App., pp. 271-272.

The above form of the argument, which is styled by Kuno Fischer (*Descartes*, trans., p. 349) the *anthropological* proof, and of which he remarks, "It is the real Cartesian proof of the existence of God," should be compared with the strictly *ontological* proof in the Fifth Meditation. The former demonstration is *a posteriori*, its principle being the law of causality; the latter is *a priori*, and finds the existence in the idea of God. See below.

pure product or fiction of my mind, for it is not in my power to diminish or to add to it ; and, consequently, there remains nothing else to be said but that this idea was born and produced with me at the time when I was created, just as was the idea of myself. And, indeed, it should not be thought strange that God, in creating me, should have put into me this idea to be, as it were, the mark of the workman impressed upon his work ; and moreover it is not necessary that this mark should be anything different from this work itself ; but from the simple fact that God created me it is very credible that he made me in some manner in his own image and likeness ; and that I conceive this resemblance, in which the idea of God is found contained, by the same faculty by which I conceive myself, that is to say that, when I reflect upon myself, not only do I take note that I am a thing imperfect, incomplete, and dependent upon another, which strives and aspires, without ceasing, toward something greater and better than I am, but I recognize also, at the same time, that he upon whom I depend possesses in himself all these great things to which I aspire, and of which I find in myself the ideas, not indefinitely and merely potentially, but that he has them in reality, actually and infinitely, and, therefore, that he is God.

And the entire force of the argument which I have here employed to prove the existence of God consists in this, that I recognize the impossibility that my nature should be what it is—that is to say, that I should have in me the idea of a God, if God did not in truth exist ; that same God, I say, of whom there is in me the idea, that is to say, who possesses all these high perfections of which our mind can have even any faint idea without being able, however, to comprehend them, who is subject to no defects, and who has none of all those things which imply imperfection. Whence it is clear enough that he cannot be a deceiver, since the natural light teaches us that deception necessarily depends on some defect.

FOURTH MEDITATION.

Of the true and the false.

.... ALREADY it seems to me that I am finding a path which will conduct us from the contemplation of this true God in whom are hid all the treasures of knowledge and wisdom to the knowledge of the rest of the universe. For, in the first place, I perceive that it is impossible for him ever to deceive me, since in all fraud and deceit there exists some sort of imperfection; and although the ability to deceive may be a mark of subtlety or of power, nevertheless the wish to deceive shows unmistakable weakness or malice; and, therefore, it cannot be found in God. In the next place, I know by my own experience that there exists in me a certain faculty of judging, or of discriminating the true from the false, which without doubt I have received from God, as well as all the rest of the things which are in me and which I possess; and since it is impossible that he should wish to deceive me, it is also certain that he has not bestowed upon me such a faculty that I could ever fall into error so long as I should use it rightly. There would remain no doubt on this point, except that, apparently, this consequence might follow, that in this case I could never deceive myself; because, if all that is in me comes from God, and if he has not put in me any faculty of error, it would appear that I should never make a mistake. And, indeed, it is true that, whenever I look upon myself solely as coming from God, and turn myself wholly toward him, I do not discover in myself any cause of error or untruth; but immediately afterward, on returning to myself, experience makes me aware that I am, nevertheless, liable to an infinitude of errors, on seeking the cause of which I observe that there is present to my thought not only a real and positive idea of God, or, rather, of a being supremely perfect; but also, so to speak, a certain negative idea of non-entity, that is to say, of that which is infinitely removed from every sort of perfection; and that I am, as it were, a mean between God and non-entity, that is to say, placed in some sort betwixt the Supreme Being and the non-existent, so that in truth there can be found in me nothing which could lead me into error, in so far as a Supreme Being has made me; but if I consider myself as participating in some sort in non-entity or non-being, that is to say in so far as I am not myself the Supreme Being, and that many things are wanting to me, I find myself exposed to an infinitude of defects; so that I ought not to be surprised if I fall into mistakes. And thus I perceive that error, in so far as it is such, is nothing real which depends upon God, but is solely a defect; and therefore, in order to err, I do not need a faculty which should be given me by God particularly for this end; but my deceiving myself arises from the fact that the power which God has given me to discriminate the false does not exist in me in an infinite degree. Nevertheless I am not yet quite satisfied, for error is not a pure negation, that is to say, it is not the simple absence or defect of some perfection which does not belong to me, but it is a privation of some knowledge which it seems as if I ought to have. But on considering the nature of God, it does not seem possible that he should have put into me any faculty which was not perfect of its kind, that is to say, which should want any perfection which belongs to it; for, if it be true that the more expert the artisan, the more perfect and complete are the works which come from his hands, what thing can have been produced by the Sovereign Creator of the universe which was not perfect and entirely finished in all its parts? And, surely, there is no doubt at all but that God might have created me such that I could never have made mistakes; it is certain, also, that he wills always that which is the best; is it, then, better that I should be able to deceive myself than that I should not have the power to do so? On considering this point attentively it occurs to my mind at once that I ought not to be surprised if I am not capable of understanding why God does what he does, and that I ought not on that account to doubt of his existence, since, perhaps, I see by experience many other things which exist, although I cannot understand for what reason or how God made them; for knowing already that my nature is extremely weak and limited, and that the nature of God, on the contrary, is boundless, incomprehensible, and infinite, I can easily see that there is an infinitude of things within his power the causes of which lie beyond the range of my mind; and this reason alone is sufficient to persuade me that all that kind of causes, which is commonly derived from the end, is of no use in things physical or natural; for it does not seem to me that I can without temerity pry into and try to discover the impenetrable purposes of God.*

* We shall not, also, stop to inquire after the ends which God proposed to himself in creating the world, and we entirely exclude

Moreover it further occurs to my mind that a single creature should not be considered separately, when inquiry is made whether the works of God are perfect, but generally all creatures taken together; because the very same thing which might with some sort of reason seem very imperfect, if it were the only thing in existence, might not fail of being very perfect, when considered as forming a part of the whole universe *; and although, since I have formed the plan of doubting everything, I might not certainly know aught beyond my own existence and that of God, nevertheless also, since I have become aware of the infinite power of God, I cannot deny that he has produced many other things, consequently that I exist and am placed in the world as forming a part of the universal whole of being.

In the next place, on looking at myself more closely, and considering what my errors are, which of themselves bear witness that there is imperfection in me, I find that they depend on the concurrence of two causes, to wit, the faculty of knowing which is in me

---

from our philosophy the investigation of final causes; for we should not be so arrogant as to presume that God desired to impart to us his plans; but, while regarding him as the author of all things, we shall attempt simply to discover, through the faculty of reasoning he has put within us, how the things which we perceive by the medium of our senses might have been produced; and we shall be warranted, by those of his attributes of which he has willed that we have some knowledge, that what we shall have once perceived clearly and distinctly to belong to the nature of these things has the perfection of being true. *Principes*, I, 28 (*Œuvres*, t. iii, p. 81).

* This thought was elaborated by Leibnitz in his *Théodicée* and forms the principal support of his optimistic theory.—Cf. Butler's Analogy, pt. i, ch. vii.

and the faculty of choosing, or rather of my free will, that is to say, upon my understanding and my will together. For by the understanding alone I do not affirm nor deny anything, but I simply conceive the ideas of things, which I can affirm or deny. But when considering the matter thus strictly, one may say that he does not find in himself any error, provided the term error is taken in its proper signification.

And although there may be an infinity of things in the world of which I have no idea in my understanding, it cannot be said on that account that it is deprived of these ideas, as of something properly belonging to its nature, but simply that it does not have them; because, in truth, there is no reason by which it could be shown that God ought to have given me a greater and more ample faculty of knowing than that which he has given me; and no matter how skillful and wise the workman I represent to myself, I am not bound for that reason to think that he ought to put into each one of his works all those perfections that he may put into some of them. Also, I cannot complain that God did not give me a free will, or a will ample and perfect enough, since in reality I find it so ample and so far-reaching that it is not inclosed within any bounds. And what appears to me here quite remarkable is that of all other things which exist within me there is none so perfect and so great that I am not well aware that it might be still greater and more perfect. For, for example, if I consider the faculty of conceiving which is in me, I find that it has a very narrow range and is greatly limited, and at the same time I represent to myself the idea of another faculty much more ample and even infinite; and from the simple fact that I can represent to myself the idea of it, I easily perceive that it belongs to the nature of God. In the same way, if I examine memory or imagination, or whatever other faculty there may be in me, I do not find any that is not very small and limited, and which in God is not immense and infinite.

It is will alone, or freedom of choice, that I find to be in me so great that I do not conceive the idea of anything else greater or of wider range ; so that it is this chiefly which makes me know that I bear the image and likeness of God. Because, although it may be incomparably greater in God than in me, whether on account of the knowledge and the power which are joined with it and which make it more steadfast and efficient, or on account of its object, inasmuch as it directs itself and extends itself to an infinitely greater number of things, nevertheless it does not seem to me to be any greater, if I consider it formally and strictly in itself. For it consists simply in this, that we are able to do a thing or not to do it, that is to say, to affirm or deny, to pursue or avoid the same thing, or rather it consists solely in this, that in affirming or denying, in pursuing or avoiding the things which understanding presents to us, we act in such a manner that we do not feel ourselves constrained by any external force. For, that I may be free, it is not necessary that I should be indifferent in choosing one or the other of two contrary things ; but rather, the more I incline toward one, whether it be that I clearly know that the good and the true meet in it, or that God thus disposes my thought within me, by so much the more freely do I choose and embrace it ; and surely divine grace and natural knowledge, far from diminishing my liberty, the rather increase and strengthen it ;

so that this indifference which I feel when I am not carried toward one side rather than toward another by the weight of any reason, is the lowest degree of liberty, and makes apparent rather a defect in knowledge than a perfection in will; for if I always knew clearly the true and the good, I should never be at any loss to decide what judgment and what choice I ought to make; and thus I should be entirely free without ever being indifferent.

From all this I perceive that neither the power of willing, which I have received from God, is of itself the cause of my errors, for it is very ample and very perfect in its kind, nor also the power of understanding or conceiving; for, not conceiving anything except by means of that power which God has given me for conceiving, without doubt, all that I conceive, I conceive as it should be, and it is not possible that in that I should deceive myself. Whence, then, arise my errors? It is from this circumstance alone, that the will being much more ample and far-reaching than the understanding, I do not keep it within the same limits, but I extend it also to things which I do not understand; to which being of itself indifferent, it very easily goes astray, and chooses the false in place of the true, and the evil in place of the good; and that is what causes me to err and to sin.*

For example, upon examining during these days just gone by whether anything truly existed in the world, and becoming aware that, from the simple fact that I had raised that question, it followed very evidently that I myself existed, I could not avoid the conclusion that what I conceived so clearly was true;

---

* Cf. Princ., Pt. I, 31–44. See Veitch, trans. pp. 207–212.

not that I found myself forced to it by any external cause, but solely because upon a great clearness in my understanding * there followed a strong inclination in my will ; and I was inclined the more freely to believe this, in proportion as I felt the less indifference. On the contrary, now I do not know solely that I exist, in so far as I am something which thinks ; but there is present also to my mind a certain idea of the corporeal nature ; which makes me question whether this nature which thinks, which is within me, or rather which I myself am, is different from this corporeal nature, or whether both are not one and the same ; and I assume here that I know as yet of no reason to incline me to the one view rather than to the other : whence it follows that I am entirely indifferent as regards a denial or an affirmation, or, indeed, as to whether I abstain from any judgment in the matter.

---

* Cf. Hobbes' objection and Descartes' reply (*Œuvres*, t. i, pp. 496-498).

Objection.—This way of speaking, *a great clearness in the understanding*, is metaphorical, and accordingly is not fit to introduce into an argument ; now he who has no doubt pretends to have such a clearness, and his will has no less inclination to affirm that of which he has no doubt than has the man who possesses perfect knowledge. This clearness, then, may very well be the cause why a man shall hold and obstinately defend any opinion, but it can never make him know with certainty that it is true.—[Cf. Mahaffy's remarks, *Descartes*, p. 96.]

Reply.—It matters little whether this way of speaking be fit or not to introduce into an argument, provided it be fit to express clearly our thought, as it does. For there is nobody who does not know that by this word, *a clearness in the understanding*, is meant a clearness or perspicuity of knowledge that not everyone who thinks possesses ; but that does not prevent its being altogether different from an obstinate opinion conceived without evident perception.

And this indifference extends not merely to things concerning which the understanding has no knowledge, but in general also to all things which it does not discover with perfect clearness at the moment when the will deliberates upon them ; for, however probable may be the conjectures which incline me to pass a judgment, the simple recognition of the fact that they are only conjectures, and not certain and indubitable reasons, is enough to afford me occasion to pass an opposite judgment, and this I have had sufficient experience of during these days just passed, when I have set down as false all that I have hitherto held to be quite true, simply because I have observed that some doubt could be entertained in regard to it.

Now if I abstain from passing judgment upon anything, so long as I do not conceive it with sufficient clearness and distinctness, it is manifest that I do well, and that I am not deceived ; but if I allow myself to deny or affirm, then I do not use my free will as I ought ; and if I affirm what is not true, it is evident that I deceive myself ; and likewise, although I judge according to truth, that happens only by chance, and I still go wrong and make bad use of my freedom ; for the natural light teaches us that the knowledge of the understanding ought always to precede the determination of the will.* And it is in this bad use of freedom that the privation is found which forms the essence of error.

Privation, I say, is found in the act so far as it proceeds from myself, but it is not found in the faculties which I have received from God, nor even in the act in so far as it depends upon him. For certainly I have

---

* Cf. Abelard's dictum : Non credendum, nisi prius intellectum. Introd. ii, 3   Shedd's Hist. of Chr. Doct., vol. i, p. 186.

no ground for complaint in that God has not given me an intelligence more ample, or a natural light more perfect, than that which he has bestowed upon me, since it is of the nature of a finite understanding not to comprehend many things, and of the nature of a created understanding to be finite; but I have every reason to render thanks to him in that, while he owed nothing whatever, he has yet given me all the few perfections there are in me; and I am far from entertaining sentiments so unjust as to imagine that he has deprived me of, or unjustly held back from me, other perfections with which he has not endowed me.

I have likewise no ground for complaint in that he has given me a will more ample in its range than my understanding, since the will consisting only in a single thing, and, as it were, in something indivisible, it appears that its nature is such that nothing could be taken from it without destroying it; and surely the more range it has, the more cause have I to thank the goodness of him who gave it me.

And finally, I ought not to complain on the ground that God concurs with me in producing the acts of this will, that is to say, judgments in which I deceive myself, because these acts are entirely true and absolutely good, in so far as they depend upon God, and there is in some sort more perfection in my nature, in that I am able to perform them, than if I were not able to do so. As for privation, in which alone consists the formal cause of error and of sin, that does not require any concurrence of God, because it is not a thing or a being, and if it be referred to God as its cause, it should not be called privation, but simply negation, according to the signification given to these terms in the school. For in reality it is no imperfection in God that he has given me the liberty of passing judgment, or of not doing so, on certain things concerning which he has not put a clear and distinct knowledge in my understanding; but, without doubt, it is in me an imperfection that I do not use well this liberty, and that I rashly give my judgment upon things which I conceive only obscurely and confusedly.

I see, nevertheless, that it would be easy for God to cause that I never should fall into error, although I still remained free and limited in my knowledge: thus, if he had given to my understanding a clear and distinct knowledge of all the things on which I should ever have to deliberate, or, if you please, if he had engraved on my memory, so deeply that I never could forget it, the resolution never to judge of anything without clearly and distinctly conceiving it. And, indeed, I admit that, in so far as I consider myself alone, as if there were no other than myself in the world, I should have been much more perfect than I am, if God had so created me that I should never have erred; but I cannot, for that, deny that it would be in some sort a greater perfection in the universe if some of its parts should not be exempt from defect, while others were, than if they all should be alike.*
And I have no right to complain that God, when he put me into the world, did not choose to put me into the rank of things most noble and most perfect; rather, I have reason to be content with this, that if he has not granted to me the perfection of not falling into error, by the first means, which I have mentioned above, which depends on a clear and certain knowledge of all the things on which I may deliberate, he has at

---

* See above, p. 150.

least left in my power the other means, which is firmly to keep the resolution never to give my judgment on things the truth concerning which is not clearly known to me ; for, although I experience in myself this weakness of not being able to hold my mind constantly to one thought, I am, nevertheless, able, by attentive and often repeated meditation, to impress it so strongly on my memory that I never fail to recollect it whenever I have need of it, and thus to acquire the habit of not making mistakes ; and, inasmuch as in this consists the greatest and principal perfection of man, I consider that I have gained not a little to-day, in having discovered the cause of error and falsity.

FIFTH MEDITATION.

Of the essence of material things ; and, again, of the existence of God.

MANY other things remain to me to be considered in regard to the attributes of God, and in regard to my own nature, that is to say, that of my mind ; but perhaps I will renew the inquiry at another time. At present, having observed what it is necessary to do or to avoid, in order to arrive at a knowledge of truth, what I have principally to do is to attempt to advance and deliver myself of all the doubts into which I have fallen in these past days, and to see if I cannot know something certain in regard to material things. But before I inquire whether there are such things existing without me, I ought to consider the ideas of them, in so far as they exist in my thought, and to see what are distinct and what are confused. In the first place, I distinctly imagine that quantity which philosophers call continuous quantity, or rather the extension in length, breadth, and thickness which is in this quantity, or rather in the thing to which they attribute it.

Moreover, I can enumerate in it many different parts, and attribute to each one of these parts all sorts of magnitudes, figures, positions, and movements ; and finally, I can assign to each of these movements all sorts of duration. And I recognize these things with distinctness not only when I consider them thus in general ; but also, for the little time that I have given my attention to it, I have come to recognize an infinitude of particulars in regard to numbers, figures, motions, and other similar things, the truth of which makes itself apparent with so much evidence, and accords so well with my nature, that when I begin to discover them it does not seem to me that I am learning anything new, but rather that I am recalling to mind something which I knew before;* that is to say, that I become conscious of things which were already in my mind, although I had not yet turned my thought toward them. And of what I find here the most important is that I discover in myself an infinitude of ideas of certain things which cannot be regarded as a pure non-entity, although perhaps they have no existence outside my thought; and things which are not mere fancies of mine, although I am at liberty to think them or not to think them; but which have a true and unchangeable nature. As, for example, when I imagine a triangle, although there may not be anywhere in the world, outside my thought, such a figure, nor ever have been, there is not wanting, nevertheless, a certain nature, form, or determinate essence of this figure, which is immutable and eternal, which I did not invent, and which does not depend in any way on my mind; as appears from the fact that there may be demonstrated divers properties of this triangle, to wit, that its three angles are equal to two right angles, that its greatest angle is subtended by its greatest side, and other similar truths, which now, whether I will or no, I recognize very clearly and very evidently as being in it, although I had not before thought of it in this way when for the first time

---

* Cf. Plato, doctrine of reminiscence. Meno, 81; Jowett's trans., vol. i. p. 282, Oxford ed.

I imagined a triangle; and accordingly it cannot be said that I have fancied or invented these things.

And I make nothing here of the objection that perhaps this idea of the triangle has come into mind through the medium of my senses, from my having seen sometimes bodies of a triangular shape ; for I can form in my mind an infinitude of other figures, of which there cannot be the least suspicion that they ever fell under the observation of my senses, and yet I should not be wanting in power to demonstrate divers properties belonging to their nature, as well as those which belong to that of the triangle ; which, certainly, must all be true, since I clearly conceive them ; and therefore they are something, and not pure non-entity ; for it is very evident that everything that is true is something, truth being identical with existence ; and I have already fully demonstrated above that all things that I clearly and distinctly know are true. And although I had not demonstrated it, nevertheless the nature of my mind is such that I cannot restrain myself from regarding them as true so long as I conceive them clearly and distinctly ; and I remind myself that at the very time when I was still strongly bound to the objects of sense I set down among the most certain truths those which I conceive clearly and distinctly in regard to figures, numbers, and the other things which belong to arithmetic and geometry.

But now, if from the simple fact that I can draw from my thought the idea of anything it follows that all that I recognize clearly and distinctly to pertain to this thing pertains to it in reality, can I not draw from this an argument and a demonstration of the existence of God?* It is certain that I do not find in me the less the idea of him, that is, of a being supremely perfect, than that of any figure or of any number whatever; and I do not know less clearly and distinctly that an actual and eternal existence belongs to his nature than I know that all that I can demonstrate of any figure or of any number belongs truly to the nature of that figure or that number: and accordingly, although all that I have concluded in the preceding meditations may not turn out to be true, the existence of God ought to pass in my mind as being at least as certain as I have up to this time regarded the truths of mathematics to be, which have to do only with numbers and figures: although, indeed, that might not seem at first to be perfectly evident, but might appear to have some appearance of sophistry. For being accustomed in all other things to make a distinction between existence and essence, I easily persuade myself that existence may perhaps be separated from the essence of God, and thus God might be conceived as not existent actually. But nevertheless, when I think more attentively, I find that existence can no more be separated from the essence of God than from the essence of a rectilinear triangle can be separated the equality of its three angles to two right angles, or, indeed, if you please, from the idea of a mountain the idea of a valley; so that there would be

---

* Cf. argument in Med. III, above, pp. 126-146.

For a statement of the difference between the ontological argument of Descartes and that of St. Thomas (of Anselm originally) see the Reply to Caterus (*Œuvres*, t. i, p. 389). The Anselmic argument (Proslogion, c. 2, 4) may be found stated in Shedd's Hist. of Chr. Doct., vol. i, p. 231 *et seq*.

no less contradiction in conceiving of a God—that is, of a being supremely perfect, to whom existence was wanting, that is to say, to whom there was wanting any perfection—than in conceiving of a mountain which had no valley.

But although, in reality, I might not be able to conceive of a God without existence, no more than of a mountain without a valley, nevertheless, as from the simple fact that I conceive a mountain with a valley, it does not follow that there exists any mountain in the world, so likewise, although I conceive God as existent, it does not follow, it seems, from that, that God exists, for my thought does not impose any necessity on things; and as there is nothing to prevent my imagining a winged horse, although there is none which has wings, so I might, perhaps, be able to attribute existence to God, although there might not be any God which existed. So far from this being so, it is just here under the appearance of this objection that a sophism lies hid; for from the fact that I cannot conceive a mountain without a valley, it does not follow that there exists in the world any mountain or any valley, but solely that the mountain and the valley, whether they exist or not, are inseparable from one another; whereas, from the fact alone that I cannot conceive God except as existent, it follows that existence is inseparable from him, and, consequently, that he exists in reality; not that my thought can make it to be so, or that it can impose any necessity upon things; but on the contrary the necessity which is in the thing itself, that is to say, the necessity of the existence of God, determines me to have this thought.

For it is not at my will to conceive of a God without existence, that is to say, a being supremely perfect without a supreme perfection, as it is at my will to conceive a horse with wings or without wings.

And it must not also be said here that it is necessarily true that I should affirm that God exists, after I have supposed him to possess all kinds of perfection, since existence is one of these, but that my first supposition is not necessary, no more than it is necessary to affirm that all figures of four sides may be inscribed in the circle, but that, supposing I had this thought, I should be constrained to admit that the rhombus can be inscribed there, since it is a figure of four sides, and thus I should be constrained to admit something false. One ought not, I say, to allege this; for although it may not be necessary that I should ever fall to thinking about God, nevertheless, when it happens that I think upon a being first and supreme, and draw, so to speak, the idea of him from the storehouse of mind, it is necessary that I attribute to him every sort of perfection, although I may not go on to enumerate them all, and give attention to each one in particular. And this necessity is sufficient to bring it about (as soon as I recognize that I should next conclude that existence is a perfection) that this first and supreme being exists: while, just as it is not necessary that I ever imagine a triangle, but whenever I choose to consider a rectilineal figure, composed solely of three angles, it is absolutely necessary that I attribute to it all the things which serve for the conclusion that these three angles are not greater than two right angles, although, perhaps, I did not then consider this in particular.

But when I inquire what figures are capable of being inscribed in the circle, it is in no way necessary that I think that all figures of four sides are of this number. On the contrary, I cannot ever fancy this to be the case, in so far as I am willing to receive into my thought only that which I can conceive clearly and distinctly. Consequently there is a great difference between false suppositions, such as this, and the true ideas, which are born with me, of which the first and principal is that of God. For, in truth, I recognize in many ways that this idea is not anything fancied or invented, depending solely on my thought, but it is the image of a veritable and immutable nature ; first, because I cannot conceive any other thing than God alone, to the essence of which existence pertains by necessity, moreover, also, because it is not possible for me to conceive two or more Gods such as he is ; and granting that there is one such who now exists, I see clearly that it is necessary that he should have existed from all eternity, and that he will exist eternally in the future, and finally, because I conceive many other things in God wherein I can diminish or change nothing whatever. As for the rest, whatever proof or argument I may employ, it is always necessary to return to this, that it is only the things which I conceive clearly and distinctly that have the force to produce complete conviction.

And although, among the things which I conceive in this manner, there are indeed some of them clearly known by everybody, and there are others also which are not discovered except by those who consider them more closely, and who investigate them more exactly, nevertheless, after they are once discovered, they are reckoned no less certain than the former. As, for example, in every right-angled triangle, although it may not at first appear so readily that the square of the base is equal to the squares of the other two sides, as it is plain that this base is opposite the greatest angle, nevertheless, after this is once recognized, one is as much persuaded of the one truth as of the other. And as respects God, surely, if my mind were not hindered by any prejudices, and my thought did not find itself diverted by the continual presence of the images of sensible things, there would be nothing which I should not sooner and more readily know than him. For is there anything of itself more clear and more evident than the thought that there is a God; that is to say, a being supreme and perfect in the idea of which alone necessary or eternal existence is comprised, and consequently who exists?

And, although, for the right conceiving of this truth, I might have need of great application of mind, nevertheless, at present, I not only consider myself as much assured of it as of anything that seems to me most certain, but I observe, in addition, that the certainty of all other things depends so absolutely upon it, that without this knowledge it is impossible to be able ever to know anything perfectly. Because, although I am of such a nature that, immediately on comprehending anything very clearly and very distinctly, I cannot help believing it to be true; nevertheless, because I am also of such a nature that I cannot keep my mind continually fixed upon the same thing, and because I remember that I have often judged something to be true, yet when I stopped thinking of the reasons which obliged me to judge it to be so, it might happen during that time that other reasons would present themselves to me, which would easily make me change my opinion, if I did not know that there was a God; and thus I should have no true and certain knowledge of anything whatever, but solely vague and wavering opinions. As, for example, when I am considering the nature of the rectilinear triangle, I perceive clearly, since I am somewhat versed in geometry, that its three angles are equal to two right angles; and it is impossible for me not to believe it, so long as I apply my mind to the demonstration of it; but as soon as I turn away from it, although I might remember having clearly comprehended it, nevertheless it might easily happen that I should doubt its truth, if I did not know that there was a God; for I might persuade myself that I had been so made by nature that I could easily deceive myself even in things that I believed I comprehended with most evidence and certitude; especially since I recollect that I have often considered many things true and certain, which, for other reasons, I have afterward been led to pronounce absolutely false.

But after I have recognized the existence of a God, and because I have at the same time recognized the fact that all things depend upon him, and that he is no deceiver, and in consequence of that I have judged that all that I conceive clearly and distinctly cannot fail to be true, although I do not think longer on the reasons on account of which I have held it to be true, provided solely that I recollect having clearly and distinctly understood it, no opposing reason can be brought against me which should make me ever call it in question; and thus I have a true and certain knowledge of it. And this same knowledge extends also to all the other things which I recollect having formerly demonstrated, as the truths of geometry and others like them; for what is there which can be objected to oblige me to call them in question? Will it be that my nature is such that I am very liable to be mistaken? But I know already that I cannot deceive myself in judgments the reasons for which I clearly perceive. Will it be that I have formerly regarded many things as true and certain which afterward I have discovered to be false? But I did not perceive any of those things clearly and distinctly, and, not knowing as yet this rule whereby I assure myself of truth, I was led to believe them for reasons that I have since recognized to be less strong than at that time I imagined them to be. What, then, can be objected further? Will it be that perhaps I am asleep (as I myself have objected heretofore), or rather that all the thoughts which I now have are no more true than the dreams that we imagine when asleep?

But even if I am asleep, all that presents itself to my mind with evidence is absolutely true. And thus I recognize very clearly that the certainty and the truth of all knowledge depend on the knowledge alone of the true God: so that before I knew him I could not perfectly know anything else. And now that I know him, I have the means of acquiring a perfect knowledge of an infinitude of things, not only of those which are in him, but also of those which belong to corporeal nature, in so far as it can be made the object of geometrical demonstrations, which do not consider it in respect to its existence.

SIXTH MEDITATION.

Of the existence of material things, and of the real distinction between the soul and the body of man.

THERE remains to me further only to inquire whether there are any material things ; and surely I know already that they can exist, at least in so far as they are regarded as the object of geometrical demonstrations, seeing that in this way I conceive them very clearly and very distinctly. For there is no doubt but that God has the power to produce everything that I am capable of conceiving with distinctness ; and I never held that it was impossible for him to do anything except on the ground alone that I discovered contradiction in the conception of it. Moreover, the faculty of imagination which exists within me, and of which I see by experience that I make use whenever I apply myself to the consideration of material things, is capable of persuading me of their existence ; for when I consider attentively the nature of imagination, I find that it is nothing else than a certain application of the faculty of knowledge to a body which is immediately present to it, and which therefore exists. And to make this very evident I observe, first, the difference between imagination and pure intellection or conception. For instance, when I imagine a triangle, not only do I conceive that it is a figure composed of three lines, but along with that I imagine these three lines as present, by the force and internal application of my mind; and it is precisely this which I call imagining. Whereas, if I desire to think of a chiliagon, I conceive indeed that it is a figure composed of a thousand sides as easily as I conceive that a triangle is a figure composed of three sides only; but I cannot imagine the thousand sides of a chiliagon as I do the three sides of a triangle, nor, so to speak, do I see them present with the eyes of my mind.

And although, in consequence of the habit I have of always using my imagination when I think of corporeal things, it happens that on conceiving a chiliagon I represent confusedly to myself some figure, nevertheless it is very evident that this figure is not a chiliagon, since it does not differ at all from that which I should represent to myself if I were thinking of a myriagon or of any other figure having a great many sides; and it would not serve in any way in the discovery of the properties which distinguish the chiliagon from other polygons. Whereas, if the subject of consideration is a pentagon, it is very true that I can conceive its figure, as indeed that of a chiliagon, without the aid of the imagination; but I can also imagine it, by giving my mind's attention to each of its five sides, and to the whole of them together, in respect to air or the space which they inclose.

Thus I see clearly that I require a particular effort of mind for imagining anything of which I do not make use for conceiving or understanding; and this particular mental effort shows clearly the difference between imagination and intellection or pure conception.* I observe, moreover, that this power of imagining which is within me, in so far as it differs from the

* Cf. Leibnitz, De Cognitione, Veritate et Ideis, Opera Philosophica, p. 79, Erdmann, 1840.

power of conceiving, is in no way necessary to my nature or to my essence, that is to say, to the essence of my mind ; for, even if I did not have it, there is no doubt I should remain always the same that I am now ; whence, apparently, we may conclude that it depends on something which is different from my mind. And I easily conceive that if some body exists, to which my mind is so joined and united that it may apply itself to the consideration of it whenever it may please, it may be by this means that it imagines corporeal things; so that this mode of thought differs from pure intellection solely in this : that the mind, in conceiving, turns itself in a manner toward itself and considers some one of the ideas which it has in itself ; but, in imagining, it turns itself toward the body and considers in it something conformed to the idea which it has formed itself, or which it has received through the senses. I easily conceive, I say, that imagination may do something of this sort, if it be true that there are bodies ; and because I cannot find any other way of explaining how it happens, I conjecture from this that probably they exist ; but only probably ; and although I carefully investigate everything, I nevertheless do not find, from this distinct idea of corporeal nature which I have in my imagination, that I can draw any argument which necessitates the conclusion that a body exists.

But I have been wont to imagine many other things besides this corporeal nature which is the object of geometry, to wit, colors, sounds, flavors, pain, and other things similar, although less distinctly ; and, inasmuch as I perceive these things much better by the senses, through the medium of which and of the memory they seem to be brought before my imagination, I think that, in order to examine them more conveniently, it is fitting that I inquire at the same time what it is to feel; and that I see whether from these ideas that I receive into my mind by this mode of thought which I call feeling, I cannot draw some certain proof of the existence of corporeal things. And, in the first place, I shall call up to mind what things I have hitherto held to be true, as having received them through the senses, and upon what foundations my belief rested; afterward I shall examine the reasons which have since obliged me to call them in question; and, finally, I shall consider what I ought at present to believe.

First, then, I felt that I had a head, hands, feet, and all the other members of which this body is composed, which I considered as a part of myself or perhaps even as the whole; moreover, I felt that this body was placed among many others, from which it was capable of receiving various impressions, favorable and unfavorable, and I took notice of the favorable through a certain feeling of pleasure or delight, and of those unfavorable through a feeling of pain. And besides this pleasure and this pain, I had the sensations within me also of hunger, thirst, and other similar appetites; as also of certain bodily inclinations toward joy and sadness, anger and other like passions. And externally, besides extension, figures, movements of bodies, I observed in them hardness, warmth, and all the other qualities which fall under touch; moreover, I observed light, colors, odors, tastes, and sounds, the variety of which afforded me means of distinguishing the sky, the earth, the sea, and, in general, all other bodies one from another. And surely, considering the ideas of all these qualities which presented themselves to my thought, and which alone I properly and immediately felt, it was not without reason that I believed that I felt things entirely different from my thought, to wit, bodies, whence proceeded these ideas; for I discovered that they presented themselves to it without requiring my consent thereto, so that I could not perceive any object, however I might desire it, if it did not happen to be present to the organ of some one of my senses; and it was not in my power not to perceive it whenever it should be present there.

And because the ideas that I received by the senses were much more lively, more vivid, and even in their way more distinct, than any of those which I could fashion of myself in meditation, or even than I found impressed upon my memory, it seemed that they could not proceed from my mind; so that it was necessary that they should be caused in me by external things. Of which things since I had no knowledge, except this, that they gave me these ideas, nothing else could occur to me but that these external things were like the ideas which they caused. And because I reminded myself also that I more frequently used my senses than my reason, and I took notice that the ideas which I formed of myself were not so vivid as those which I received through the senses, and also that they were oftener made up of parts than the latter were, I easily persuaded myself that I had no idea in my mind which had not first passed through my senses. It was not without reason, also, that I believed that this body, which by a certain peculiar right I called my own, belonged to me more properly and more strictly than any other; for, in reality, I could never be separated from it as from other bodies;

I experienced in it and on account of it all my appetites and all my passions; and, finally, I was affected with feelings of pleasure and of pain in its members, and not in those of other bodies which were separate from it. But when I inquired why, from this indefinite feeling of pain sadness arose in the mind, and from the feeling of pleasure joy sprang up, or, if you please, why this vague feeling of the stomach, which I call hunger, should cause us to desire to eat, and the dryness of the throat should cause us to desire to drink, and so of the rest, I could assign no reason for it except that nature had so taught me; for there is, surely, no affinity nor relationship, at least none that I could comprehend, between this feeling of the stomach and the desire to eat, no more than between the feeling of the thing which causes pain and the thought of sadness to which this feeling gives birth.

And in the same way it seemed to me that I had learned from nature all the other things that I judged to be true concerning the objects of my senses; because I observed that the judgments that I was accustomed to make of these objects formed themselves in me before I had time to deliberate and consider any reasons which should oblige me to make them.

But afterward many experiences destroyed, little by little, all the confidence I had reposed in my senses; for I observed many times that towers, which from a distance seemed to me to be round, near at hand appeared to me to be square, and that colossal figures raised upon the very high summits of these towers appeared to me to be small statues when looked at from below; and so, in a multitude of other experiences, I have discovered error in judgments based upon the external senses; and not only upon the external senses, but even upon the internal; for is there anything more personal or more internal than pain? and, nevertheless, I have sometimes heard of persons who had their arms and legs cut off, that it still seemed to them sometimes that they felt pain in the part which no longer belonged to them; which circumstance has given me ground to think that I myself could not be quite sure that anything was the matter with any of my members even if I did feel pain in it.

And to these reasons for doubt I further added, not long since, two others quite general; the first is that I never believed myself to perceive anything when awake that I could not also believe I perceived when asleep; and as I did not believe that the things that I thought I perceived when asleep proceeded from any objects outside of me, I did not see why I ought any more to have this confidence in respect to those which I thought I perceived when awake; and the second, that not knowing yet, or rather feigning that I did not know, the author of my being, I did not see anything to hinder that I might not have been so made by nature that I might deceive myself even in things which appeared to me the most certain.

And as for the arguments which hitherto persuaded me of the truth of sensible things, I had no great difficulty in answering them; for nature appearing to carry me toward many things from which reason turned me aside, I did not believe I ought to trust very much to the teachings of this nature.

And although the ideas which I received by the senses did not depend upon my will, I did not conclude on that account that they proceeded from things different from myself, since, perhaps, there might be found in me some faculty, although it might be up to the present unknown to me, which was the cause of them, and which produced them. But now that I am beginning to understand myself better, and to discover more clearly the source of my being, I do not think in truth that I ought rashly to admit all the things which the senses appear to teach me, but I do not think also that I ought to call them universally in question.

And in the first place, because I know that all things which I conceive clearly and distinctly may be produced by God such as I conceive them, it is sufficient that I can conceive clearly and distinctly one thing without another, to make it certain that the one is distinct or different from the other, because they might be separated at least by the almighty power of God; and it makes no difference by what power this separation is effected, to make the judgment necessary that they are different; and because, from the fact itself that I know with certainty that I exist, and, nevertheless, I do not observe that there necessarily belongs to my nature or to my essence anything else, but that I am a thing which thinks, I very properly conclude that my essence consists in this alone that I am a thing which thinks, or a substance the whole essence or nature of which is only to think. And although, perhaps, or rather, certainly, as I shall show directly, I may have a body to which I am very closely united; nevertheless, because I have, on the one side, a clear and distinct idea of myself, in so far as I am solely a thing which thinks, and is not extended, and on the other I have a distinct idea of body, in so far as it is solely a thing extended, and which does not think, it is certain that I, that is to say, my soul, by which I am what I am, is entirely and truly distinct from my body, and that it may be, or exist, without it.*

Moreover, I find within me divers faculties of thought, each of which has its peculiar mode ; for example, I find within me the faculties of imagination and perception, without which I can easily conceive myself as a whole clearly and distinctly, but not reciprocally these without myself, that is to say, without an intelligent substance, to which they are attached or to which they belong : because, in the notion which we have of these faculties, or—to make use of the scholastic terms—in their formal concept, they include some sort of intellection ; whence I conclude that they are distinct from me as modes are from things. I am conscious, also, of certain other faculties, as those of locomotion, of assuming various positions, and others similar, which cannot be conceived, any more than the preceding, without some substance to which they are attached, nor consequently exist without it ; but it is very evident that these faculties, if it be true that they exist, must belong to some corporeal or extended substance, and not to an intelligent substance, since in the clear and distinct concept of them there is indeed found contained some sort of extension, but no intelligence whatever.

Moreover, I cannot doubt that there is within me a certain passive faculty of perception—that is to say, of receiving and of recognizing the ideas of sensible things ; but it would be useless to me, and I could not in any way avail myself of it, if there were not also in me, or in some other thing, another active faculty,

---

*Cf. *Princ.*, i, 51-56 (*Œuvres*, t. 3, p. 94, Lat. p. 13). below p. 194, and Geom. proof, Prop. IV., *Œuvres*, t. 3, p. 464. Veitch, p. 273.

capable of forming and producing these ideas. But this active faculty cannot be in me in so far as I am only a thing which thinks, seeing that it does not presuppose my thought, and that these ideas are often represented in me without my contributing to it in any manner, and even often against my desire ; it must, therefore, necessarily be in some substance different from me, in which all the reality, which is objectively in the ideas produced by this faculty, is contained formally or eminently, as I have already observed ; and this substance is either a body, that is to say, a corporeal nature, in which is contained formally and in reality all that is objectively and representatively in the ideas ; or else it is God himself, or some other created thing more noble than the body, in which the body itself is contained eminently.

But, God being no deceiver, it is very manifest that he did not impart these ideas to me immediately from himself, nor even by the medium of some created existence in which their reality was not contained formally, but solely, eminently. For as he has not given me any faculty for knowing what this might be, but, on the contrary, a very strong disposition to believe that they come from corporeal things, I do not see how he could be acquitted of deception if in reality these ideas come from elsewhere, or were produced by any other causes than corporeal things ; and, accordingly, it must be concluded that corporeal things exist.* Nevertheless they are, perhaps, not altogether such as we perceive them by the senses, for there are many things which make this perception of the senses very obscure and confused ; but at least it must be ad-

* Cf. *Princ.*, pt. II, 1, *Œuvres*, t. 3, p. 120. Veitch's *Descartes*, p. 232.

mitted that all things that I conceive clearly and distinctly—that is to say, all things, speaking generally, which are comprised in the field of speculative geometry—actually exist.

But as for other things, which either are merely particular [perceptions] for example, that the sun is of such a size and of such a figure, etc.; or which are less clearly and less distinctly conceived, as light, sound, pain, and the like, it is certain that although they are very doubtful and uncertain, nevertheless, from the fact alone that God is no deceiver, and, consequently, that he did not permit that there should be any falsity in my opinions which he has not also given me some faculty capable of correcting, I believe I may assuredly conclude that I have within me the means of knowing them with certainty.*

And in the first place, there is no doubt that all that nature teaches me contains some truth, for by nature, considered in general, I now understand nothing else than God himself,† or, rather, the order and disposition which God has established in the creation; and by my nature in particular I understand nothing else than the constitution or assemblage of all the things which God has given me. But there is nothing which this nature teaches me more distinctly or more sensibly than that I have a body which is out of order when I feel pain, which has need of food or drink when I have the sensations of hunger, or thirst, etc. And therefore I cannot doubt that there is in this some truth.

* Cf. Kant's *Critique of Pure Reason*, Transcendental Dialectic, Book ii, ch. ii, § 4, Professor Watson's *Selections*, p. 166.

† Deus sive natura—Spinoza. Notice, however, this corrected statement.

Nature teaches me also by these sensations of pain, hunger, thirst, that I am not merely lodged in my body as a pilot in his ship, but, besides, that I am very closely conjoined with it, and so mixed and mingled with it that I compose, as it were, one whole with it. For if it were not so, whenever my body is hurt, I should not on that account feel any pain—I who am only a thing which thinks—but I should perceive this injury by the understanding alone, as a pilot perceives by sight if anything is giving way in his vessel. And when my body needs drink or food, I should be simply aware of this, without being apprised of it by the confused sensations of hunger and thirst; for in reality all these sensations of hunger, thirst, pain, etc., are nothing but certain confused forms of thought which spring from and are dependent upon the union and, as it were, the blending of the mind with the body. Besides this, nature teaches me that many other bodies exist around my own, some of which I have to seek after and others to avoid. And surely, from the fact that I perceive divers sorts of colors, odors, tastes, sounds, warmth, hardness, etc., I readily conclude that there are in the bodies whence these divers perceptions of sense proceed certain changes which correspond to them, although perhaps these changes do not in reality resemble them; and from the fact that, among these divers perceptions of the senses, some of them are agreeable and others disagreeable, there is no doubt that my body, or, rather, my entire self, in so far as I am composed of body and soul, might receive divers benefits or injuries from other bodies which surround me.

But there are many other things which apparently nature has taught me, which nevertheless I did not really learn from her, but which have introduced themselves into my mind through a certain habit I have of judging of things inconsiderately; and so it can easily happen that they contain some falsity; as, for example, the opinion I have that every space, in which there is nothing which moves and makes impression upon my senses, is empty; that in a body which is warm there is anything resembling the idea of warmth which is in me; that in a white or black body there is the same whiteness or blackness which I perceive; that in a bitter or sweet body there is the same taste, or the same flavor, and so of the rest; that stars, towers, and other distant bodies are of the same figure and size as they appear from afar to be to our eyes, etc.

But in order that there may be nothing in this that I do not distinctly conceive, I ought precisely to define what I mean when I say that nature teaches me anything. For I use the term nature here in a more restricted sense than when I called it an assemblage or constitution of all the things which God has given me; seeing that this assemblage or constitution comprises many things which pertain to the mind alone, of which I do not here intend to speak while speaking of nature; as, for example, the notion which I have of this truth, that what has once been done can no longer be as not having been done, and a multitude of others like it, which I know by the natural light without the aid of the body; and that it comprises, also, many others which belong to body alone, and are not here contained under the term nature—as the quality it has of being heavy, and many others similar; of which, also, I do not speak, but solely of the things which

God has given me as being composed of mind and body.

But this nature teaches me, indeed, to avoid the things which cause in me the sensation of pain and carries me toward those which make me have some pleasurable sensation; but I do not see that beyond this it teaches me that, from these divers perceptions of the senses, we ought ever to conclude anything in respect to the things which are external to us, unless the mind has carefully and maturely considered them; for, it seems to me, it pertains to the mind alone, and not to the mind as blended with the body, to know the truth of these things.

Thus, although a star makes no greater impression upon my eye than the flame of a candle, there is, nevertheless, in me no faculty, real or natural, which leads me to believe that it is not greater than this flame, but I have judged it to be so from my earliest years without rational grounds. And although in approaching fire I feel the heat, and also by drawing a little nearer to it I feel pain, there is, nevertheless, no reason which could persuade me that there is anything in the fire resembling this heat, any more than this pain; but, merely, I have reason to believe that there is something in it, whatever it may be, which excites in me these sensations of heat or pain. Likewise, although there may be spaces in which I do not find anything which excites and stirs my senses, I ought not, on that account, to conclude that these spaces contain no bodies within them; but I see that in this, as in many other things similar, I have been in the habit of perverting and confounding the order of nature, because these sensations, or perceptions of the senses, having been put in me merely to indicate to my mind what things are beneficial or harmful to the composite whole of which it is a part, and being for that purpose sufficiently clear and distinct, I have nevertheless made use of them as if they were very certain rules, whereby I might immediately know the essence and the nature of bodies outside of me, concerning which, notwithstanding, they can teach me nothing except very obscurely and confusedly. . . . .

Beginning then this inquiry, I observe in the first place that there is a great difference between the mind and the body, in that the body, from its nature, is always divisible, while the mind is entirely indivisible. For in truth, when I consider it, that is to say, when I consider myself, in so far as I am simply a thing which thinks, I cannot distinguish within me any parts, but I know and conceive very clearly that I am a thing absolutely one and entire. And although the entire mind seems to be united to the entire body, nevertheless, whenever a foot, or an arm, or any other part has been separated from it, I know very well that nothing for that reason has been cut off from my mind. And the faculties of willing, of feeling, of conceiving, etc., can not properly be called its parts ; for it is the same mind which is active as one whole in willing, and as one whole in feeling and in conceiving, etc.

But quite the contrary is the case with things corporeal or extended, for I cannot imagine any one of them, however small it may be, that I could not easily take to pieces in my thought, or that my mind could not readily divide into many parts, and, consequently, that I should not know to be divisible. This is sufficient to teach me that the mind or soul of man is entirely different from the body, if I had not already learned this truth well enough from other sources.

I observe, also, that the mind does not receive immediately impressions from all parts of the body, but solely from the brain, or perhaps even from one of its smallest parts, to wit, from that where it exercises this faculty which it calls the common sense, which, whenever it is disposed in the same way, causes the mind to perceive the same thing, although, nevertheless, the other parts of the body may be differently disposed, as testify a multitude of experiences which there is no need here to recount.

I observe, further, that the nature of the body is such that no one of its parts can be moved by another part a little remote from it, except as it might be moved, in the same way, by each of the parts which are between the two, although the most distant part did not act. As for example, in the cord A B C D, which is completely tense, if one should draw and move the last part, D, the first, A, will not be moved any otherwise than it would be if one of the middle parts, B or C, were drawn, while the last, D, remained unmoved.

In the same way, when I feel pain in the foot physics teaches me that this sensation communicates itself by means of the nerves spread through the foot, which, being stretched like cords from that point up to the brain, whenever they are excited in the foot, excite also at the same time that part of the brain from whence they come and at which they terminate, and cause there a certain motion which nature has instituted for the purpose* of making the pain to be felt by the mind, as if this pain were in the foot ; but because these nerves must pass through the shank, the

---

* Note the admission of final cause, which Descartes excludes from his philosophy. See above, p. 149 n.

thigh, the loins, the back, and the neck, in order to reach from the foot to the brain, it may happen that although their extremities in the foot may not be moved, but merely some of their parts which pass through the loins or the neck, that nevertheless excites the same motions in the brain which would be excited there by a wound received in the foot ; in consequence of which the mind will necessarily feel a pain in the foot just as it would had there been an injury there ; and we must judge the same to be true of all the other perceptions of our senses.

Finally I observe that since each one of the motions which are made in that part of the brain where the mind immediately receives the impression can make it sensible of but a single sensation, nothing better can be desired or imagined than that this motion should cause the mind to feel, among all the sensations which it is capable of causing, that one which is the most suitable and the most commonly useful to the preservation of the human body when it is in full health. But experience teaches us that all the sensations which nature has bestowed upon us are such as I have just described, and accordingly there is nothing to be found in them which would not make manifest the power and the goodness of God. Thus, for example, when the nerves which are in the foot are violently and extraordinarily disturbed, their motion, passing through the spinal marrow to the brain, makes there an impression on the mind which causes it to feel something ; to wit, a pain as being in the foot, whereby the mind is warned and aroused to do its utmost to drive away the cause of it, as being very dangerous and injurious to the foot. It is true that God might have so constituted the nature of man that this same motion in the brain might have caused something quite different to be felt by the mind; for example, that it should have caused it to feel itself, either in so far as it is in the brain, or as it is in the foot, or, indeed, as it is in any place between the foot and the brain, or, finally, something else, whatever it might be, but nothing of all that could so well have contributed to the preservation of the body as that which it does cause it to feel.

Likewise, when we need to drink, there arises therefrom a certain dryness in the throat which sets its nerves in motion, and by means of them the interior parts of the brain; and this motion causes the sensation of thirst to be felt in the mind, because, under those circumstances, there is nothing which can be more useful for us to know than that for the preservation of our health we need to drink; and so of the rest.

Whence it is quite plain that, notwithstanding the sovereign goodness of God, the nature of man, in so far as it is composed of mind and body, cannot but be sometimes misleading and deceptive. For if there is any cause which excites not in the foot, but in some part of the nerve which extends from the foot to the brain, or even within the brain, the same motion which it ordinarily causes when something is the matter with the foot, pain will be felt as if it were in the foot, and the sense will naturally be deceived; because the same motion in the brain being able to cause only the same sensation in the mind, and this sensation being oftener excited by a cause which injures the foot than by another which may be felt elsewhere, it is much more reasonable that it carry to the mind pain of the foot than that of any other part.

And if it happen that sometimes dryness of the throat does not proceed, as ordinarily, from the fact that drink is needed for the health of the body, but from some cause quite opposite, as happens to those who are dropsical, nevertheless it is much better that it deceive in this condition, than it would be if it should deceive always when the body is in health; and so of the rest. And certainly this consideration is of great service to me, not only for recognizing all the errors to which my nature is subject, but, also, for the more easy avoidance or correction of them, because, knowing that all my senses indicate more commonly what is true than what is false in respect to the things which are favorable or unfavorable to the body, and being almost always able to make use of several of them to examine the same thing, and besides that, being able to use my memory to connect present knowledge with past, and my understanding, which has already discovered all the causes of my errors, I ought not henceforward to fear to meet with falsity in the things which are most commonly presented by my senses.

And all the doubts of these past days I ought to reject as absurd and ridiculous, and particularly that uncertainty in general about sleep, and my not being able to distinguish the state of being awake ; for now I find a most notable difference, in that our memory can never bind and join together our dreams one with another, and with the whole course of our life, as it is accustomed to join together the things which happen to us while we are awake. And, in truth, if anyone, when I am awake, should appear all of a sudden and disappear in the same way as do the phantoms which I see when I am asleep, so that I could not tell whence he came or whither he went, it would not be without reason if I thought him a specter or a phantom fashioned within my brain, and like those which are formed there when I am asleep, rather than a real man.

But when I perceive things of which I know distinctly both the place whence they come and where they are, and the time at which they appear to me, and am able, without any break, to connect the perception which I have of them with the remaining course of my life, I am perfectly certain that I perceive them being awake, and not in my sleep, and I ought not in any manner to doubt the truth of these things if, after I have summoned all my senses, my memory, and my understanding, to the examination of them, there is nothing reported to me by any of them which disagrees with what is reported to me by the rest. Because, from the fact that God is no deceiver, it follows necessarily that I am not deceived in this. But because exigency of circumstances often obliges us to decide before we have had the leisure to examine so carefully, it must be admitted that human life is liable to very frequent mistakes in particular instances; and, in fine, the infirmity and weakness of our nature must be confessed.

SELECTIONS
FROM THE PRINCIPLES OF PHILOSO-
PHY, TRANSLATED FROM THE
LATIN: OPERA PHILOSOPHICA,
EDITIO ULTIMA, AMSTELO-
DAMI, APUD DANIE-
LEM ELZEVIRIUM,
MDCLXXVII.

PRINCIPLES OF PHILOSOPHY.

PART FIRST.*

.... There are very many persons who never in their whole life perceive anything so correctly as to warrant a certain judgment upon it. For, in order that a certain and incontestable judgment may be based upon the perception of anything, it is requisite that the perception be not only clear but distinct. I call a perception clear which is present and manifest to an attentive mind; just as we say that those things are clearly seen by us, which, being present to the gazing eye, affect it with sufficient strength and plainness. But I call a perception distinct which, while it is clear, is also so separated and distinguished from all others that it plainly contains nothing but what is clear.

Thus, when anyone feels any great pain, this perception of pain is, indeed, most clear to him, but it is not always distinct, for men usually confound it with an obscure judgment of their own concerning the nature of something in the part affected which they think to be similar to the feeling of the pain which alone they clearly perceive. And thus a perception may be clear which is not distinct, but no perception can be distinct which is not clear.

But, indeed, in our earliest years the mind was so

* §§ 45-70. Translated from the Latin: *Opera Philosophica*, editio ultima, Amstelodami, Apud Danielem Elzevirium, MDCLXXVII.

immersed in the body that although it perceived many things clearly it did not perceive anything distinctly; and as, nevertheless, it formed its judgments concerning many things, we imbibed many prejudices which, in the case of many persons, never afterward have been laid aside. In order that we may be able to free ourselves from these, I will make a complete enumeration of all the simple notions of which our thoughts are composed, and will distinguish what in each is clear and what is obscure, or in what we may err.

Whatever falls under our perceptions we consider as being either things or certain affections of things, or as being eternal truths having no existence beyond our thought. Among those which we consider as things, the most general notions of them are substance, duration, order, number, and any others of this sort which relate to all classes of things. But I recognize only two highest classes [*summa genera*] of things; one is of things intellectual, or having the power of thought, that is, pertaining to mind or the thinking substance; the other of material things, or which pertain to extended substance, that is, to body. Perception, volition, and all modes both of perceiving and of willing, are referred to thinking substance; but to extended substances [are referred] magnitude —or extension in length, breadth, and depth—figure, motion, position, divisibility of parts, and such like. But there are certain other modes also, which we experience in ourselves, which are to be referred neither to the mind alone, nor yet to the body alone, but arise from the close and intimate union of our mind with the body, namely the appetites of hunger, thirst, etc., likewise emotions, or passions of the mind, which consist not in thought alone, as the emotions of anger, joy, sadness, love, etc., and finally, all sensations, as of pain, pleasure, of light and colors, sounds, odors, tastes, heat, hardness, and other tangible qualities.

And all these we consider as things or qualities or modes of things. But when we recognize anything as being impossible, as that something should arise from nothing, then this proposition, *Ex nihilo nihil fit*, is considered not as an existing thing, nor yet as a mode of a thing, but as a certain eternal truth which has its seat in our mind, and is called a common notion, or axiom.* Of this sort are : It is impossible that the same thing should at once be and not be ; Whatever has been done cannot be not done ; He who thinks cannot be non-existent while he thinks ; and innumerable others which, indeed, cannot all be easily enumerated, but neither can they be ignored, whenever the occasion arises that we think of them, and are blinded by no prejudices.

And, indeed, as respects these common notions, there is no doubt but that they can be clearly and distinctly perceived, for otherwise they could not be called common notions ; although it is true that certain of them do not merit that title in regard to all men, because they are not equally perceived by all. Not, however, as I think, because the knowing faculty of one man has wider range than that of another ; but because these common notions happen to be opposed to the pre-formed opinions of some men who, for that reason, cannot easily grasp them ; while others, who are

---

* For a list of such axioms (10 in all) see Geom. proof, Axioms or Common Notions, in Reply to 2d Obj., *Œuvres*, t. i, pp. 458–460 ; Veitch's *Descartes*, p. 270.

free from these prejudices, perceive them most plainly.*

In respect to what we regard either as things or as modes of things, it is worth while to consider each in succession. <u>By substance we can understand nothing else than a thing which so exists that it needs no other thing in order to exist.</u> And, indeed, the substance which evidently needs no other thing can be thought of as being one only, namely, God.† But all others we perceive can exist only by the help of the concourse of God.‡ And therefore the name, substance, cannot belong to God and to them *univocally*, as they say in the schools, that is, no signification of this name can be distinctly understood as common to God and to creatures.

But corporeal substance and mind, or thinking substance, as created, can be comprehended under this common conception, because they are things which require only the concourse of God for their existence. Nevertheless, substance cannot be first known by this alone—that a thing exists; because this by itself alone does not affect us; but we easily recognize it by any one of its attributes, through that common notion that nothing can have no attributes or properties or qualities. For from this, that we perceive some attribute to be present, we conclude some existing thing, or substance, to which that can be attributed, to be necessarily present also.

And indeed, from any attribute whatever, a substance can be recognized; but, nevertheless, there is of

---

* Cf. Hobbes' objection and Descartes' reply (Med. iv, 302), Obj. et Rép., *Œuvres*, i, p. 496. See above, p. 154 n.

† Deus est substantia una et unica—Spinoza.

‡ Occasionalism—Geulincx.

any substance one principal property, which constitutes its nature and essence, and to which all the rest are related ; namely, extension in length, breadth, and depth constitutes the nature of corporeal substance ; and thought constitutes the nature of thinking substance. For everything else which can be attributed to body presupposes extension, and is only a certain mode of an extended thing ; as, also, all that we can discover in mind are only divers modes of thinking. Thus, for example, figure cannot be understood except in an extended thing, nor motion except in a space extended ; nor imagination, nor sense, nor will, except in a thinking thing. But, on the other hand, extension can be understood without figure or motion, and thought without imagination, or sense, and so of the rest ; as is plain to anyone who reflects upon it. And thus we can easily have two clear and distinct notions or ideas, one of created thinking substance, the other of corporeal substance ; if, namely, we distinguish accurately all attributes of thought from attributes of extension. So, also, we can have a clear and distinct idea of a thinking substance uncreated and independent, that is, of God ; only we must not suppose that it adequately represents all that is in God, nor must we introduce anything fictitious, but simply attend to what in truth is contained in it, and what we plainly perceive to belong to the nature of a being supremely perfect. And surely no one can deny that such an idea of God exists within us, unless he thinks that there is no knowledge of God whatever in human minds.

Duration, order, and number are also most distinctly known by us, provided we assign to them no conception of substance, but think the duration of anything to be merely a mode under which we conceive this thing, in so far as it continues to exist. And in a similar way we are to conceive of order and number as not being anything distinct from things ordered and numbered, but as being merely modes under which we consider them.

And, indeed, here we are to understand by modes what elsewhere we mean by attributes or qualities. But when we consider substance to be affected or changed by them, we call them modes; and again, when we consider them more generally, as simply existing in substance, we call them attributes. Therefore we say that, properly speaking, there are in God no modes or qualities, but attributes only, because no variation is known in him.* And also, in created things, those characters which are not subject to change, such as existence and duration, in a thing existing and enduring, should not be called qualities or modes, but attributes.

But some of these are in things themselves, of which they are said to be attributes or modes; others in our thought only. Thus, when we distinguish time from duration taken generally, and say that it is the number of motion, it is merely a mode of our thought; nor do we know, indeed, any other duration in motion than in things not moved; as is evident from this, that, if two bodies are moved, one slowly, the other swiftly, for an hour, we count no more time in one than in the other, although there is much more motion. But in order to measure the duration of all things, we compare it with the duration of those greatest and in the highest degree equable motions by which the years and days arise; and this duration

* Cf. Spinoza's views of attribute and mode. See above, p. 29

we call time, which, accordingly, is nothing superadded to duration taken generally, but a mode of thought.*

So also number, when considered not in any created things, but only in the abstract or in kind, is a mode of thought only; so are all other notions which we call universals.

These universals arise from this, merely, that we use one and the same idea in thinking of all the individuals which are similar among themselves; as also we impose one and the same name upon all the things represented by this idea, which name is a universal. Thus, when we see two stones, and do not attend to their nature, but to this only that they are two, we form an idea of that number which we call the binary; and when afterward we see two birds or two trees, and do not consider their nature, but only that they are two, we repeat the same idea as before, which, accordingly, is a universal, and we call this number by the same universal name, binary. In the same manner, when we consider a figure bounded by three lines, we form a certain idea of it, which we call triangle; and we use this afterward as a universal to represent to our mind all other figures bounded by three lines. And when we observe among triangles that some have one right angle and others have not, we form a universal idea of right-angled triangles, which, being related to the preceding as more general, is called a species; and this character of being right-angled is the universal difference by which all right-angled triangles are distinguished from others; and that in these the square of the base is equal to the square of the sides is a property belonging to all of

---

* See above, p. 34.

them, and to them only; and finally, if we suppose some triangles of this sort to be in motion, and others not to be moved, this will be in them a universal accident. And in this way there are commonly reckoned five universals, genus, species, difference, property, and accident.

But number arises in things themselves from distinction in regard to them, which distinction is threefold : real, modal, and logical. The real properly exists only between two or more substances, and these we perceive to be really mutually distinct in themselves by this alone, that we are able to know one from the other clearly and distinctly. For, knowing God, we are certain that he can bring to pass whatever we distinctly know, so that, for example, from this alone, that we have the idea of extended or corporeal substance, although we do not yet certainly know that any such substance really exists, nevertheless we are certain that it can exist, and, if it exist, every part of it distinguished by us in thought is in reality distinct from the other parts of the same substance. Likewise, from this alone, that each one of us knows himself to be a thinking thing, and is able in thought to exclude from himself every other substance, both thinking and extended, it is certain that everyone, so regarded, is really distinct from every other thinking substance, and from every corporeal substance. And even if we suppose that God has joined in the closest manner possible to such a thinking substance a certain corporeal substance, and so from these two has produced one, they nevertheless remain really distinct; because, however closely he may have united them, he cannot dispossess himself of the power which he had before of separating them, or of preserving one without the other ; and whatever substances either can be separated by God, or preserved independently, are really distinct.

Modal distinction is twofold ; the one between mode properly so called, and the substance of which it is the mode ; the other between two modes of the same substance. The former is known by this, that we can clearly perceive a substance indeed without a mode, which we say is distinct from it, but we cannot, *vice versa*, comprehend that mode without the substance. So figure and motion are distinguished modally from corporeal substance, to which they belong ; so also an affirmation and a recollection, from the mind. But the latter is known from this, that we can indeed apprehend one motion apart from another, and *vice versa*, but neither apart from the substance to which they belong ; as, if a stone be moved, and be square, I can, indeed, apprehend its square figure without its motion ; and, *vice versa*, its motion without its square figure ; but neither that motion nor that square figure can I apprehend without the substance of the stone. But the distinction whereby the mode of one substance differs from another substance, or from a mode of another substance, as the motion of one body from another body, or from the mind, and motion from doubt, would seem to be properly called real rather than modal, because those modes are not clearly known apart from substances really distinct, of which they are modes.

Finally, distinction of reason exists between substance and any attribute of it without which the substance itself cannot be known ; or between two such attributes of the same substance. And it is recognized by this, that we cannot form a clear and distinct idea of the substance itself if we exclude from it that attribute; or that we cannot clearly apprehend the idea of one of its attributes if we separate that one from another. Inasmuch as any substance whatever, if it cease to endure, ceases also to exist, it is distinguished from its own duration by intellect only. And all modes of thinking, which we regard as if they were in objects, differ only for the intellect, now from the objects concerning which they are thought, and now from one another in one and the same object. I remember, indeed, that I have elsewhere conjoined this sort of distinction with the modal; namely, at the end of the Reply to the First Objections in the Meditations on the First Philosophy; but in that case there was no occasion for accurate distinction of them, and it was sufficient to my purpose to distinguish both from the real.

Thought and extension may be regarded as constituting the nature of substance, intelligent and corporeal; and accordingly they should not be otherwise conceived than as the thinking substance itself and the corporeal substance, that is, as mind and body; thus we know them most clearly and most distinctly. Moreover, we know extended substance or thinking substance more easily than substance alone, abstracting the quality that it thinks or is extended. For there is some difficulty in abstracting the notion of substance from the notions of thought and extension, which, indeed, are diverse from it only by this very reason; * and a conception does not become more distinct, because we comprehend in it fewer things, but only because the things which we do com-

---

* Namely, that we thus mentally abstract them from substance; in reality they are inseparable from substance.

prehend in it we distinguish accurately from all the rest.

Thought and extension may be taken as modes of substance in so far, indeed, as one and the same mind may have many different thoughts; and one and the same body, while retaining the same magnitude, may be extended in many different modes; now more in length, and less in breadth or depth, and again, on the contrary, more in breadth and less in length. And then they are distinguished modally from substance, and may be known not less clearly and distinctly than [substance] itself; only they are not to be regarded as substances, or things separate from others, but solely as modes of things. For it is by considering them as being in the substances of which they are the modes, that we distinguish them from those substances and know them as they really are. But, on the contrary, if we choose to consider them as existing apart from the substances in which they inhere, by this very fact we regard them as things subsistent [by themselves] and thus confound the ideas of mode and substance.

In the same way we shall best understand the different modes of thought, such as intellection, imagination, memory, will, etc., and also the different modes of extension, or, as belonging to extension, all figures, and positions of parts, and motions of these, if only we regard them as modes of the things in which they inhere; and, as respects motion, [we shall best unstand it] if we consider none but local motion and force, if we do not inquire what excites it (which, however, I shall attempt to explain in its proper place).

There remain the senses, the affections, the appetites, which also can be clearly understood if we carefully avoid passing any judgment upon them except in regard to precisely that which is contained in our perception and of which we are inwardly conscious. But this precaution it is very difficult to exercise, at least in regard to the senses, because there is no one of us who has not from infancy judged that all those things which he perceives are things existing outside his mind and quite similar to his sensations, that is to say, to the perceptions which he has of them; so that when, for example, we see a color, we think we see something situated outside of us and quite similar to that idea of color of which we then have experience within ourselves; and, on account of our habit of so judging, we seem to see this so clearly and distinctly that we hold it certainly and undoubtedly true.

The same thing is evident in respect to all other sensations, even of pleasure and pain. For although these are not thought to be outside of us: neither yet are they wont to be regarded as in the mind alone, or in our perception, but as in the hand, or in the foot, or in some other part of our body. Nor, indeed, is it more certain when, for example, we perceive a pain as if in the foot, that this is something existing outside our mind in the foot, than, when we see light as if in the sun, that this light exists outside of us in the sun; but both these are prejudices of our early years, as shall clearly be made apparent below.

But in order that we may distinguish at this point what is clear from what is obscure, it is most carefully to be noted that pain, indeed, and color, and other [qualities] of this kind are clearly and distinctly understood, provided only they are regarded as affections of sense or as thoughts; but when they are judged to be things existing outside our minds, we are able in no way to understand what sort of things they are, and it is just the same when anyone says that he sees in any body a color, or feels in any member a pain, as if he should say that he sees or feels there something of which he is quite ignorant, that is, that he does not know what he sees or feels. For although, if he attend but little, he may easily persuade himself that he has some notion of it, from the fact that he supposes it to be something similar to that sensation of color or of pain which he experiences within himself, yet if he examine into the nature of that which this sensation of color or of pain represents to him as being in a colored body, or as existing in the part affected, he will find that he knows nothing at all about it.

[This will be apparent] if he considers that he knows in a manner entirely different the nature of magnitude in a visible body, or of figure, or motion (at least of motion from place to place; for philosophers who feign that there are other forms of motion different from this have shown that they little understood the nature of this), or position, or duration, or number, and the like, which it has just been said are clearly perceived in bodies; [that he knows these in a manner entirely different from that] in which he knows what in the same body color is, or pain, or smell, or taste, or any of those [qualities] which are said to be referred to the senses. For although in seeing any body we are not more certain that it exists in so far as it appears as having figure than as it appears colored; yet we know far more clearly what it is as having figure than what it is as colored.

Manifestly, therefore, when we say that we perceive colors in objects, it is in reality the same as saying that we perceive something in objects, the nature of which we do not know, but something by which there is produced in us a certain very clear and vivid sensation which is called a sensation of color. But in the mode of our judging there is a very great difference, for so long that we judge only that there is something in objects (that is, in things, whatever they may be, from which the sensation comes to us) of which something we are indeed ignorant, we are so far from falling into error that on the other hand we avoid it, in that by admonishing ourselves that we are ignorant of this something we are the less prone to judge rashly concerning it.

But when we think we perceive colors in objects, although, indeed, we are ignorant what that may be, which we then call by the name of color, nor are able to recognize any similarity between the color which we suppose to be in objects and that which we experience in the sense, nevertheless, because we do not pay attention to this fact, and there are many other things, such as magnitude, figure, number, etc., which we clearly perceive to be felt or understood by us not otherwise than as they are, or, at least, may be, in objects, we easily lapse into this error, that we judge that that which in objects we call color is altogether like the color which we have in sensation, and so that what we in no manner perceive we think we clearly perceive. . . . .

THE WORLD;
OR, ESSAY ON LIGHT.

THE WORLD; OR, ESSAY ON LIGHT.*

CHAPTER I.

Of the difference between our sensations and the things which produce them.

PROPOSING, as I do, to treat of the nature of light, the first thing of which I wish you to take note is, that there may be a difference between the sensation which we have in ourselves, that is to say, the idea which is formed within our imagination by the help of our eyes, and that which exists in the objects that produce within us the sensation, namely, that which exists in the flame, or in the sun, and is called by the name of light; because, although everyone is commonly persuaded that the ideas that we have in our thought are altogether similar to the objects whence they proceed, I see no reason, nevertheless, to assure us that this is true; but, on the contrary, I observe many facts which should incline us to question it.

You know that words, while having no resemblance to the things which they signify, do not fail to make them intelligible to us, and often, even without our paying attention to the sound of the words, or to their syllables; so that it may happen that after having listened to a discourse, the meaning of which we have

---

* This is a fragment of the Treatise referred to in the Discourse on Method as having been suppressed by the author. See *Œuvres*, t. i, p. 168, Veitch's *Descartes*, p. 42; and above, pp. 10-12.

completely understood, we are not able to say in what language it was spoken. But if words, which signify nothing except by human institution, are capable of making conceivable for us things to which they have no resemblance, why may not nature also have established a certain sign which should make us feel the sensation of light, although this sign should have nothing in itself resembling sensation? Has she not thus appointed laughter and tears to make us read joy and sadness in the human countenance?

But you will say, perhaps, that our ears make us perceive in reality merely the sound of the words, and our eyes only the face of him who laughs or who weeps, and that it is our mind, which, having retained what these words and this countenance signify, represents it to us at the same time. To that I may reply that, just in the same way, it is our mind which represents to us the idea of light whenever the action which signifies it touches our eye; but, without wasting time in dispute, I will at once bring forward another illustration.

Do you think that when we pay no attention to the meaning of words, and only hear the sound of them, that the idea of this sound, which is formed within our thought, is anything like the object which is the cause of it? A man opens his mouth, moves his tongue, expels his breath; I see nothing in all these motions which is not quite different from the idea of the sound which they cause us to imagine. And most philosophers assure us that the sound is nothing but a certain trembling of the air which has just struck our ears; so that, if the sense of hearing brought to our thought the true image of its object, it would be necessary, in place of making us conceive the sound, that it should make us conceive the motion of the portions of the air which is trembling at the time against our ears. But because, perhaps, everybody will not believe what the philosophers say, I will adduce still another example. Touch is the one of all the senses which we consider the least deceptive and the most trustworthy ; so that, if I prove to you that even touch makes us conceive many ideas which do not at all resemble the objects which produce them, I do not think you ought to consider it strange if I say that sight may do the same.

But there is no one who does not know that the ideas of pleasure and of pain which are formed within our thought on occasion of bodies touching us externally have no resemblance to them. A person gently passes a feather over the lips of a child asleep, and he perceives the tickling; do you suppose that the idea of the tickling which he conceives has any resemblance to anything there is in the feather? A soldier returns from a fight; during the heat of the combat he might have been wounded without perceiving it, but now that he begins to cool off he feels pain, he thinks he has been wounded; a surgeon is called, his uniform is stripped off, he is examined, and at last it is found that what he felt was nothing but a buckle or a strap, which, being twisted underneath his uniform, pressed upon him and hurt him. If his sense of touch, while making him feel the strap, had impressed the image of it on his thought, he would not have needed a surgeon to tell him what he felt.

But I see no reason which obliges us to think that what is in the objects from which the sensation of light comes to us is any more like that sensation than the action of a feather and a buckle is like the tickling and the pain ; and yet I have not adduced these examples in order to make you believe absolutely that this light is something different in the objects from what it is in our eyes, but simply that you may question it, and that, being on your guard against a prejudice to the contrary, you may now the better inquire with me into the true state of the case.

CHAPTER II.

In what the heat and light of a fire consist.

I KNOW only two kinds of bodies in the universe in which light is found, namely, the stars, and flame or fire ; and because the stars are without question further removed from the knowledge of men than fire or flame is, I will attempt to explain in the first place what I observe in respect to flame. When it burns wood or any similar material, we can see at a glance that it removes small particles of this wood, and separates them one from another, transforming thus the finer parts into fire, into vapor and smoke, and leaving the grosser parts as ashes. Anyone else, if he pleases, may imagine in this wood the form of fire, the quality of heat, and the energy which burns it, as all different things ; as for me, who am afraid of deceiving myself if I suppose anything more to be there than what I see must necessarily be present, for my part, I am content with conceiving there the movement of its parts : because, put the fire there, put the heat there, and make it burn as much as you please, if you do not suppose, along with that, that there are some of its parts in motion, and that they detach themselves from their neighbors, I cannot imagine that it receives any alteration or change ; and, on the contrary, remove the fire, remove the heat, prevent it from burning, provided only that you grant me that there is some power which sets in violent motion its minutest parts, and which separates them from the grosser parts, I find that that by itself could effect in it all the changes which take place when it burns.

But, inasmuch as it does not seem to me possible to conceive that one body can move another, unless it is also in motion itself, I conclude from this that the body of flame, which acts upon the wood, is composed of small parts which are in motion separately one from another, with a motion very rapid and very violent, and which, thus moving themselves, push and move with themselves the parts of the bodies which they touch, and which do not offer them too great resistance. I say that the parts move separately one from another, because, although they often accord and conspire, many together, to produce a single effect, we see nevertheless that each of them acts in its own particular way upon the bodies which they touch. I say, also, that their motion is very rapid and very violent; because, being too small for sight to distinguish, they would not have the force they do for acting on other bodies, if the rapidity of their motion did not make up for the want of its extent.

I add nothing in respect to the direction which each part takes; for if you consider that the power of moving itself, and that which determines the direction which the movement shall take, are two entirely different things, one of which might exist without the other (as I have explained in the second discourse of the Dioptrics*), you will readily decide that each moves in the way that is made the least difficult to it by the disposition of the bodies which surround it, and that in the same flame there may be parts which would move up and others down, in a straight line and in a curve, and in all directions, without thereby changing its nature at all; so that, if you see almost

* Œuvres, t. 5, p. 17, et seq.

all of them tending upward, it need not be supposed that this happens so for any other reason than that the other bodies which touch them are almost in every case disposed to offer them more resistance on every other side.

But having taken note that the parts of the flame move in this manner, and that it is sufficient to conceive its motions in order to comprehend how it has the power to consume wood and to burn, let us inquire, pray, whether the same [conception] will not enable us also to comprehend how it warms us and how it illuminates us: for, if this should prove to be the case, it will not be necessary that there should exist in it any other quality, and we can say that it is this motion alone which, according to the different effects which it produces, is called now heat and now light.

But as concerns the nature of heat, the sensation which we have of it may, as it seems to me, be regarded as a kind of pain when it is violent, and sometimes as a kind of pleasure when it is moderate; and as we have said before that there is nothing external to our thought which is like the ideas that we conceive of pleasure and pain, we can easily believe also that there is nothing like that which we conceive of as heat, but that whatever can put in motion in divers ways the minute particles of our hands, or any other portion of our body, may excite in us this sensation. Many things which we experience also favor this view; for, in simply rubbing the hands, they become warm, and every other body also may be made warm without putting it before the fire, provided only it be moved and shaken so that many of its minute particles are set in motion, and along with them those of our hands.

As for what light is, it can easily be conceived that the same motion which exists in the flame may be sufficient to enable us to perceive it; but inasmuch as it is in this that the principal part of my design consists, I wish to attempt to explain it at length, and to carry on my discourse further.

CHAPTER III.

Of solids and fluids.

I CONSIDER that there is an infinity of different motions which are perpetually going on in the universe, and after having observed the greater, which make the days, the months, and the years, I take note that the vapors of the earth do not cease to rise toward the clouds and to descend from them, that the air is always moved by the winds, that the sea is never at rest, that the springs and the rivers flow without ceasing, that the firmest buildings fall at last in decay, that plants and animals do nothing but grow up and perish; in short, that there is nothing anywhere which does not change. Whence I certainly know that it is not in flame only that there is a multitude of minute particles in incessant motion, but that they exist also in all other bodies, although their actions are not so violent, and, because of their minuteness, they cannot be perceived by any of our senses.

I am not going to stop to inquire into the cause of their movements, because it is sufficient for my purpose to suppose that they began to be in motion as soon as the world began to exist, and, this being so, I find by my reasonings that it is impossible that their movements should ever cease, nor even change otherwise than in the subject of them; that is to say, that the virtue or power of moving itself, which exists in a body, may indeed pass, either wholly or in part, into another, and thus no longer exist in the first, but that it cannot be no longer at all in the world. My reasonings, I say, satisfy my own mind with regard to this, but there is no need that I state them to you at present; and still, if you please, you may imagine, as do the majority of the learned, that there is some *primum mobile* which, revolving about the world with inconceivable velocity, is the origin and source of all other movements which occur in it.

Now, in accordance with this view, there is afforded an explanation of the cause of all the changes which happen in the universe, and of all the varied phenomena which appear upon the earth; but I shall here content myself with speaking of those which relate to my subject.

The difference which exists between hard bodies and those which are liquid is the first that I desire you to observe; and, to this end, suppose that every body be divisible into parts extremely small. I do not wish to decide whether the number of them is infinite or not; but it is certain, at least in relation to our knowledge, that the number is indefinitely great, and that we may suppose that there are many millions in the smallest grain of sand which can be perceived by our eyes. And observe, that if two of these minute parts touch each other without being in action, in order to remove them the one from the other, some force, however slight, is necessary to separate them; for when once they are so situated they will never think of arranging themselves otherwise. Observe, also, that twice as much force is necessary to separate two of them as to separate one, and a thousand times as much to separate a thousand; so that if many millions are to be separated all at once—as, perhaps, might be necessary to be done in order to break a single hair—it is no wonder if there is needed a force great enough to be appreciable by the senses.

On the other hand, if two or more of these minute particles touch only in passing and while they are in motion, the one in one direction, the other in another, it is certain that there will be required less force to separate them than if they were entirely motionless; and even none at all, if the motion with which they tend of themselves to separate is equal to or greater than that with which one seeks to separate them. Now I find no other difference between solid and liquid bodies save that the particles of the one can be separated from the mass much more easily than those of the other. So that, to constitute the hardest body imaginable, I hold that it is enough that all its parts touch, without there remaining any space between them, and without any of them having a tendency to move, for what glue or what cement could be imagined besides that, which could make them better hold together?

I suppose, also, that it is enough to constitute the most liquid body which could be found, that all its most minute particles should be moving in the most various directions from one another and with the utmost possible velocity, although at the same time they do not lose the power of touching one another on every side and of occupying as little space as if they were motionless. In fine, I believe that every body approaches more or less these two extremes, in proportion as its particles have more or less the tendency to withdraw from one another; and all the phenomena upon which I cast my eyes confirm me in this opinion.

Flame, of which I have already said that all its particles are in perpetual motion, is not only liquid, but it also liquefies most other bodies. And observe that when it melts metals it acts with no other power than when it burns wood; but because the particles of metals are a little more nearly equal, it cannot separate one without another, and thus make of them bodies entirely liquid, whereas the particles of wood are so unequal that it can separate the smallest particles and liquefy them; that is to say make them fly off in smoke, without thus moving the grosser ones.

Next to flame there is nothing more liquid than air; and one may see at a glance that its particles move separately one from another; for, if you will condescend to notice those minute particles which are commonly called motes, and which appear in sunbeams, you will see, even if there is no wind moving them, that they are incessantly flying hither and thither in a thousand different directions. The same thing can be shown in all the grosser liquids, if they are mixed of divers colors the one with the other, so as better to distinguish their movements. And finally, this appears very clearly in strong acids, when they move and separate particles of any metal.

But you may ask me at this point why, if it is the motion only of the flame which makes it burn and be liquid, the motion of the particles of the air, which renders it also extremely liquid, does not impart to it just the same power to burn, but, on the contrary, makes it almost imperceptible to our hands. To which I reply that it is necessary not only to take account of the swiftness of the motion, but also of the size of the particles, and that those are the smallest which constitute the most liquid bodies, but those are the largest which have the greatest power to burn, and, in general, to act on other bodies.

Observe, in passing, that I mean here, and that I shall always mean hereafter, by a single particle, all that is joined together and which has no tendency to separate itself, although those which have very little magnitude might easily be divided into many others still smaller; thus, a grain of sand, a stone, a rock, the whole earth even, will be taken hereafter as a single particle, in so far as we shall consider therein only a motion entirely simple and uniform.

Now, between the particles of the air, if there are any of them very large in comparison to the rest, as are these motes which are seen in it, they move also more slowly, and if there are any which move more swiftly, they are also smaller; but between the parts of a flame, if there are any which are smaller than those in the air, there are also greater ones, or at least there is a greater number of those which are equal to the greatest in the air, which at the same time move much more swiftly, and it is only these last which have power to burn. That it has smaller ones may be conjectured from the fact that they penetrate through many bodies the pores of which are so small that the air even cannot enter them; that it has greater, or at least the large ones in greater number, is evident from this, that the air alone is not sufficient to support it; that they move more rapidly the violence of their action sufficiently attests; and finally, that it is the largest of these particles which have the power to burn, and not the others, appears in this, that the flame which comes from brandy or other highly rarefied substances scarcely burns at all, and on the other hand that which proceeds from hard and heavy substances is very hot.

CHAPTER IV.

Of vacuum;* and how it happens that our senses do not perceive certain substances.

BUT we must inquire more particularly why the air, being a substance as well as others, cannot as well be perceived as they, and by this means deliver ourselves from an error which has held possession of our minds from infancy, since we have believed that there are no other bodies about us than those which can be perceived, and, accordingly, that although the air be a substance, because we perceive it slightly, it cannot, at any rate, be so material or so solid as those which we perceive more sensibly.

In regard to which I desire first that you observe that all bodies, solid as well as liquid, are composed of one and the same matter, and that it is impossible to conceive that the particles of this matter ever compose a substance more solid, or which occupies less space, than those do where each one of them is touched on all sides by those which environ it; whence it follows, as it seems to me, that if there is a vacuum anywhere, it must rather be in solid than in liquid bodies; for it is evident that the particles of these latter may be more easily compressed and brought to bear upon one another, because they are in motion, than would be possible in the case of those of others which are motionless.

**Princ.*, pt. ii, 16, 17, 18 (*Œuvres*, t. 3, p. 133, *seq.*); Veitch's *Descartes*, p. 241.

For example, if you put a powdered substance into a vase, you shake the vase and strike it, in order to get in more; but if you pour into it any liquid, it immediately takes up as little space as it can be made to occupy. And, also, if you consider in this relation some of the experiments which philosophers are wont to make use of in order to show that there is no void in nature, you will easily see that all those spaces which people think are empty, and where they perceive nothing but air, are at least as full, and filled with the same matter, as those where they perceive other bodies.

For, tell me, pray, what likelihood there is that nature would make the heavier bodies rise and the harder ones break, as we find that she does in certain machines, rather than suffer that any of their parts should fail to be in contact with each other, or with some other bodies; and that, nevertheless, she should permit the particles of the air, which are so ready to yield and to dispose themselves in every way, to remain, some next others without being in contact on all sides, or without there being any body between them which they could touch? Is it easy to believe that the water in a well would rise upward, contrary to its natural inclination, merely that the tube of a pump might be filled, and to suppose that the water in the clouds should not descend to fill the spaces below, if there were never so little void between the particles of the bodies which they contain?

But you might here present a difficulty of considerable weight, namely, that the particles which compose liquid bodies cannot, apparently, be in incessant motion, as I have said they were, if there do not exist empty space between them, at least in the places from which they start, in proportion to the distance which they move. I should have some trouble in meeting this objection had I not satisfied myself, by various experiments, that all the motions which take place on the earth are of a circular form; that is to say, that when a body quits its place, it always enters that of another, and that one into that of another, and so on up to the last, which takes, at the same instant, the place left by the first, so that there exists a void between them no more when they are in motion than when they are at rest. And notice here that it is not on this account necessary that all the particles of a body which are in motion together should be exactly arranged in a round line in the form of a true circle, nor even that they should be of the same size and figure; for these inequalities may easily be compensated by other inequalities in their velocity.

Now we do not ordinarily notice these circular movements when bodies are moving in the air, because we are accustomed to conceive the air only as an empty space; but watch the fish swimming in the basin of a fountain; if they do not come too near the surface of the water they do not disturb it at all, although they pass beneath it with very great swiftness; whence it manifestly appears that the water which they push before them does not push indiscriminately all the water of the basin, but only that which can best serve to complete the circle of their movement and re-enter into the place which they leave behind. And this example is enough to show how easy and familiar to nature these circular movements are; but I will now adduce another, to show that there is never any other than a circular movement. When the wine in a cask does not flow out at the opening below, because the one above is closed, it is incorrect to say, as is commonly said, that this is due to the "horror of a vacuum." It is well understood that the wine has no mind whereby it can fear anything ; and if it had, I do not see what occasion it would have to fear that vacuum, which is really nothing but a chimera ; but it must be said rather that it cannot pass out of the cask because the outside is as full as it can be, and that the portion of the air, the place of which it would occupy if it should descend, could find no other where to bestow itself in all the rest of the universe, unless an opening were made at the top of the cask, by which this air might remount in a circle to the place left.

As for the rest, I will not affirm that there is no void at all in nature ; I fear my discourse would run on too long if I should undertake to explain what there is of void ; and the facts I have just mentioned are not sufficient to prove it, although they are sufficient to convince us that the spaces where we perceive nothing are filled with the same matter, and contain at least as much of this matter as those which are occupied with bodies which we perceive ; so that, when a vase, for example, is full of gold or lead, it does not, on that account, contain more matter than when we think it is empty. This may seem very strange to many whose mind does not reach beyond their fingers, and who think there is nothing at all except what they touch.

But when you shall have taken into consideration what it is that makes us perceive a body or not perceive it, I am sure you will not find anything incredible in this, for you will clearly understand that, so far from it being true that all the things which are about us are perceptible, on the contrary it is those which are most commonly present which are the least so, and those which are always present are never perceptible.

The heat of the heart is very great, but we do not perceive it, because it is uniform; the weight of the body is not small, but it does not inconvenience us; we do not notice even that of our garments, because we are accustomed to wear them; and the reason for this is clear enough, for it is certain that we cannot perceive any body unless it cause some change in the organs of our senses; that is to say, unless it set in motion in some way the minute particles of matter of which these organs are composed; which objects that are not always present may easily do, provided they have sufficient force; for if they consume something in their action, nature can repair this afterward, when they are no longer acting; but as for those substances with which we are continually in contact, if they have never had the power to produce any change in our senses, and to set in motion any particles of their matter, it may be they have so powerfully excited them at the beginning of our existence as to disunite them entirely from the rest, and so they may have left there only those which entirely resist their action, and by means of which they could not in any way be perceived; whence you see that is no marvel that there should be many spaces around us where we do not perceive any substance, although they may contain no fewer than those where we perceive many.

But it is not necessary on that account to suppose that this grosser air, which we draw into our lungs in breathing, which becomes wind when set in motion, which appears hard to us when confined in a balloon, and which is composed only of exhalations and vapors, is as solid as water or the earth. We must follow in this the common opinion of philosophers, all of whom assure us that it is more rare. And this is easily ascertained by experience, for the particles of a drop of water being separated from one another by the agitation of heat can make much more of this air than the space where the water was could contain; whence it certainly follows that there is a great number of minute interspaces between the particles of which it is composed; for there is no way of conceiving, otherwise, a rare body. But because these interspaces cannot be empty, as I have said above, I conclude from all this that there are of necessity some other bodies, one or many, mixed with this air, which fill as completely as possible the minute interspaces which exist between its particles. There now remains only to consider what these other bodies may be, and after that I hope it will not be difficult to comprehend the probable nature of light.

CHAPTER V.

Of the number of elements and their qualities.

PHILOSOPHERS assure us that there is, above the clouds, a certain air far more rare than ours, and which is not composed of vapors of the earth, as this is, but constitutes an element by itself. They say, also, that above this air there is still another substance yet more rare, which they call the element of fire. They add further that these two elements are mingled with the water, the air, and the earth in the composition of all inferior bodies; so that I only follow their opinion if I say that this more subtle air and this element of fire fill the interspaces which are between the particles of the grosser air which we breathe, so that these substances, intermixed with one another, compose a mass which is as solid as any substance can be.

But in order that I may make you better understand my thought upon this subject, and that you may not suppose that I would have you believe all that philosophers tell us about the elements, I must describe them to you in my own way.

I conceive the first, which may be called the element of fire, as a liquid the most subtle and penetrating in the universe; and, in accordance with what has been said above concerning the nature of liquid bodies, I imagine its particles much smaller and as moving much more swiftly than those of other bodies; or rather, in order not to be compelled to admit any vacuum in nature, I do not attribute to it particles having any size or determinate figure, but I am persuaded that the impetuosity of its movement is sufficient to cause it to be divided in every form and manner on meeting with other bodies, and that its particles change their form at every instant to accommodate themselves to the spaces which they enter, so that there is never a passage so narrow, nor any angle so small, between the particles of other bodies, where those of this element cannot penetrate without difficulty, and which they cannot fill completely.

As for the second, which may be taken for the element of air, I conceive it, indeed, also, as a very rare liquid, when compared with the third : but, when compared with the first, it is necessary to attribute some magnitude and some figure to each of its particles, and to imagine them almost entirely round and joined together, like grains of sand and dust; so that they cannot so easily come in contact nor press so much against one another but that there always remain about them many small interstices, into which it is the easier for the first element to glide, because they have to undergo no change of form in order exactly to fill them. And so I am persuaded that this second element cannot be so pure in any part of the universe that it has not always in it some small part of the matter of the first.

Besides these two elements I recognize only a third, namely that of earth, the particles of which I suppose to be as much larger and as moving with as much less rapidity in comparison to those of the second, as the latter do in comparison with those of the first; and, also, I think it sufficient to conceive it as one or as many great masses, the parts of which have very little or no motion whatever, which should make them change their position with respect to one another.

If you are surprised that, for the explanation of these elements, I make no use of the qualities called heat, cold, moisture, dryness, as do the philosophers, I will inform you that these qualities appear to me to need explanation themselves, and that, if I am not mistaken, not only these four qualities, but also all the rest, and, indeed, all the forms of inanimate bodies, can be explained without the necessity of supposing for this purpose anything else in their matter than the motion, size, figure, and arrangement of these particles; accordingly, I can easily make you understand why I accept no other elements than those I have described; for the difference which would exist between them and the bodies which philosophers call mixed, or mingled, and composite, consists in this, that the forms of those composite bodies always contain in themselves some qualities which are hostile and harmful, or, at least, which do not tend to mutual preservation; whereas the forms of elements should be simple and have no qualities which do not perfectly agree together—so perfectly that each should tend to the preservation of all the rest. Examine, as much as you please, all the forms which the various motions, the various figures, and sizes, and the different arrangement of the particles of matter can impart to composite bodies, and I assure you that you will not find one which has not in it qualities which cause it to change, and which, in changing, would reduce itself to some one of those of the elements.

As for example, flame—the form of which requires it to have particles which move very swiftly and which, at the same time, must have some magnitude, as has been said above—cannot exist long without consuming itself; for either the magnitude of its particles, imparting to them energy of action upon other substances, will cause their motion to be diminished, or the violence of their motion, shattering them when they clash against other substances, will cause them some loss of magnitude; and, in this way, they might, little by little, be reduced to the form of the third element, or to that of the second, and even, also, some of them to that of the first. And thereby you may understand the difference between this flame, or common fire, as we know it, and the element of fire which I have described. And you should also know that the elements of air and of earth, that is to say the second and third elements, are not more similar to the grosser air which we breathe and this earth upon which we walk; but that, in general, all the substances which exist about us are mixed or composite, and subject to decay.

And yet it must not be supposed on that account that the elements have no places in the universe particularly assigned to them, and where they can perpetually preserve themselves in their native purity; but, on the contrary, since each particle of matter tends always to reduce itself to some one of its forms, and, once being reduced thereto, it never tends to leave it, although indeed God might have created at the beginning only composite bodies; nevertheless, during the time the universe has existed, all bodies have had sufficient time to leave their own forms and take those of the elements; so that now there is great probability that all bodies, which are large enough to be reckoned among the more important parts of the universe, have each of them only the quite simple form of one of the elements, and that composite substances exist nowhere else than upon the surfaces of these great bodies : but they must necessarily exist there ; for, the elements being hostile by nature, two of them cannot come into contact without each acting upon the surface of the other, and thus imparting to the matter which is there the different forms of composite substances.

In reference to which, if we consider, in general, all the bodies of which the universe is composed, we shall find only three kinds which can be called great and be reckoned among its principal portions : that is to say, the sun and fixed stars for the first, the heavens for the second, and the earth, with the planets and the comets, for the third ; we have, therefore, good reason for thinking that the sun and fixed stars have no other form than that of the first element quite pure ; the heavens, that of the second ; and the earth, with the planets and the comets, that of the third.

I put the planets and the comets with the earth, because seeing that they resist the light as it does, and reflect its rays, I can perceive no difference. I put the sun with the fixed stars, and attribute to them a nature quite opposite to that of the earth, for the action of their light alone convinces me that their substance is of a matter extremely rare and mobile.

As for the heavens, inasmuch as they cannot be perceived by our senses, I think I am right in attributing to them an intermediate nature, between that of the luminous bodies, the action of which we perceive, and that of the hard and heavy substances, the resistance of which we feel.

Finally, we are not aware of the existence of composite bodies in any other place than upon the surface of the earth; and when we consider that the whole space which contains them—namely, all that which lies between the highest clouds and the deepest mines which the greed of man has dug to extract the metals—is extremely small in comparison of the earth and the immense expanse of the sky, we can easily imagine that these composite bodies, all taken together, are only the outside rind which has been formed upon the surface of the earth by the motion and mixture of the matter of the heavens which surround it.

And thus we shall have occasion to think that not only in the air that we breathe, but also in all other composite substances, even to the hardest stones and the heaviest metals, there are particles of the element of air mixed with those of the earth, and consequently, also, particles of the element of fire, because this is always found in the pores of that of the air.

But it is to be observed that, although there are particles of these three elements mingled with each other in all these substances, it is, properly speaking, only those which on account of their size or the difficulty with which they move, are to be referred to the third, which compose all the substances which we perceive around us; for the particles of the two other elements are so rare that they cannot be perceived by our senses; and thus all these substances can be imagined as being sponges, in which, although there are a quantity of pores or holes which are always full of air or water, or some similar liquid, it is, nevertheless, not supposed that these liquids enter into the composition of the sponge. There still remain many other things for me to explain, and I should be very glad to add some reasons to make my views seem more probable, but in order that the length of this discourse may seem the less tedious to you, I wish to clothe a part of it in the guise of a fable, through which I hope the truth will not fail sufficiently to appear, and will be no less agreeable to look upon than if I should present it quite naked.

CHAPTER VI.

Description of a new world and of the qualities of the matter of which it is composed.

LET, then, your thought pass for a little while beyond this world, that you may behold another wholly new one, which I shall cause to rise to view in imaginary spaces. Philosophers tell us that these spaces are infinite; and they surely ought to be believed, since it is themselves who have made them; but that this infinity may not hinder us or prove an embarrassment, let us not try to get to the end of it: let us proceed so far only as to lose sight of all the creatures God has made in five or six thousand years; and when we have come to a stand there at some fixed point, let us imagine that God creates anew all around us so much matter as that, whatever direction our imagination may take, it shall discover no empty place. Grant that the ocean is not infinite, those who are upon a ship in the middle of it can extend their view apparently to infinity, and nevertheless there is water beyond what they can see; thus, although our imagination seems to be able to stretch to infinity, and this new matter may not be supposed to be infinite, we may nevertheless well suppose that it fills spaces far greater than all those we shall have imagined; and yet, in order that there may be no ground for objection in all this, let us not allow our imagination to stretch itself as far as it can, but let us purposely confine it within a certain space, which need not be very great—for example, the distance between the earth and the principal stars of the firmament; and let us suppose that the matter which God shall have created stretches far beyond, to an indefinite distance in all directions; for this is, indeed, more likely, and we can more easily prescribe limits to the activity of our thought than to the works of God.

Now, since we take the liberty to fashion this matter according to our fancy, we will attribute to it, if you please, a nature in which there is nothing at all that anyone cannot know as perfectly as possible; and, in order to this, let us suppose expressly that it has not the form of earth, or fire, or air, or of any other thing in particular, as wood, stone, or metal; nor the qualities of being hot or cold, dry or moist, light or heavy; or that it has any taste, or odor, or sound, or color, or light, or other similar quality, in the nature of which it could be said there was something which is not clearly known by everybody.

And, on the other hand, let us not think of it as being that primary matter of philosophers, which has been so stripped of all its forms and qualities that there is nothing remaining which can be clearly conceived; but let us conceive of it as a true substance perfectly solid, which uniformly fills all the length, breadth, and depth of that great space, in the midst of which we have stayed our thought, so that each one of its particles always occupies a portion of that space so related to its magnitude that it could not fill a greater, nor contract itself into a less, nor allow, while it remains there, any other to enter it.

Add to this, that this matter can be divided into all the parts and according to all the figures we can imagine, and that each one of its parts is capable of taking on also all the motions which we can conceive of; and suppose, further, that God has actually divided it into many such parts, some greater, some smaller; some of one figure, others of another, whatever we may be pleased to fancy; not that, in doing so, he has separated them from one another, so that there should be any empty space between two of them; but let us suppose that the only distinction to be met with consists in the variety of the motions he gives to them, in causing that, at the very instant that they are created, some of them begin to move in one direction, others in another; some more swiftly, others more slowly (or, if you please, not at all), and that they continue thereafter their motions according to the ordinary laws of nature; for God has so marvelously ordained these laws that, although we should suppose that he had created nothing more than what I have said, and even that he had established therein no order or proportion, but that he had made a chaos the most confused and the most perplexed that poets could describe, they would be sufficient to cause the parts of this chaos to disentangle themselves, and to arrange themselves in such good order that they would take the form of a very perfect world, and one in which not only light would be seen, but also all other things, in general and particular, which appear in this real world.

But, before I go on to explain this more at length, pause to consider yet a little further this chaos, and observe that it contains nothing which is not so perfectly known to you that you cannot even pretend to be ignorant of it; for as to the qualities I have assigned to it, if you have attended, you have noticed that I have supposed such only as you could conceive.

And as for the matter of which I have composed it, there is nothing more simple or more easy to understand in the inanimate world ; and the idea of it is so comprehended in all those objects which our imagination can frame that it must necessarily be that you conceive it, or that you could never conceive anything. Nevertheless, since philosophers are so acute that they know how to find difficulties in things which seem extremely clear to other men, and the recollection of their primary matter—which they know to be very hard to conceive of—might prevent them from understanding that of which I am speaking, I must tell them just here that, if I am not mistaken, the whole difficulty which they experience in regard to it arises from their desire to distinguish it from its quantity and extension, that is to say, from its property of occupying space ; wherein, indeed, I am quite willing that they should think themselves to be right, for I do not mean to stop to refute them ; but on their part they ought not to find it strange if I suppose that the quantity of the matter which I have described does not differ from its substance any more than number does from things numbered, and if I conceive its extension,—or its property of occupying space,—not at all as an accident, but as its true form and its essence ; for they cannot deny that it is very easy to conceive it in this way.

And my purpose is not to explain, like them, things which really exist in the actual world ; but simply to fancy one at pleasure, in which there should be nothing which the dullest minds are not capable of conceiving, and which might not, nevertheless, be created just as I have imagined it. If I should introduce therein the least thing which should prove obscure, it would be owing to the fact that included in that obscurity there was some concealed contradiction of which I had not been aware, and thus, without knowing it, I had supposed something impossible ; whereas, on the other hand, if I am able distinctly to conceive all I include in it, it is certain that, although there may be nothing like it in the old [real] world, God might nevertheless create it in a new one, for it is certain that he can create everything we can conceive.

CHAPTER VII.

Of the natural laws of this new world.

But I will not longer delay to tell you by what reasons nature alone will be able to disentangle the confusion of the chaos of which I have spoken, and what are the laws which God has imposed upon it.

Know, then, in the first place, that by nature I do not here understand any goddess or any other sort of imaginary power, but I make use of this word to signify matter itself, in so far as I consider it with all the qualities I have attributed to it, taken as a whole, and under this condition, that God continues to preserve it in the same way that he has created it ; for, from the simple fact that he continues thus to preserve it, it necessarily follows that there must be many changes in its parts, which not being, as it seems to me, properly attributed to the Divine activity,—because that does not change,—I attribute them to nature ; and the rules in accordance with which these changes occur I call the laws of nature.

In order the better to understand this, remember that among the qualities of matter we have supposed that its particles have had various motions from the instant of their creation, and, besides that, they are all in contact on every side, so that there is no empty space between any two of them ; whence it follows of necessity that at the time they began to move they began to change also and to vary their movements as they encountered one another ; and thus, even if God preserved them thereafter in the same manner as he created them, he does not preserve them in the same condition—that is to say, while God always acts in the same way, and consequently always produces the same effect in substance, there result, as it were by accident, many diversities in this effect. And it is easy to believe that God, who, as everybody ought to know, is immutable, acts always in the same way. But without involving myself further in these metaphysical considerations, I will lay down two or three principal rules in accordance with which it must be thought that God causes the nature of this new world to act, and which are sufficient, as I believe, to enable you to comprehend all the rest.

The first is, that each individual particle of matter remains always in one and the same state, so long as contact with others does not compel it to change it; that is to say, if it have a certain magnitude it will never become smaller, unless others divide it; if it be round or square, it will never change this figure, unless the rest compel it to do so; if it be at rest in any place, it will never leave it, unless others drive it therefrom; and if it have once begun to move, it will continue always to move with uniform energy until others stop or retard it.

There is no one who does not believe that this same rule is of force in the old [real] world, in respect to magnitude, figure, rest, and a thousand other matters of like kind; but philosophers have made an exception in the case of motion, which is, nevertheless, the thing which I desire most expressly to include in it. Do not think, however, that I intend to oppose them: the motion of which they speak is so very different from that which I have in mind, it may easily happen that what is true of the one should not be so of the other. They admit themselves that the nature of theirs is very little understood, and to render it intelligible in any way they have been unable to explain it more clearly than in these terms: *motus est actus entis in potentia prout in potentia est*, which are so obscure to me that I am constrained to leave them here in their own language, because I cannot interpret them (and indeed these words, *le mouvement est l'acte d'un être en puissance, en tant qu'il est en puissance*, are no clearer in French). But, on the other hand, the nature of the motion I intend here to speak of is so easy to comprehend, that the geometers themselves, who, of all men, have made the greatest efforts to conceive very distinctly the things they have treated of, have judged the nature of motion more simple and more intelligible than that of their surfaces and their lines, as appears in the fact that they have explained the line by the motion of a point, and the surface by that of a line.

The philosophers suppose, also, many motions which they think could occur without a body changing its place, as those which they call *motus ad formam, motus ad calorem, motus ad quantitatem* (motion as to form, motion as to heat, motion as to quantity), and a thousand others: for my part, I know of none more easy to conceive than the lines of the geometers, which bodies make in passing from one place to another and successively occupying all the spaces between the two.

Besides, they attribute to the least of these motions an existence much more substantial and real than they do to rest, which they say is merely privation; for my part, I conceive that rest is as much a quality to be attributed to matter, so long as it remains in one place, as motion is, so long as it changes its place.

Finally, the motion of which they speak is of a nature so strange that, whereas all other things have for their end their perfection, and aim only to preserve themselves, this has no other end or aim but rest, and, contrary to all the laws of nature, it aims at its own destruction; but, on the contrary, that which I have in mind follows the same laws of nature which bring about in general all the arrangements and all the qualities which are found in matter, as well as those which the learned call *modos et entia rationis cum fundamento in re* (modes and entities of reason with foundation in things), together with *qualitates reales* (real qualities), in which I candidly confess that I find no more reality than in the rest.

I suppose, for the second rule, that when one body impels another, it cannot impart to it any motion without at the same time losing so much of its own, nor take from it but so much as its own is thereby increased. This rule, together with the preceding, agrees very well with all the facts which we observe when a body begins or ceases to move, on account of being pushed or stopped by another. For, having assumed the preceding rule, we are free from the difficulty in which the learned find themselves when they wish to give a reason why a stone continues to move for some time after it has left the hand of one who has thrown it; for we ought rather to ask ourselves why it should not continue to move on forever. But the reason is easy to give; for who can deny that the air in which it is moving offers it some resistance? We can hear the air whistle when it is parted, and if set in motion by a fan, or any other very light and very broad body, it can be sensibly felt by the hand that it hinders the movement rather than helps it, as some would have us say. But if the effect of its resistance is not explained according to our second rule, and it is thought that the more a body can resist the more capable it becomes of stopping the movement of others, as perhaps one might at first be inclined to think, there would be considerable difficulty in giving a reason why the movement of this stone is sooner overcome when it meets a soft body, the resistance of which is moderate, than when it meets a harder one which resists it more ; as, also, why, as soon as it has made a slight effort against this last, it instantly returns upon its path rather than arrest or interrupt its motion on account of it. Whereas, admitting this rule, there is no difficulty at all ; for it instructs us that the motion of a body is not retarded on meeting another in proportion to the degree with which this resists it, but only in proportion to the degree in which its own resistance of it is overcome, and that, in submitting to it, it receives into itself the energy of motion which the other loses.

Now, although in most of the movements which we observe in the real world, we might not perceive that the bodies which begin or cease to move are impelled or arrested by any others, we have no ground on that account to conclude that these two rules are not exactly observed ; for it is certain that these bodies may frequently be set in motion by the two elements of air and fire, which are always intermixed with them, though they cannot be perceived there, as was said a while ago ; or even by this grosser atmosphere, which also cannot be perceived ; and that they may be able to transmit it presently to this grosser air, and again to the whole mass of the earth, in which, being dispersed, it may also not be perceived.

But although all that our senses have ever experienced in the real world might appear contrary to these two rules, the reason which has indicated them to me seems so strong that I cannot help thinking myself obliged to admit them in the new one which I am describing to you; for what firmer or more solid foundation could be found to establish a truth, although one were at liberty to choose what he would, than the constancy and immutability of God?

Now these two rules follow manifestly from the simple fact that God is immutable, and that, acting always in the same way, he produces always the same effect: for granting that he has put a certain quantity of motion into all matter universally at the first instant that he created it, it must be admitted that he also preserves as much of it there, or else it cannot be thought that he acts always in the same way; and granting with this that from that first instant the various parts of matter, in which these motions are found unequally distributed, have begun to retain them or to transfer them one to another, according as they had power to do, it must necessarily be thought that he makes them always continue to do the same thing; and this is what these two rules contain.

I will add, for the third, that when a body moves, although its movement is most frequently in a curved line, and can never be otherwise than circular in some degree, as has been said above, nevertheless each one of its particles in particular tends always to continue its own motion in a straight line. And so their action —that is to say, their inclination to move—is different from their movemen*

For example, if a wheel be turned on its axle, although all its parts move in a circle, because being joined together they could not move otherwise, nevertheless their tendency is to move in a right line, as plainly appears if by chance any one is detached from the rest; for as soon as it is set free, its movement ceases to be circular, and it continues on in a straight line. Likewise, when a stone is whirled in a sling, not only does it go in a straight line as soon as it leaves it, but further, all the time it is in it, it presses upon the center of the sling, and stretches the cord, thus showing plainly that it always has a tendency to go in a straight line, and that it moves in a circle only by constraint.

This rule rests on the same foundation as the other two, and depends only on the fact that God preserves each thing by one continuous activity, and that, consequently, he does not preserve it such as it may have been some time before, but precisely such as it is at the very instant that he preserves it. Now the case is that, among all movements, that which is in a straight line is the only one which is entirely simple, and one the whole nature of which may be embraced in a single instant; for, in order to conceive it, it is enough to think of a body actually moving in one fixed direction, which is the case in every one of the instants which can be determined during the time it is in motion; whereas, to conceive circular movement, or any other that can exist, it is necessary to consider at least two of these instants, or rather two of its parts, and the relation between them; but in order that philosophers, or sophists rather, may not take occasion here to practice their superfluous subtleties, notice that I do not say that movement in a straight line can take place in an instant, but simply that all that is required to produce it exists in the body in every instant which can be determined during its movement, and not all that is required to produce the circular. .... It must then be said, according to this rule, that God alone is the author of all the movements in the universe, in so far as they exist, and in so far as they are in straight lines; but that there are various arrangements of matter which render them irregular and curved, just as theologians teach us that God is the author of all our actions, in so far as they exist, and in so far as they have any goodness in them, but that it is the various dispositions of our wills which make them bad.

I might add here many rules to determine in particular when, and how, and how much the movement of any body can be deflected, and increased or diminished, by meeting others, in which are summarily comprehended all natural phenomena; but I shall content myself with informing you that, besides the three laws which I have explained, I do not intend to assume any others except those which follow infallibly from the eternal verities upon which mathematicians are wont to found their most certain and most evident demonstrations; those verities, I say, in accordance with which God himself has taught us that he has disposed all things by number, weight, and measure, and the knowledge of which is so natural to our minds that we cannot help knowing them infallibly when we conceive them distinctly, nor doubting that, had God created many worlds, they would be no less true in all than in this.

So that those who shall have sufficiently examined the consequences of these verities, and of our rules, will be able to know effects by their causes, and, to express myself in the language of the school, may have *a priori* demonstrations of all that can come to pass in this new world. And, in order that there may be no exception whatever to embarrass us, we will add to our assumptions, if you please, that God will never work any miracle there, and that the intelligences, or reasonable minds, which we shall hereafter assume to be there, will never interfere in any way with the ordinary course of nature. In what follows, nevertheless, I do not promise to place before you exact demonstrations of all that I have to say; it will be enough that I open the way by which you shall be able to find them out for yourselves, when you will take pains to seek them. Most minds are displeased when things are made too easy for them. And to paint a picture here which shall please you, I must make use of shadows as well as colors. Accordingly, I shall content myself with following out the description which I have begun, having no other design than to tell you a story.

CHAPTER VIII.

Of the formation of the sun and the stars of this new world.

WHATEVER inequality and confusion we might suppose God had introduced at the beginning among the particles of matter, it is necessary, according to the laws which he has imposed upon nature, that nearly all of them should afterward be reduced to one size and one moderate motion, and thus that they should take the form of the second element, such as I have explained it above. For, considering this matter in the state in which it might have been before God had set it in motion, it should be conceived of as being like the hardest and most solid body in the world. And as one could not push a single particle of such a body without also, by the same means, pushing or drawing all the rest, so it must be thought that the action or force of motion, or division, which at the first had been placed in any of its particles, would have expanded and distributed itself at the same instant to all the rest as uniformly as possible.

It is true that this uniformity could not have been absolutely perfect, for, in the first place, because there is no void at all in this world, it would have been impossible that all the particles of matter should move in a straight line ; but being very nearly equal, and one being almost as easily deflected as another, they should all agree together in a circular motion of some sort. And nevertheless, inasmuch as we suppose that God has moved them variously at the first, we must not think that they would all agree in revolving about a single center, but about many different ones, which we may conceive of as being differently situated with respect to one another.

Accordingly, we must conclude that they would naturally be in less rapid motion, or smaller, or both at once, in the places nearer these centers than in those more remote; for all having a disposition to continue their movement in a straight line, it is certain that those are the strongest—that is, the largest, among those which may be equally swift in their motion, and the swiftest among those which may be equal in size—which have to describe the greater circles, as being the nearest to the straight line. And as for the matter contained between three or more of these circles, it might well be at first much less divided and less swift in its motion than all the rest; and what is more, inasmuch as we suppose that God at the beginning has put all sorts of inequality into the different parts of this matter, we ought to think that from that time it has had all sorts of sizes and shapes, and has been disposed to move, or not to move, in every way and manner.

But this does not prevent them afterward becoming nearly all uniform, especially those which remain at an equal distance from the centers around which they revolve; for, being unable to move independently, it was necessary that the swifter communicate of their motion to those which had less, and that the greater break up and divide, in order to be able to pass over the same spaces as those which preceded them, or, at least, that they mount higher; and thus they would arrange themselves, in a short time, all in order, so that each one would find itself more or less distant from the center around which it had taken its course, according as it had more or less of size or swiftness than the rest; and also, inasmuch as size always conflicts with speed, it must be thought that the most distant from each center were those which, being a little smaller than those nearer, have been also much swifter.

The same would be true of their figures. Although we may suppose that these at the beginning were of every sort, and that they had, for the most part, many angles and many sides, like the pieces which split off from a stone when it is broken, it is certain that afterward, in moving and striking against one another, they would have rubbed off, little by little, the small points of their angles, and blunted the edges of their sides, until they became by degrees almost all round, as grains of sand and flint do when rolled about in running water ; so that there might not now be any noticeable difference between those which are near enough together, nor even between those which are very distant, except in the fact that they can move a little faster, and be a little smaller or larger, one than the other ; and this does not prevent our attributing to all of them the same form. Only an exception must be made of some which, having been from the first much larger than the rest, have not so easily become divided, or which, having had very irregular and resistant shapes, have tended to unite in a mass rather than to break up and become round, and thus they have retained the form of the third element, and have served to compose the planets and the comets, as I shall hereafter explain to you.

Further, it is to be noted that the matter which has

come off from the surface of the parts of the second element, in proportion as they have broken up and blunted the sharp corners of their angles in becoming round, has necessarily acquired a motion much swifter than theirs, and at the same time a facility of dividing and changing its shape at every moment to accommodate itself to that of the places where it happens to be, and so it has taken the form of the first element.

It is also to be noted that what there is of this first element, more than is needed to fill the small interspaces that the particles of the second, which are spherical, necessarily leave around them, must move toward the centers about which they [the particles of the second element] revolve, because these occupy all the other places more distant, and that it must there form round bodies perfectly liquid and rare, which, turning incessantly much more rapidly and in the same direction as the particles of the second element which environ them, have power to increase the motion of those to which they are nearest, and also to push them all in every direction, drawing them from the center toward the circumference, so that they also push one another, and this by a mode of action which it is necessary that I presently describe as exactly as I am able to do; for I apprise you here in advance that it is this action which we take to be light, just as we take those round bodies composed of matter of the first element quite pure, the one to be the sun, the others to be the fixed stars, of the new world I am describing to you, and the matter of the second element, which revolves around them, to be the heavens. . . . .

CHAPTER IX.

Of the origin and course of the planets and comets in general, and in particular of the comets.

Now,—to begin to speak to you of the planets and comets,—consider that as respects the diversity o.́ the parts of the matter which I have assumed, although the larger part of them, through clashing and breaking up on encountering one another, would take the form of the first or second element, there would still be found two sorts which have necessarily retained the form of the third, namely, those whose figure was so extended and so resistant that, on meeting one another, it was easier for several of them to join together and by this means to become larger, than to break up and become smaller; and those which were from the beginning the largest and most massive of all were well able to break and shatter the others on striking them, but not, reciprocally, to be broken and shattered. If now, you should conceive that these two sorts of parts were at first in very rapid motion, or even that they moved very slowly, or not at all, it is certain that afterward they would have to move at the same rate as the matter of the heavens which contained them; for, if at first they were moved more swiftly than this matter, as they would unavoidably push it forward as they encountered it in their path, they must in a short time have transferred to it a part of their own momentum; and if, on the contrary, they had not in themselves any disposition to move, nevertheless, being surrounded on all sides by this matter of the heavens, they would necessarily have followed its course; just as we see every day that boats and various other bodies which float upon the water, the largest and most massive, as well as the smallest, follow the current of the water in which they are, whenever there is nothing else to prevent them.

And observe that, among the various bodies which thus float upon the water, those which are solid and massive enough, as boats commonly are, especially the larger and more heavily laden, have always much more force than it to continue their movement, even though it may be from it alone that they have received it; and that, on the contrary, those which are very light, such as the masses of white foam which are seen floating along on rivers during a storm, have less of it. So that if you imagine two rivers which unite at a certain point and separate soon after, before their waters, which must be conceived as very calm and quite uniform in force, but also very rapid, have had time to mingle, boats or other bodies massive and heavy enough, which are carried along by the current of one, might easily pass into the other, whereas the lighter ones would keep separate from it, and be borne by the force of this stream toward parts where it is less rapid. . . . .

From this illustration it is easy to understand that, in whatever place there may be found, at the beginning, parts of matter which could not take the form of the second element, nor of the first, all the largest and most massive among them would have been compelled in a short time to take their course toward the outer circle of the heavens which contain them, and to pass continually thereafter from one of these heavens into another, without ever stopping for any long time together in the same heavens; and that, on the contrary, all the less massive must have been pushed in turn toward the center of the heavens which contained them, by the current of the matter of those heavens; and that, considering the forms I have attributed to them, they must, on meeting, have united themselves many of them together, and formed those great globes which, revolving in the heavens, have there a motion the resultant of all those which their parts would have when moving separately, so that some of them would tend toward the circumferences of these heavens, and others toward their centers. And understand that it is those which tend thus to move toward the center of any heavens that we must here call the planets, and those which pass across the different heavens we must call comets.

Now, in the first place, in regard to the comets, it must be observed that there would be but few of them in this new world, in comparison to the number of the heavens; for although, indeed, there might have been many of them at the beginning, they must, in course of time, in their passage across the different heavens, nearly all of them have struck against one another and gone to pieces, as I have said two vessels might do by running into one another, so that only the biggest might now remain. It is necessary, also, to observe that, when they pass thus from one heaven into another, they always push before themselves a little of the matter of that which they leave, and remain for some time enveloped in it, until they have entered pretty well within the borders of the next heavens; on being there, they finally free themselves of it all at once, as it were, and without taking any more time perhaps than the sun does to rise in the morning above our horizon ; so that they move much more slowly when they tend to pass out of any heaven than they do a little after entering it. . . .

CHAPTER X.

Of the planets in general, and in particular of the earth and the moon.

THERE are, likewise, in regard to the planets, many things to be noted: the first of which is that, although they all tend toward the centers of the heavens which contain them, they never can reach those centers ; for, as I have already said above, it is the sun and the fixed stars which occupy them. . . . .

If I have not yet made you sufficiently understand the cause which makes the parts of the heaven which are outside [the orbits of the planets], being incomparably smaller than the planets, have greater power than these to continue their movement in a straight line, consider that this force does not depend solely on the quantity of the matter in each body, but also on the extent of its surface. For although when two bodies are moving with equal velocity, it may be correct to say that if one contain twice as much matter as the other, it has, also, twice as much momentum ; it cannot on that account be said that it has twice as much power to continue to move in a straight line ; but it will have just twice as much if, along with that, its surface be exactly twice as great, because it will always meet twice as many other bodies which will resist it ; and it will have much less if its surface is much more than twice as great.

Now you know that the particles which compose the heavens are almost quite spherical, and so they have that figure which of all others contains the most matter within the least surface ; and that, on the contrary, the planets, being composed of small parts which are of very irregular and extended figure, have great surface in proportion to the quantity of their matter, so that they may have much more than most of the parts of the heaven, and yet also have less than some of the smaller parts and those nearer the centers ; for it must be understood that, as between two globes quite solid—as are those parts of the heaven—the smaller has always more surface, in proportion to its quantity, than the larger has.

And all this may easily be confirmed by experience. For if a great globe, made of the boughs of trees all matted together, as the parts of the matter composing the planets may be conceived as being, should be set in motion, it is certain that it would not continue its movement so far, although impelled by a force entirely proportionate to its size, as would another globe much smaller and made of the same wood, but quite solid ; it is certain, also, quite to the contrary, that another globe might be made of the same wood and quite solid, but which should be so extremely small that it would have much less power to continue its movement than the first ; finally, it is certain that this first would have more or less power to continue its movement, according as the boughs which composed it were more or less large and compacted together. From this you see how different planets may be suspended within the outermost circle at different distances from the sun, and how it is not those simply which appear the largest outside, but those which are in their interior most solid and massive, which must be the more distant.

It is to be observed, further, that as we find that boats which follow the current of a river never move so swiftly as the water which bears them, nor the largest among them so fast as the smallest; so, although the planets follow the course of the matter of the heavens without resistance, and move by the same impetus as that, it cannot be said, on that account, that they ever move so swiftly; and, also, the inequality of their movement must have some relation to that which exists between the greatness of their mass and the smallness of the parts of the heavens which environ them. The reason of which is this, that, generally speaking, the larger a body is, the easier it is for it to communicate a part of its motion to other bodies, and the more difficult for other bodies to communicate to it any of theirs; for although many small bodies, when combining together to act upon a greater, might have as much force as it, nevertheless they never could make it move so fast in every way as they move themselves; because, if they agree in certain of their movements which they communicate to it at the same time, they inevitably differ in others which they do not communicate to it.

Now, there follow from this two things, which seem to me to be of considerable importance: the first is that the matter of the heavens must not only cause the planets to revolve about the sun, but also about their own center (except when there is any particular cause to hinder them), and, accordingly, that it must be composed of small heavens around them which move in the same way as the greater. And the second is that, if there meet together two planets unequal in size, but so situated as to take their course in the heavens at the same distance from the sun, so that one were exactly so much more solid than the other was large, the smaller of these two, having a motion more rapid than the larger, will unite itself with the small heaven which is around this larger one and revolve continually with it.* . . . .

* This celebrated theory of the vortices (*les tourbillons*) is more fully set forth, and illustrated by diagrams, in *Les Principes de la Philosophie*, iii, §§ 30-157 (*Œuvres*, t. 3, pp. 198-329).

CHAPTER XI.

Of Gravity.

BUT I desire now that you consider what the gravity of this earth is, that is to say, the force which unites all its parts, and which makes them all tend toward its center, everyone more or less according as they are more or less large and solid; which is nothing else and consists only in this, that the parts of the small heaven which surrounds it, turning much more swiftly than its own do around its center, tend also with much more force to withdraw themselves from it, and consequently push them back there.

In which if you find any difficulty from the fact that I have said so many times that the more massive and solid bodies, such as I have assumed the comets to be, would tend toward the circumference of these heavens, and it would be only the less so which would be pushed back toward their centers, as if it should follow from that it would be only the less solid parts of the earth which could be pushed toward its center, and the others would necessarily withdraw from it; observe that, when I said that the most solid and massive bodies tend to withdraw from the center of a heaven, I assumed that they were moving already with the same impetus as the matter of that heaven : because it is certain that if they had not yet begun to move, or if they were in motion, provided this motion were less rapid than was necessary to follow the current of this matter, they must be forced by it toward the center around which it turned; and, also, it is certain that, in proportion as they were greater and more solid, they would be pushed with more force and swiftness.

And nevertheless, this would not prevent that, if they were solid enough to compose comets, they would tend but little toward the exterior circles of the heavens, inasmuch as the energy which they should have acquired in descending toward any one of their centers would inevitably impart to them force to pass beyond it and reascend toward its circumference. . . . .

Now it is evident that a stone, containing in itself more of the matter of the earth, and in return containing much less of that of the heaven, than a quantity of air of equal extent, and also its parts being less impelled by the matter of this heaven than that of this air, it would not have power to mount above it, but rather, on the contrary, it would have power to make this descend below it, so that the air would be light when compared with the stone; but heavy when compared with the heaven itself. . . . .

And you can understand from this that the arguments which many philosophers employ, to refute the motion of the real earth, have no force at all against that of the earth which I am describing to you; as when they say that if the earth were in motion heavy bodies would not fall plumb toward its center, but rather would stray this way and that toward the sky, and that cannon pointed toward the west would carry much further than when pointed toward the east, and that great winds would be felt and great noises heard in the air, and such like things, which could happen only on the supposition that the earth is not carried forward by the current of the heaven which surrounds it, but is moved by some other force and in some other way than this heaven moves.

[Chapter xii., Of the Ebb and Flow of the Sea, requiring diagrams, is omitted.]

CHAPTER XIII.

Of Light.

I HAVE repeatedly said that bodies which revolve in a circle tend always to withdraw from the centers of the circles which they describe ; but I must here determine more precisely in what directions the parts of the matter of which the heavens and the stars are composed have a tendency to move. And accordingly, it must be understood that when I speak of a body tending to move in any direction, I do not wish it to be supposed on that account that it has in it any thought or design which carries it hither, but simply that it is disposed to move that way, whether it actually does move thither, or some other body prevents it from doing so ; and it is principally in this latter signification that I employ the word "tend," because it seems to signify some effort, and all effort presupposes resistance. Now, inasmuch as there are often various causes which, acting together upon the same body, counteract one another, it may be said, for various reasons, that the same body tends to move in different directions at the same time, as has just been said that the particles of the earth tend to withdraw from its center, so long as they are considered independently, and that they tend on the contrary to approach it when the force of the particles of the heavens which push them thither is considered ; and again that they tend to withdraw from it when contrasted with other terrestrial particles which compose bodies more massive than they are. As, for example, a stone whirled in a sling.* . . . .

Still further I reply† that their other motions which continue in them [the particles of the second element], while thus advancing toward the circumference, not allowing them to remain a single instant arranged in the same way, prevent them from coming in contact, or at least cause that as soon as they touch they instantly separate again, and thus they do not cease to advance without interruption toward the circumference until the whole space is filled. Accordingly we can draw from this no other conclusion than that the force by which they tend toward [the circumference] is probably, as it were, a tremulous one, and increases and diminishes in varying minute vibrations, according as they change their situation, which seems to me a property very well agreeing with light. . . . . Finally, the particles of the first element which . . . compose the body of the sun, revolving in a circular manner very swiftly about [its center], tend to scatter themselves in every direction in straight lines. . . . . As for the rest, although they must thus advance toward [the circumference] if this space be occupied only by the first element, it is certain that they tend to move thither just the same if it be filled with any other body, and that, consequently, they push and strive against this body, as it were, to drive it from its place. So that if the eye of a man should be at [a point in this circumference] it would be really pushed upon by the sun as much as by any of the matter [in the intervening space.] Now

---

* The various tendencies to move in different directions are then described and illustrated by diagrams.

† In response to an objection suggested by the author himself.

it is to be understood that the inhabitants of this new world are of such a nature that, when their eyes are thus pushed upon, they have a sensation in every respect resembling that which we have of light.

CHAPTER XIV.

Of the properties of light.

BUT I wish to delay a little longer at this point to explain the properties of the energy (*de l'action*) by which their eyes can be excited. For they agree so perfectly with those which we observe in light, that when you shall have considered them, I am sure that you will declare, as I do, that there is no need of conceiving in the stars, nor in the heavens, any other quality than this energy, which is called by the name of light.*

The principal properties of light are : 1, That it spreads itself around on all sides about bodies which we call luminous ; 2, and to every degree of distance ; 3, and instantaneously ; 4, and usually in straight lines, which must be understood as rays of light ; 5, and that many of these rays, coming from different points, may gather at one point ; 6, or, coming from the same point, may proceed to different points ; 7, or, coming from different points, and going toward different points, may pass by the same point without interference with one another ; 8, and that they may also sometimes hinder one another, to wit, when their force is very unequal, and that of some is very much greater than that of others ; 9, and finally, that they can be turned aside by reflection ; 10, or by refraction ; 11, and that their force may be increased ; 12, or diminished by the different dispositions or qualities of the matter which receives them.

* Cette action, qui s'appelle du nom de lumière.

These are the principal properties observed in light, all of which agree with this energy, as you shall see:

1. That this energy must spread itself in all directions around luminous bodies, the reason whereof is evident, because it is from the circular movement of their particles that it proceeds.

2. It is also evident that it can extend itself to every degree of distance; because, for example, supposing that the particles of the heavens which are contained in the space between [the sun and some point in the circumference of those heavens] are already of themselves disposed to move toward [the circumference], as we have said they are, it cannot be doubted that the force with which the sun impels those which are [about it] must make them reach as far as the [circumference], even although it were a distance greater than that between the most distant stars of the firmament and ourselves.

3. And considering that the particles of the second element which are between [the sun and some point on the circumference] touch upon and press each other as much as possible, it cannot be doubted also that the energy by which the first are impelled must pass in an instant as far as the last, just as that by which one end of a stick is pushed passes in the same instant to the other end. . . . .

4. In regard to the lines along which this energy is communicated, and which are properly rays of light, it must be observed that they differ from the particles of the second element, by the medium of which this same energy is propagated, and that they are nothing material in the medium through which they pass, but that they signify simply in what way and in what di-

rection the luminous body acts upon that which it illuminates ; and thus they are not to be conceived otherwise than as exactly straight, although the particles of the second element, which serves to transmit this energy or light, might almost never be so directly situated one after another as to compose perfectly straight lines. . . . .

9, 10. As for reflection and refraction, I have already sufficiently explained them elsewhere.* Nevertheless, because for the illustration of the movement, I then made use of a ball instead of speaking of rays of light, in order by this means to make my discourse more intelligible ; it remains to me here to bring to your attention the fact that the energy, or inclination to move, which is transmitted from one place to another by means of many bodies which are in contact and which exist without break throughout all the space between both, follows precisely the same path wherein this same energy might cause the first of these bodies to move, if the others were not in its way, with no other difference except that time would be required for this body to move, whereas the energy which is in it may, through the intervention of those which are in contact with it, extend itself to all distances in an instant ; whence it follows that, in like manner as a ball is reflected when it hits against the wall of a tenniscourt, and that it suffers refraction when it enters obliquely into water, or passes out of it, so also when the rays of light meet a body which does not allow them to pass through, they must be reflected ; and when they enter obliquely into any place through which they can extend themselves more or less easily than through that whence they proceed, they must

* *La Dioptrique*, Discours second. *Œuvres*, t. v, p. 17.

also, at the point of this change, be deflected and suffer refraction.

11, 12. Finally, the energy of light is not only more or less great in each place, according to the quantity of rays which meet there, but it can also be increased and diminished by the different dispositions of the bodies which happen to be in the places through which it passes, just as the velocity of a ball or stone thrown into the air may be increased by the winds which blow in the same direction in which it is moving, and diminished by those which oppose it.

CHAPTER XV.

That the heavens of this new world must appear to its inhabitants the same as ours.

HAVING thus explained the nature and properties of that energy which I understand light to be, it is necessary also that I explain how by means of it the inhabitants of the planet, which I have assumed for the earth, may see the face of their heavens as one quite like ours. In the first place, there is no doubt that they must see the [central body] all full of light and like our sun, seeing that that body sends its rays from every point of its surface toward their eyes ; and because it is much nearer them than the stars, it must appear much larger. . . . .

It must be understood that the great heavens, that is to say, those which have a fixed star or sun for their center, although, perhaps, quite unequal in extent, must always be of exactly equal energy ; for, if this equilibrium did not exist, they would inevitably perish in a short time, or at least they would change until they acquired this equilibrium. . . . . But it is necessary that you further observe, in regard to their situation, that the stars can never appear in the places where they really are. . . . . The reason of this is that the [different] heavens being unequal in extent, the surfaces which separate them never happen to be so disposed that the rays, which cross them in going from these stars toward the earth, meet them at right angles; and, meeting them obliquely, it is certain, according to what has been shown in the "Dioptrics,"* that they must be bent and suffer considerable refraction, inasmuch as they pass much more easily through one of the sides of this surface than through the other. . . . .

Consider, also, as regards the number of these stars, that frequently the same one might appear in several places, because of the different surfaces which deflect its rays toward the earth . . . just as objects are multiplied when seen through glasses or other transparent bodies cut with many faces.

Further consider, in regard to their size, that although they must appear much smaller than they are, because of their extreme distance, and also that, for the same reason, the larger part of them cannot appear at all, and others can appear only as the rays of many uniting together make the parts of the firmament through which they pass a little whiter, and like certain stars which astronomers call nebulous, or that great belt of our heavens which the poets feign was washed in the milk of Juno; nevertheless, as for those which are less distant, it is enough to assume them to be about equal to our sun, in order to conclude that they would appear as large as the largest in our world. . . . . . Besides that, it is very probable that the [limiting] surfaces of the heavens being of an extremely fluid matter, which is incessantly in motion, would constantly shake and undulate somewhat; and, consequently, that the stars which are seen through it would appear scintillating and trembling, as it were, as do our own, and also, because of their trembling, a little larger, as does the image of the moon upon a

* Discours second, *Œuvres*, t. v, p. 21.

lake, the surface of which is not greatly disturbed nor tossed, but only slightly ruffled by a breeze.

And finally, it may come about that in course of time these limiting surfaces change a little, or even again that some [of them] bend as much in a short time—on occasion, it may be, of a comet approaching them—and, by this means, many stars appear, after a long time, to be a little changed in position without being so in magnitude, or slightly changed in magnitude without being so in position; or even that some begin suddenly to appear or to disappear, as is seen to happen in the real world.

As for the planets and comets which are in the same heavens as the sun, remembering that the particles of the third element of which they are composed are so large, or so many of them compacted together, that they can resist the action of light, it is easy to understand that they must shine by means of the rays that the sun sends toward them, and which they reflect thence toward the earth; just as opaque or dark objects in a chamber can be seen by means of the rays which a torch lighted there sends toward them, and which return thence toward the eyes of the observers. And besides, the rays of the sun have a very considerable advantage over those of a torch, which consists in this, that their energy is preserved or even increased more and more in proportion to their distance from the sun, until they reach the exterior surface of its heavens, because all the matter of those heavens tends thither; whereas the rays of a torch grow feebler as they recede, in proportion to the extent of the spherical surfaces which they illuminate, and also, in some small degree, on account of the resistance of the air through which they pass. Whence it arises that objects which are in the vicinity of the torch are noticeably brighter than those which are at a distance from it ; and that the inferior planets are not in the same proportion more illuminated by the sun than the superior, nor even than the comets, which are, beyond comparison, more distant.

Now, experience shows that the same thing happens, also, in the real world; and, nevertheless, I do not believe it possible to give a reason for it, if it be assumed that light be anything else in objects than an energy [*une action*] or disposition, such as I have explained it to be. I say an energy or disposition ; for if you have paid good attention to what I have recently proved, that, if the space where the sun is were quite empty, the particles of its heavens would not cease to tend toward the eyes of observers in the same way as when they are impelled by its matter, and even with almost as much force, you may easily conclude that there would be hardly any need of its having in it any activity, or even, as it were, any being, other than pure space, in order to appear such as we see it. As to the rest, the movement of these planets about their center is the cause of their scintillating, yet much less strongly and in a different way from the fixed stars ; and, because the moon is devoid of this movement, it does not scintillate at all.* . . . .

*The remainder of the treatise, about six pages, requiring diagrams, is omitted.

SELECTIONS FROM THE TRACT ON MAN, ETC.

MAN.*

THESE men shall be composed, as we are, of a soul and a body ; and I must describe to you first the body by itself, afterward the soul, also by itself, and finally I must show you how both these natures are to be joined and united to compose men which resemble us.

I assume that the body is nothing else than a statue or machine of clay which God forms expressly to make it as nearly like as possible to ourselves, so that not only does he give it externally the color and the form of all our members, but also he puts within it all the parts necessary to make it walk, eat, breathe, and in fine imitate all those of our functions which may be supposed to proceed from matter and to depend merely on the arrangement of organs.

We see clocks, artificial fountains, mills, and other similar machines, which, although made by men, are not without the power of moving of themselves in many different ways ; and it seems to me that I should not be able to imagine so many kinds of movements in this one, which I am supposing to be made by the hand of God, nor attribute to it so much of artifice that you would not have reason to think there might still be more.

Now, I will not stop to describe to you the bones, nerves, muscles, veins, arteries, stomach, liver, spleen, heart, brain, nor all the other different parts of which

* *Œuvres*, t. iv, p. 335, *seq.*

it is to be composed; for I assume them to be in every respect similar to the parts of our own body which have the same names, and which you can have shown to you by any learned anatomist, at least those which are large enough to be seen, if you do not already know them well enough yourselves; and as for those which, because of their minuteness, are invisible, I shall be able to make you more easily and clearly understand them, by speaking of the movements which depend upon them; so that it is only necessary here for me to explain in order these movements, and to tell you by the same means what functions of our own they represent. . . . .

But what is here to be chiefly noted is that all the most active, vigorous, and finest particles of the blood tend to run into the cavities of the brain, inasmuch as the arteries which carry them are those which come in the straightest line of all from the heart, and, as you know, all bodies in motion tend, as far as possible, to continue their motion in a straight line. . . . .

In regard to the particles of blood which penetrate to the brain, they serve not only to nourish and support its substance, but chiefly, also, to produce there a certain very subtle breath, or rather flame, very active and very pure, which is called the *animal spirits*. For it must be understood that the arteries which carry them from the heart, after being divided into an infinitude of small branches, and having formed those small tissues which are spread like tapestries at the base of the cavities of the brain, collect about a certain small *gland* situated nearly at the middle of the substance of the brain, just at the entrance of its cavities, and have at this place a great number of small openings through which the finest particles of the blood they contain can run into this gland, but which are too narrow to admit the larger.

It must also be understood that these arteries do not end there, but that—many of them there joined together in one—they mount directly upward and empty into that great artery which is like a Euripus [aqueduct] by which the whole exterior surface of the brain is irrigated. And, moreover, it is to be noted that the larger particles of the blood may lose much of their onward motion in the winding passages of the small tissues through which they pass, inasmuch as they have the power to push on the smaller ones among them, and so transfer it to them; but that these smaller ones cannot in the same way lose their own, inasmuch as it is even increased by that which the larger transfer to them, and there are no other bodies around them to which they can so easily transfer it.

Whence it is easy to conceive that, when the larger ones mount straight toward the exterior surface of the brain, where they serve for the nourishment of its substance, they cause the smaller and more rapidly moving particles all to turn aside and enter into this gland, which is to be conceived of as a very copious fountain, whence they flow on all sides at once into the cavities of the brain; and thus, with no other preparation or change, except that they are separated from the larger, and that they still retain the extreme swiftness which the heat of the heart has imparted to them, they cease to have the form of blood and are called the animal spirits.

Now, in proportion as these spirits enter thus the cavities of the brain, they pass thence into the pores of its substance, and from these pores into the nerves;

where, according as they enter, or even only as they tend to enter, more or less into some rather than into others, they have the power to change the form of the muscles into which their nerves are inserted and by this means to cause all the limbs to move ; just as you may have seen in grottoes and fountains in the royal gardens that the force alone with which the water moves, in passing from the spring, is enough to move various machines, and even to make them play on instruments, or utter words, according to the different arrangement of the pipes which conduct it.

And, indeed, the nerves of the machine that I am describing to you may very well be compared to the pipes of the machinery of these fountains, its muscles and its tendons to various other engines and devices which serve to move them, its animal spirits to the water which sets them in motion, of which the heart is the spring, and the cavities of the brain the outlets. Moreover, respiration and other such functions as are natural and usual to it, and which depend on the course of the spirits, are like the movements of a clock or a mill, which the regular flow of the water can keep up. External objects which, by their presence alone, act upon the organs of its senses, and which by this means determine it to move in many different ways, according as the particles of its brain are arranged, are like visitors who, entering some of the grottoes of these fountains, bring about of themselves, without intending it, the movements which occur in their presence ; for they cannot enter without stepping on certain tiles of the pavement so arranged that, for example, if they approach a Diana taking a bath, they make her hide in the reeds ; and, if they pass on in pursuit of her, they cause a Neptune to appear before them, who menaces them with his trident ; or if they turn in some other direction they will make a marine monster come out, who will squirt water into their faces, or something similar will happen, according to the fancy of the engineers who construct them. And finally, when the *reasonable soul* shall be in this machine, it will have its principal seat in the brain, and it will be there like the fountain-maker, who must be at the openings where all the pipes of these machines discharge themselves, if he wishes to start, to stop, or to change in any way their movements.* . . . .

I desire you to consider next that all the functions which I have attributed to this machine, such as the digestion of food, the beating of the heart and arteries, the nourishment and growth of the members, respiration, waking, and sleeping ; the impressions of light, sounds, odors, tastes, heat, and other such qualities on the organs of the external senses ; the impression of their ideas on the common sense† and the imagination ; the retention or imprinting of these ideas upon the memory ; the interior motions of the appetites and passions ; and, finally, the external movements of all the members, which follow so suitably as well the actions of objects which present themselves to sense, as the passions and impressions which are found in the memory, that they imitate in the most perfect manner possible those of a real man ; I desire, I say, that you consider that all these functions follow naturally in this machine simply from the arrangement of its parts, no more nor less than do the movements

---

* What intervenes is illustrated by diagrams and is therefore omitted here.

† *Sensus communis.*

of a clock,* or other *automata*, from that of its weights and its wheels; so that it is not at all necessary for their explanation to conceive in it any other soul, vegetative or sensitive, nor any other principle of motion and life, than its blood and its spirits, set in motion by the heat of the fire which burns continually in its heart, and which is of a nature no different from all fires in inanimate bodies.

* Apparently the first suggestion of the comparison afterward employed by Bontekoe (?) and by Leibnitz. See above, pp. 26 and 31.

AUTOMATISM OF BRUTES.

Letter to the Marquis of Newcastle.*

. . . . As for the understanding or thought attributed by Montaigne and others to brutes, I cannot hold their opinion; not, however, because I am doubtful of the truth of what is commonly said, that men have absolute dominion over all the other animals; for while I allow that there are some which are stronger than we are, and I believe there may be some, also, which have natural cunning capable of deceiving the most sagacious men; yet I consider that they imitate or surpass us only in those of our actions which are not directed by thought; for it often happens that we walk and that we eat without thinking at all upon what we are doing; and it is so much without the use of our reason that we repel things which harm us, and ward off blows struck at us, that, although we might fully determine not to put our hands before our heads when falling, we could not help doing so. I believe, also, that we should eat as the brutes do, without having learned how, if we had no power of thought at all; and it is said that those who walk in their sleep sometimes swim across rivers, where, had they been awake, they would have been drowned.

As for the movements of our passions, although in ourselves they are accompanied with thought, because we possess that faculty, it is, nevertheless, very evident that they do not depend upon it, because they often

* *Œuvres*, t. ix, p. 423.

arise in spite of us, and, consequently, they may exist in brutes, and even be more violent than they are in men, without warranting the conclusion that brutes can think ; in fine there is no one of our external actions which can assure those who examine them that our body is anything more than a machine which moves of itself, but which also has in it a mind which thinks—excepting words, or other signs made in regard to whatever subjects present themselves, without reference to any passion. I say words or other signs, because mutes make use of signs in the same way as we do of the voice, and these signs are pertinent ; but I exclude the talking of parrots, but not that of the insane, which may be apropos to the case in hand, although it is irrational ; and I add that these words or signs are not to relate to any passion, in order to exclude, not only cries of joy or pain and the like, but, also, all that can be taught to any animal by art ; for if a magpie be taught to say " good-morning " to its mistress when it sees her coming, it may be that the utterance of these words is associated with the excitement of some one of its passions ; for instance, there will be a stir of expectation of something to eat, if it has been the custom of the mistress to give it some dainty bit when it spoke those words ; and in like manner all those things which dogs, horses, and monkeys are made to do are merely motions of their fear, their hope, or their joy, so that they might do them without any thought at all.

Now, it seems to me very remarkable that language, as thus defined, belongs to man alone ; for although Montaigne and Charron have said that there is more difference between one man and another than between a man and a brute, nevertheless there has never yet been found a brute so perfect that it has made use of a sign to inform other animals of something which had no relation to their passions; while there is no man so imperfect as not to use such signs; so that the deaf and dumb invent particular signs by which they express their thoughts, which seems to me a very strong argument to prove that the reason why brutes do not talk as we do is that they have no faculty of thought, and not at all that the organs for it are wanting. And it cannot be said that they talk among themselves, but we do not understand them; for, as dogs and other animals express to us their passions, they would express to us as well their thoughts, if they had them. I know, indeed, that brutes do many things better than we do, but I am not surprised at it; for that, also, goes to prove that they act by force of nature and by springs, like a clock, which tells better what the hour is than our judgment can inform us. And, doubtless, when swallows come in the spring, they act in that like clocks. All that honey-bees do is of the same nature; and the order that cranes keep in flying, or monkeys drawn up for battle, if it be true that they do observe any order, and, finally, the instinct of burying their dead is no more surprising than that of dogs and cats, which scratch the ground to bury their excrements, although they almost never do bury them, which shows that they do it by instinct only, and not by thought. It can only be said that, although the brutes do nothing which can convince us that they think, nevertheless, because their bodily organs are not very different from ours, we might conjecture that there was some faculty of thought joined to these organs, as we experience in ourselves, although theirs be much less perfect, to which I have nothing to reply, except that, if they could think as we do, they would have an immortal soul as well as we,* which is not likely, because there is no reason for believing it of some animals without believing it of all, and there are many of them too imperfect to make it possible to believe it of them, such as oysters, sponges, etc.

Letter to Henry More, 1649.†

. . . . But the greatest of all the prejudices we have retained from infancy is that of believing that brutes think. The source of our error comes from having observed that many of the bodily members of brutes are not very different from our own in shape and movements, and from the belief that our mind is the principle of the motions which occur in us ; that it imparts motion to the body and is the cause of our thoughts. Assuming this, we find no difficulty in believing that there is in brutes a mind similar to our own ; but having made the discovery, after thinking well upon it, that two different principles of our movements are to be distinguished,—the one entirely mechanical and corporeal, which depends solely on the force of the animal spirits and the configuration of the bodily parts, and which may be called corporeal soul, and the other incorporeal, that is to say, mind or soul, which you may define a substance which thinks,—I have inquired with great care whether the motions of animals proceed from these two principles or from one alone. Now, having clearly perceived that they can proceed from one only, I have held it demonstrated tha we are not able in any manner to prove that there is in

* Cf. *Butler's Analogy*, Pt. i, chap. i.
† *Œuvres*, t. x, p. 204.

the animals a soul which thinks. I am not at all disturbed in my opinion by those doublings and cunning tricks of dogs and foxes, nor by all those things which animals do, either from fear, or to get something to eat, or just for sport. I engage to explain all that very easily, merely by the conformation of the parts of the animals. Nevertheless, although I regard it as a thing demonstrated that it cannot be proved that the brutes have thought, I do not think that it can be demonstrated that the contrary is not true, because the human mind cannot penetrate into the heart to know what goes on there; but, on examining into the probabilities of the case, I see no reason whatever to prove that brutes think, if it be not that having eyes, ears, a tongue, and other organs of sense like ours, it is likely that they have sensations as we do, and, as thought is involved in the sensations which we have, a similar faculty of thought must be attributed to them. Now, since this argument is within the reach of everyone's capacity, it has held possession of all minds from infancy. But there are other stronger and more numerous arguments for the opposite opinion, which do not so readily present themselves to everybody's mind; as, for example, that it is more reasonable to make earth-worms, flies, caterpillars, and the rest of the animals, move as machines do, than to endow them with immortal souls.

Because it is certain that in the body of animals, as in ours, there are bones, nerves, muscles, blood, animal spirits, and other organs, disposed in such a manner that they can produce of themselves, without the aid of any thought, all the movements which we observe in the animals, as appears in convulsive movements, when, in spite of the mind itself, the machine of the body moves often with greater violence, and in more various ways than it is wont to do with the aid of the will; moreover, inasmuch as it is agreeable to reason that art should imitate nature, and that men should be able to construct divers *automata* in which there is movement without any thought, nature, on her part, might produce these *automata*, and far more excellent ones, as the brutes are, than those which come from the hand of man, seeing no reason anywhere why thought is to be found wherever we perceive a conformation of bodily members like that of the animals, and that it is more surprising that there should be a soul in every human body than that there should be none at all in the brutes.

But the principal argument, to my mind, which may convince us that the brutes are devoid of reason, is that, although among those of the same species, some are more perfect than others, as among men, which is particularly noticeable in horses and dogs, some of which have more capacity than others to retain what is taught them, and although all of them make us clearly understand their natural movements of anger, of fear, of hunger, and others of like kind, either by the voice or by other bodily motions, it has never yet been observed that any animal has arrived at such a degree of perfection as to make use of a true language; that is to say, as to be able to indicate to us by the voice, or by other signs, anything which could be referred to thought alone, rather than to a movement of mere nature; for the word is the sole sign and the only certain mark of the presence of thought hidden and wrapped up in the body; now all men, the most stupid and the most foolish, those even who are deprived of the organs of speech, make use of signs, whereas the brutes never do anything of the kind; which may be taken for the true distinction between man and brute. I omit, for the sake of brevity, the other arguments which deny thought to the brutes. It must, however, be observed that I speak of thought, not of life, nor of sensation; for I do not deny the life of any animal, making it to consist solely in the warmth of the heart. I do not refuse to them feeling even, in so far as it depends only on the bodily organs. Thus, my opinion is not so cruel to animals as it is favorable to men; I speak to those who are not committed to the extravagances of Pythagoras, which attached to those who ate or killed them the suspicion even of a crime. . . . .

Letter to Mersenne, July 30, 1640.*

As for the brute beasts, we are so accustomed to persuade ourselves that they feel just as we do, that it is difficult to rid ourselves of this opinion; but, if we were also accustomed to see *automata* which should imitate perfectly all those of our actions which they could imitate and remain *automata*, we should have no doubt whatever that all animals without reason are also *automata*, because we should find just the same differences between ourselves and them as between ourselves and *automata*, as I have written on page 56 † of the Method; and I have very particularly shown in my World ‡ how all the organs which are required to produce all those actions which occur in *automata* are found in the bodies of animals.

* *Œuvres*, t. viii, p. 299.
† *Œuvres*, t. i, p. 184; Veitch's *Descartes*, page 54.
‡ In the part not published.

SELECTIONS FROM THE PASSIONS OF
THE SOUL.

THE PASSIONS OF THE SOUL.*

PART I.

ARTICLE I.

Passion, as respects the subject, is always action in some other respect.

THERE is nothing which better shows how defective the sciences are which we have received from the ancients than what they have written upon the passions ; for, although it is a subject the knowledge of which has always been much sought after, and which does not appear to be one of the more difficult sciences, because everyone, feeling the passions in himself, stands in no need whatever of borrowing any observation elsewhere to discover their nature, nevertheless, what the ancients have taught on this subject is of so little consequence, and for the most part so untrustworthy, that I cannot have any hope of reaching the truth, except by abandoning the paths which they have followed. That is the reason why I shall be obliged to write now in the same way as I should if I were treating a topic which no one before me had ever touched upon ; and, to begin with, I take into consideration the fact that an event is generally spoken of by philosophers as a passion as regards the subject to which it happens, and an action in respect to that which causes it ; so that, although the agent and the patient may often be very different,

* *Œuvres*, t. iv, p. 37, *seq.*

action and passion are always one and the same thing, which has these two names because of the two different subjects to which it can be referred.

Article II.

In order to understand the passions of the soul, it is necessary to distinguish its functions from those of the body.

Next I take into consideration that we know of no subject which acts more immediately upon our soul than the body to which it is joined, and that consequently we must think that what in the one is a passion is commonly in the other an action; so that there is no better path to the knowledge of our passions than to examine into the difference between the soul and the body, in order to know to which of them is to be attributed each of our functions.

Article III.

The rule to be observed to this end.

No great difficulty will be found in this, if it be borne in mind that all that which we experience in ourselves which we see can also take place in bodies entirely inanimate is to be attributed only to our body; and, on the contrary, all that which is in us and which we cannot conceive in any manner possible to pertain to a body is to be attributed to our soul.*

---

* "This utter disanimation of Body and its, *not* opposition, but contrariety, *sicuti omnino heterogeneum*, to soul, as the assumed Basis of Thought and Will; this substitution, I say, of a merely logical *negatio alterius in omni et singulo*, for a philosophic antithesis necessary to the manifestation of the identity of both— 2═1—as the only form in which the human understanding can re-

Article IV.

That heat and the movement of the limbs proceed from the body, thoughts from the mind.

Thus, because we cannot conceive that the body thinks in any manner whatever, we have no reason but to think that all forms of thought which are in us belong to the mind; and because we cannot doubt that there are inanimate bodies which can move in as many or more different ways than ours, and which have as much or more heat (as experience teaches us in the case of flame, which alone has more heat and motion than any of our members), we must believe that all the heat and all the motions which are in us, in so far as they do not depend at all on thought, belong only to the body.

Article V.

That it is an error to think that the soul imparts motion and heat to the body.

By this means we shall avoid a very great error, into which many have fallen, an error which I consider to be the principal hindrance, up to the present time, to a correct explanation of the passions and other properties of the soul. It consists in this, that, seeing that all dead bodies are deprived of heat and, consequently, of motion, it is imagined that the absence of the soul causes these movements and this heat to cease; and thus it has been thought, without reason,

present to itself the I=2, is the *peccatum originale* of the Cartesian system."

Marginal jotting by Coleridge in a copy of Descartes' *Opera Philosophica*, once owned by him, and now in the library of the University of Vermont.

that our natural heat and all the motions of our body depend upon the soul; instead of which it should be thought, on the contrary, that soul departs, when death occurs, only because this heat fails and the organs which serve to move the body decay.

Article VI.

The difference between a living and a dead body.

In order, then, that we may avoid this error, let us consider that death never takes place through the absence of a soul, but solely because some one of the principal parts of the body has fallen into decay; and let us conclude that the body of a living man differs as much from that of a dead man as does a watch or other automaton (that is to say, or other machine which moves of itself), when it is wound up, and has within itself the material principle of the movements for which it is constructed, with all that is necessary for its action, from the same watch or other machine, when it has been broken, and the principle of its movement ceases to act.

Article VII.

*Brief explanation of the parts of the body and of some of its functions.**

In order to render this more intelligible, I will explain here in a few words how the entire mechanism of our body is composed. There is no one who does not already know that there is in us a heart, a brain, a stomach, muscles, nerves, arteries, veins, and such things; it is known also that the food we eat descends

---

* Cf. Discourse on Method, pt. v. (*Œuvres*, t. i, p. 173); Veitch, p. 46.

into the stomach and the bowels, where their juices, flowing through the liver and through all the veins, mix themselves with the blood they contain, and by this means increase its quantity. Those who have heard the least talk in medicine know, further, how the heart is constructed, and how all the blood of the veins can easily flow through the *vena cava* on its right side, and thence pass into the lung, by the vessel which is called the arterial vein, then return from the lung on the left side of the heart, by the vessel called the venous artery, and finally pass thence into the great artery, the branches of which are diffused through the whole body. Also, all those whom the authority of the ancients has not entirely blinded, and who are willing to open their eyes to examine the opinion of Hervæus * in regard to the circulation of the blood, have no doubt whatever that all the veins and arteries of the body are merely channels through which the blood flows without cessation and very rapidly, starting from the right cavity of the heart by the arterial vein, the branches of which are dispersed throughout the lungs and joined to that of the venous artery, by which it passes from the lungs into the left side of the heart; next, from thence it passes into the great artery, the branches of which, scattered throughout all the rest of the body, are joined to the branches of the vein, which carry once more the same blood into the right cavity of the heart; so that these two cavities are like sluices, through each of which all the blood passes every time it makes the circuit of the body. Still further, it is known that all the movements of the limbs depend upon the muscles, and that these muscles are opposed to one another in such a

* Harvey. See tribute to Harvey, *Œuvres*, t. ix, p. 361.

way that, when one of them contracts, it draws toward itself the part of the body to which it is attached, which at the same time stretches out the muscle which is opposed to it ; then, if it happens, at another time, that this last contracts, it causes the first to lengthen, and draws toward itself the part to which they are attached. Finally, it is known that all these movements of the muscles, as also all the senses, depend upon the nerves, which are like minute threads, or small tubes, all of which come from the brain, and contain, like that, a certain subtle air or breath, which is called the animal spirits.

Article VIII.

The principle of all these functions.

But it is not commonly known in what manner these animal spirits and these nerves contribute to the movements of the limbs and to the senses, nor what is the corporeal principle which makes them act; it is for this reason, although I have already touched upon this matter in other writings,* I shall not omit to say here briefly, that, as long as we live, there is a continual heat in our heart, which is a kind of fire kept up there by the blood of the veins, and that this fire is the corporeal principle of the movements of our limbs. . . . .

Article XVI.

How all the limbs can be moved by the objects of the senses and by the spirits without the aid of the soul.

Finally, it is to be observed that the machine of our body is so constructed that all the changes which

* On Man, see above p. 280; also Discourse, etc.; Veitch, p. 52.

occur in the motion of the spirits may cause them to open certain pores of the brain rather than others, and, reciprocally, that when any one of these pores is opened in the least degree more or less than is usual by the action of the nerves which serve the senses, this changes somewhat the motion of the spirits, and causes them to be conducted into the muscles which serve to move the body in the way in which it is commonly moved on occasion of such action ; so that all the movements which we make without our will contributing thereto (as frequently happens when we breathe, or walk, or eat, and, in fine, perform all those actions which are common to us and the brutes) depend only on the conformation of our limbs and the course which the spirits, excited by the heat of the heart, naturally follow in the brain, in the nerves, and in the muscles, in the same way that the movement of a watch is produced by the force solely of its mainspring and the form of its wheels.* . . . .

Article XXX.

That the soul is united to all parts of the body conjointly.

But, in order to understand all these things more perfectly, it is necessary to know that the soul is truly joined to the entire body, and that it cannot properly be said to be in any one of its parts to the exclusion of the rest, because the body is one, and in a manner

---

* " Can the Bruckers and the German Manualists have read this work of Descartes—which yet was his most popular treatise—that they should (one, I guess, copying from the other) talk of Spinoza's having given Leibnitz the *hint* of his pre-established Harmony ? What is this XVIth Article, if not a clear and distinct statement of this theory ?"—*Marginal note by Coleridge.*

indivisible, on account of the arrangement of its organs, which are so related to one another, that when any one of them is taken away, that makes the whole body defective : and because the soul is of a nature which has no relation to extension, or to dimensions, or other properties of the matter of which the body is composed, but solely to the whole collection of its organs, as appears from the fact that we cannot at all conceive of the half or the third of a soul, nor what space it occupies, and that it does not become any smaller when any part of the body is cut off, but that it separates itself entirely from it when the combination of its organs is broken up.

Article XXXI.

That there is a small gland in the brain in which the soul exercises its functions more particularly than in the other parts.

It is, also, necessary to know that, although the soul is joined to the entire body, there is, nevertheless, a certain part of the body in which it exercises its functions more particularly than in all the rest ; and it is commonly thought that this part is the brain, or, perhaps, the heart : the brain, because to it the organs of sense are related ; and the heart, because it is as if there the passions are felt. But, after careful examination, it seems to me quite evident that the part of the body in which the soul immediately exercises its functions is neither the heart, nor even the brain as a whole, but solely the most interior part of it, which is a certain very small gland, situated in the middle of its substance, and so suspended above the passage by which the spirits of its anterior cavities communicate with those of the posterior, that the slightest motions in it may greatly affect the course of these spirits, and, reciprocally, that the slightest changes which take place in the course of the spirits may greatly affect the motions of this gland.

ARTICLE XXXII.

How this gland is known to be the principal seat of the soul.

The reason which convinces me that the soul cannot have in the whole body any other place than this gland where it exercises its functions immediately, is the consideration that the other parts of our brain are all double, just as also we have two eyes, two hands, two ears, and, in fine, all the organs of our external senses are double; and inasmuch as we have but one single and simple thought of the same thing at the same time, there must necessarily be some place where the two images which by means of the two eyes, or the two other impressions which come from a single object by means of the double organs of the other senses, may unite in one before they reach the mind, in order that they may not present to it two objects in place of one; and it may easily be conceived that these images or other impressions unite in this gland, through the medium of the spirits which fill the cavities of the brain; but there is no other place whatever in the whole body, where they can thus be united, except as they have first been united in this gland.

[*Letter to Mersenne, July* 30, 1640.*

As for the letter of the physician De Sens, it contains no argument to impugn what I have written upon the gland called *conarium*, except that he says that it can be changed like all the brain, which does not at all prevent its being the principal seat of the soul;

*Œuvres, t. viii, p. 301.

for it is certain that the soul must be joined to some part of the body, and there is no point which is not as much or more liable to alteration than this gland, which, although it is very small and very soft, nevertheless, on account of its situation, is so well protected, that it can be almost as little subject to any disease as the crystalline humor of the eye; and it happens more frequently indeed that persons become troubled in mind, without any known cause, in which case it may be assigned to some disorder of this gland, than it happens that sight fails by any defect of this crystalline humor, besides that all the other changes which happen to the mind, as when one falls asleep after drinking, etc., may be ascribed to some changes occurring in this gland.

As for what he says about the mind's being able to make use of double organs, I agree with him, and that it makes use also of the spirits, all of which cannot reside in this gland; but I do not at all conceive that the mind is so restricted to it that it cannot extend its activity beyond it; but it is one thing to make use of, and another thing to be immediately joined and united to it; and our mind not being double, but one and indivisible, it seems to me that the part of the body to which it is most immediately united must also be one and not divided into two similar parts, and I find nothing of that kind in the whole brain except this gland.*

* It is needless to say that modern physiology fails to confirm the view of Descartes concerning the pineal gland as the seat of the soul. "Its nervous nature is doubtful, and its function in man obscure or absent, but it is constant among vertebrates, and in several, especially lizards, it is connected with a more or less rudimentary eye in the middle of the top of the head." Foster's *Medical Dictionary*, p. 1724.]

Article XXXIII.

That the seat of the passions is not in the heart.

As for the opinion of those who think that the soul experiences its passions in the heart, it is of no great account, because it is founded only on the fact that the passions cause some stir to be felt there; and it is easy to see that this change is felt, as if in the heart, only through the medium of a small nerve, which descends to it from the brain, just as pain is felt as if in the foot through the medium of the nerves of the foot, and the stars are perceived as in the heavens by the medium of their light and the optic nerves; so that it is no more necessary that our soul exercise its functions immediately in the heart in order to feel there its passions, than it is necessary that it should be in the heavens in order to see the stars there.

Article XXXIV.

How the soul and the body act one upon the other.

Let us conceive, then, that the soul has its principal seat in this little gland in the middle of the brain, whence it radiates to all the rest of the body by means of the spirits, the nerves, and even of the blood, which, participating in the impressions of the mind, can carry them by means of the arteries into all the members; and, bearing in mind what has been said above concerning the machine of our body, to wit, that the minute filaments of our nerves are so distributed throughout all its parts that, on occasion of the different motions which are excited there by means of sensible objects, they open in divers manners the pores of the brain, which causes the animal spirits contained in these cavities to enter in various ways into the muscles, by means of which they can move the limbs in all the different ways of which they are capable, and, also, that all the other causes, which in other ways can set the spirits in motion, have the effect to turn them upon various muscles [keeping all this in mind], let us add here that the little gland which is the principal seat of the soul is so suspended between the cavities which contain the spirits, that it can be affected by them in all the different ways that there are sensible differences in objects ; but that it can also be variously affected by the soul, which is of such a nature that it receives as many different impressions—that is to say, that it has as many different perceptions—as there occur different motions in this gland ; as also, reciprocally, the machine of the body is so composed that from the simple fact that this gland is variously affected by the soul, or by whatever other cause, it impels the spirits which surround it toward the pores of the brain, which discharge them by means of the nerves upon the muscles, whereby it causes them to move the limbs. . . . .

Article XL.
The principal effect of the passions.

It is to be noted that the principal effect of all the passions in man is that they incite and dispose the mind to will the things to which they prepare the body, so that the sentiment of fear incites it to will to fly ; that of courage, to will to fight ; and so of the rest.

Article XLI.
The power of the mind over the body.

But the will is so free in its nature that it can never be constrained ; and of the two kinds of thoughts which I have distinguished in the mind—of which one is its actions, that is, its volitions; the other its passions, taking this word in its most general signification, comprehending all sorts of perceptions—the first of these are absolutely in its power, and can be changed only indirectly by the body, while, on the contrary, the last depend absolutely on the movements which give rise to them, and they can be affected only indirectly by the mind, except when it is itself the cause of them. And the whole action of the mind consists in this, that by the simple fact of its willing anything it causes the little gland, to which it is closely joined, to produce the result appropriate to the volition.

ARTICLE XLII.

How the things we wish to recall are found in the memory.

Thus, when the mind wills to recall anything, this volition causes the gland, by inclining successively to different sides, to impel the spirits toward different parts of the brain, until they come upon that where the traces are left of the thing it wills to remember; for these traces are due to nothing else than the circumstance that the pores of the brain, through which the spirits have already taken their course, on presentation of that object, have thereby acquired a greater facility than the rest to be opened again in the same way by the spirits which come to them; so that these spirits coming upon these pores, enter therein more readily than into the others, by which means they excite a particular motion in the gland, which represents to the mind the same object, and causes it to recognize that it is that which it willed to remember.

Article XLIII.

How the mind can imagine, attend, and move the body.

Thus, when it is desired to imagine something which has never been seen, the will has the power to cause the gland to move in the manner requisite to impel the spirits toward the pores of the brain by the opening of which that thing can be represented; so, when one wills to keep his attention fixed for some time upon the same object, this volition keeps the gland inclined during that time in the same direction; so, finally, when one wills to walk or to move his body in any way, this volition causes the gland to impel the spirits toward the muscles which serve that purpose.

Article XLIV.

That each volition is naturally connected with some motion of the gland, but that, by intention or by habit, the will may be connected with others.

Nevertheless, it is not always the volition to excite within us a certain motion, or other effect, which is the cause of its being excited; but this varies according as nature or habit has variously united each motion of the gland to each thought. Thus, for example, if one desires to adjust his eyes to look at a very distant object, this volition causes the pupil of the eye to expand, and if he desires to adjust them so as to see an object very near, this volition makes it contract; but if he simply thinks of expanding the pupil, he wills in vain—the pupil will not expand for that, inasmuch as nature has not connected the motion of the gland, which serves to impel the spirits toward the optic nerve in the manner requisite for expanding or contracting the pupil, with the volition to expand or contract, but with that of looking at objects distant or near. And when, in talking, we think only of the meaning of what we wish to say, that makes us move the tongue and lips much more rapidly and better than if we thought to move them in all ways requisite for the utterance of the same words, inasmuch as the habit we have acquired in learning to talk has made us join the action of the mind—which, through the medium of the gland, can move the tongue and the lips—with the meaning of the words which follow these motions rather than with the motions themselves. . . . .

ARTICLE XLVII.

Wherein consist the conflicts which are imagined to exist between the inferior and the superior parts of the soul.

It is only in the opposition between the motions that the body through the spirits, and the soul through the will, tend to excite at the same time in the gland, that all the conflicts consist which are commonly imagined to arise between the inferior part of the soul, which is called sensitive, and the superior part, which is rational, or rather between the natural appetites and the will; for there is but one soul within us, and that soul has in it no diversity of parts whatever; the same which is sensitive is rational, and all its appetites are volitions. The error which is committed in making it play the parts of different persons commonly opposed to each other arises only from the want of a right distinction of its functions from those of the body, to which is to be attributed all that which may be observed within us to be hostile to our reason, so that there is in this no other conflict whatever, except that the little gland which is in the middle of the brain may be pushed on the one side by the soul and on the other by the animal spirits, which are only corporeal, as I have said above, and it often happens that these two impulses are contrary, and the stronger hinders the effect of the other. Now there may be distinguished two kinds of motion excited by the spirits in the gland ; the one represents to the soul the objects which move the senses, or the impressions which meet in the brain, and produce no effect upon the will ; the other kind is those which produce some effect upon it, namely, those which cause the passions or the movements of the body which accompany them ; and as for the first, although they often hinder the actions of the soul, or perhaps may be hindered by them, nevertheless, because they are not directly opposed, no conflict is observed. . . . .

PART II.

Article LI.

The primary causes of the passions.

IT is understood, from what has been said above, that the last and proximate cause of the passions of the soul is nothing but the motion imparted by the spirits to the little gland in the middle of the brain. But this is not enough to enable us to distinguish them from one another; it is necessary to trace them to their sources and to inquire into their primary causes; now, although they may sometimes be caused by the action of the mind, which determines to think upon such or such objects, and also by the mere bodily temperament or by the impressions which happen to present themselves in the brain, as occurs when one feels sad or joyous without being able to assign any reason for it, it should appear, nevertheless, according to what has been said, that the same passions may all be excited by objects which move the senses, and that these objects are their most ordinary and principal causes; whence it follows that, to discover them all, it is sufficient to consider all the effects of these objects.

Article LII.

What service they render, and how their number may be determined.

I observe, further, that the objects which move the senses do not excite in us different passions by reason of all the diversities which are in them, but solely on account of the different ways in which they can injure or profit us, or, in general, be important to us; and that the service which all the passions render consists in this alone, that they dispose the mind to choose the things which nature teaches us are useful, and to persist in this choice, while also the same motion of the spirits which commonly causes them disposes the body to the movements which serve to the performance of those things; this is why, in order to determine the number of the passions, it is necessary merely to inquire, in due order, how many different ways important to us there are in which our senses can be moved by their objects; and I shall here make the enumeration of all the principal passions in the order in which they may thus be found.

Article LIII.
Wonder.

When on first meeting an object we are surprised, and judge it to be novel, or very different from what we knew it before, or from what we supposed it should be, this causes us to wonder at it and be astonished; and since this may happen before we could know whether this object was beneficial to us or not, it seems to me that wonder is the first of all the passions; and it has no contrary, because, if the object which presents itself has nothing in it which surprises us, we are not at all moved by it, and we regard it without emotion.

Article LXVIII.

Why this enumeration of the passions differs from that commonly received.

Such is the order which seems to me the best in enumerating the passions. I know very well that in this my position is different from that of all who have hitherto written upon them, but it is so not without important reason. For they derive their enumeration from their distinction in the sensitive part of the soul of two appetites, one of which they call *concupiscible*, the other *irascible*.* And, inasmuch as I recognize in the soul no distinction of parts, as I have said above, this seems to me to signify nothing else but that it has two faculties: one of desiring, the other of being angry; and because it has in the same way the faculties of admiring, of loving, of hoping, of fearing, and of entertaining each of the other passions, or of performing the actions to which these passions incline it, I do not see why they have chosen to refer all to desire or to anger. Moreover, their enumeration does not include all the principal passions, as I believe this does. I speak only of the principal ones, because there may still be distinguished many other more special ones, and their number is indefinite.

ARTICLE LXIX.

That there are only six primary passions.

But the number of those which are simple and primary is not very great. For, on reviewing all those which I have enumerated, it is readily observed that there are only six of this sort; to wit, wonder, love, hate, desire, joy, and sadness, and that all the rest are made up of some of these six, or at least are species of them. This is why, in order that their number may not embarrass my readers, I shall here treat separately of the six primaries; and afterward I shall show how all the rest derive their origin from these.

* Plato, *Republic*, bk. iv.

Article LXXIV.
In what respect the passions are of service and in what they are harmful.

Now it is easy to see, from what has been said above, that the usefulness of all the passions consists only in this, that they strengthen and make enduring in the mind the thoughts which it is well for it to keep, and which but for that might easily be effaced from it. As, also, all the evil they can cause consists in their strengthening and preserving those thoughts in the mind more than there is any need of, or else that they strengthen and preserve others which it is not well for the mind to attend to.

Article LXXIX.
Definitions of love and hatred.

Love is an emotion of the soul, caused by the motion of the spirits, which incites it to unite itself voluntarily to those objects which appear to it to be agreeable. And hatred is an emotion, caused by the spirits, which incites the mind to will to be separated from objects which present themselves to it as harmful. I say that these emotions are caused by the spirits, in order to distinguish love and hatred, which are passions, and depend upon the body, as well as the judgments which also incline the mind to unite itself voluntarily with the things which it regards as good, and to separate itself from those which it regards as evil, as the emotions which these judgments excite in the soul.

Article LXXX.
What is meant by voluntary union and separation.

For the rest, by the word *voluntarily*, I do not here intend desire, which is a passion by itself, and relates to the future, but the consent wherein one considers himself for the moment as united with the beloved object, conceiving as it were of one whole of which he thinks himself but one part, and the object beloved the other. While on the contrary, in the case of hatred, one considers himself alone as a whole, entirely separated from the object for which he has aversion.

ARTICLE LXXXVI.

Definition of desire.

The passion of desire is an agitation of the soul, caused by the spirits, which disposes it to wish for the future the objects which it represents to itself to be agreeable. Thus one desires not only the presence of absent good, but also the preservation of the present good, and, in addition, the absence of evil, as well that which is already experienced, as that which it is feared the future may bring.

ARTICLE XCI.

Definition of joy.

Joy is an agreeable emotion of the soul in which the enjoyment consists which it has in any good that the impressions of the brain represent to it as its own. I say that it is in this emotion that the enjoyment of good consists, for in reality the soul receives no other fruit of all the goods it possesses ; and so long as it has no joy in them, it may be said that it has no more fruition of them than if it did not possess them at all. I add, also, that it is of good which the impressions of the brain represent to it as its own, in order not to confound this joy, which is a passion, with the purely intellectual joy, which arises in the mind by the simple activity of the mind, and which may be said to be an agreeable emotion excited within itself, in which consists the enjoyment which it has of the good which its understanding represents to it as its own. It is true that, so long as the mind is joined to the body, this intellectual joy can scarcely fail to be accompanied with that joy which is passion ; for, as soon as our understanding perceives that we possess any good, although that good may be as different as imaginable from all that pertains to the body, the imagination does not fail on the instant to make an impression on the brain, upon which follows the motion of the spirits which excites the passion of joy.

Article XCII.

Definition of sadness.

Sadness is a disagreeable languor, in which consists the distress which the mind experiences from the evil or the defect which the impressions of the brain represent as pertaining to it. And there is also an intellectual sadness, which is not the passion, but which seldom fails to be accompanied by it.

Article XCVI.

The motions of the blood and the spirits which cause these five passions.

The five passions which I have here begun to explain are so joined or opposed to one another, that it is easier to consider them all together than to treat of each separately (as wonder has been treated) ; and the cause of them is not as is the case with wonder, in the brain alone, but also in the heart, the spleen, the liver, and in all other parts of the body, in so far as they serve in the production of the blood, and thereby of the spirits; for although all the veins conduct the blood they contain toward the heart, it happens, nevertheless, that sometimes the blood in some of them is impelled thither with more force than that in others; it happens, also, that the openings by which it enters into the heart, or else those by which it passes out, are more enlarged or more contracted at one time than at another. . . . .

ARTICLE CXXXVII.

Of the utility of these five passions here explained, in so far as they relate to the body.

Having given the definitions of love, of hatred, of desire, of joy, of sadness (and treated of all the corporeal movements which cause or accompany them*) we have only to consider here their utility. In regard to which it is to be noted that, according to the appointment of nature, they all relate to the body, and are bestowed upon the mind only in so far as it is connected with it; so that their natural use is to incite the mind to consent and contribute to the actions which may aid in the preservation of the body, or render it in any way more perfect; and, in this sense, sadness and joy are the first two which are employed. For the mind is immediately warned of the things which harm the body only through the sensation of pain, which produces in it first the passion of sadness; next, hatred of that which causes this pain; and thirdly, the desire to be delivered from it; likewise the mind is made aware immediately of things useful to the body only by some sort of pleasure,

---

* In the intervening Articles.

which excites in it joy, then gives birth to love of that which is believed to be the cause of it, and, finally, the desire to acquire that which can make the joy continue, or else that the like may be enjoyed again. Whence it is apparent that these five passions are all very useful as regards the body, and also that sadness is, in a certain way, first and more necessary than joy, and hatred than love, because it is more important to repel things which harm and may destroy us, than to acquire those which add a perfection without which we can still subsist. . . . .

Article CXLIV.

Of desires where the issue depends only on ourselves.

But because the passions can impel us to action only through the medium of the desire which we must take pains to regulate—and in this consists the principal use of morality ; now, as I have just said, as it is always good when it follows a true knowledge, so it cannot fail to be bad when it is based on error. And it seems to me that the error most commonly committed in regard to desires is the failure to distinguish sufficiently the things which depend entirely upon ourselves and those which do not ; for, as for those which depend only upon ourselves, that is to say, upon our free will, it is sufficient to know that they are good to make it impossible for us to desire them with too great ardor, since to do the good things which depend upon ourselves is to follow virtue, and it is certain that one cannot have too ardent a desire for virtue, and moreover, it being impossible for us to fail of success in what we desire in this way, since it depends on ourselves alone, we shall always attain all the satisfaction that we have expected. But the most common fault in this matter is not that too much, but too little, is desired; and the sovereign remedy against that is to deliver the mind as much as possible from all other less useful desires, then to try to understand very clearly, and to consider attentively, the excellence of that which is to be desired.

ARTICLE CXLV.

Of those which depend only on other things.

As for the things which depend in no wise upon ourselves, however good they may be, they should never be desired with passion ; not only because they may not come to pass, and in that case we should be so much the more cast down, as we have the more desired them, but principally because by occupying our thoughts they divert our interest from other things the acquisition of which depends upon ourselves. And there are two general remedies for these vain desires; the first is high-mindedness (*la générosité*), of which I shall speak presently ; the second is frequent meditation on Divine Providence, with the reflection that it is impossible that anything should happen in any other manner than has been determined from all eternity by this Providence ; so that it is like a destiny or an immutable necessity, which is to be contrasted with chance in order to destroy it as a chimera arising only from an error of our understanding. For we can desire only those things which we regard as being in some way possible, and we do not regard as possible things which do not at all depend upon ourselves, except in so far as we think that they depend on chance, that is to say, as we judge that they can happen, and that similar things have happened before. Now this opinion is based only on the fact that we do not know all the causes which have contributed to each effect; for when anything which we have thought depended upon chance has not taken place, this shows that some one of the causes necessary to produce it was wanting, and, consequently, that it was absolutely impossible, and the like of it never took place; that is to say, to the production of the like a similar cause was also wanting, so that, had we not been ignorant of that beforehand, we never should have thought it possible, and consequently should not have desired it.

ARTICLE CXLVI.

Of those things which depend upon ourselves and others.

It is necessary then utterly to reject the common opinion that there is externally to ourselves a chance which causes things to happen or not to happen, at its pleasure, and to know, on the other hand, that everything is guided by Divine Providence, whose eternal decree is so infallible and immutable, that, excepting the things which the same decree has willed to depend upon our free choice, we must think that in regard to us nothing happens which is not necessary, and, as it were, destined, so that we cannot, without folly, wish it to happen otherwise. But because most of our desires extend to things, all of which do not depend upon ourselves, nor all of them upon others, we should distinguish precisely that in them which depends only on ourselves in order to confine our desires to that; and, moreover, although we should consider success therein to be altogether a matter of immutable destiny, in order that our desires may not be taken up with it, we ought not to fail to consider the reasons which make it more or less to be hoped for, to the end that they may serve to regulate our conduct ; as, for example, if we had business in a certain place to which we might go by two different roads, one of which was ordinarily much safer than the other, although perhaps the decree of Providence was such that if we went by the road considered safest we should certainly be robbed, and that, on the contrary, we might travel the other with no danger at all, we ought not on that account to be indifferent in choosing between them, nor rest on the immutable destiny of that decree ; but reason would have it that we should choose the road which was ordinarily considered the safer, and our desire should be satisfied regarding that when we have followed it, whatever be the evil that happens to us, because that evil, being as regards ourselves inevitable, we have had no reason to desire to be exempt from it, but simply to do the very best that our understanding is able to discover, as I assume we have done. And it is certain that when one thus makes a practice of distinguishing destiny from chance, he easily accustoms himself so to regulate his desires that, in so far as their accomplishment depends only upon himself, they may always afford him entire satisfaction.

ARTICLE CXLVII.

Of the interior emotions of the mind.

I will simply add a consideration which appears to me of much service in averting from us the disturbance of the passions : it is that our good and our evil principally depend upon the interior emotions, which are excited in the mind only by the mind itself, in which respect they differ from its passions, which always depend upon some motion of the spirits ; and although these emotions of the mind are often united with the passions which resemble them, they may often also agree with others, and even arise from those which are contrary to them. .... And when we read of strange adventures in a book, or see them represented on the stage, this excites in us sometimes sadness, sometimes joy, or love, or hatred, and, in general, all the passions, according to the diversity of the objects which present themselves to our imagination ; but along with that we have the pleasure of feeling them excited within us, and this pleasure is an intellectual joy, which can arise from sadness as well as from any other passion.*

Article CXLVIII.

That the practice of virtue is a sovereign remedy for all the passions.

Now, inasmuch as these interior emotions touch us more nearly, and in consequence have much greater power over us than the passions from which they differ, which occur with them, it is certain that, provided the mind have that within wherewith it may be content, all the troubles which come from elsewhere have no power whatever to disturb it, but rather serve to augment its joy, in that, seeing that it cannot be troubled by them, it is thereby made aware of its own superiority. And to the end that the mind may have that wherewith to be content, it needs but to follow

* Cf. Aristotle, *Poetics*, 6.

virtue perfectly. For whoever has lived in such a manner that his conscience cannot reproach him with ever having failed to do any of those things which he has judged to be the best (which is what I call here following virtue), he enjoys a satisfaction so potent in ministering to his happiness, that the most violent efforts of the passions never have power enough to disturb the tranquillity of his mind.

PART III.

Article CXLIX.

Of esteem and contempt.

HAVING explained the six primitive passions, which are, as it were, genera, of which all the rest are species, I will here notice briefly what special ones there are in each of the others, and will observe the same order in accordance with which I have enumerated them above. The first two are esteem and contempt; for, although these names ordinarily signify only the opinion held, without passion, concerning the value of anything, nevertheless, because from these opinions there often arise passions to which no particular names have been given, it seems to me that these may be assigned to them. And esteem, in so far as it is a passion, is an inclination which the mind has to represent to itself the value of the thing esteemed, which inclination is caused by a particular motion of the spirits, so converged into the brain as to strengthen the impressions which relate to this subject; while, on the contrary, the passion of contempt is an inclination which the mind has to dwell upon the baseness or littleness of that which it despises, caused by the motion of the spirits which strengthens the idea of this littleness.

Article CL.

Thus these two passions are only species of wonder.

Article CLI.

Now these two passions may, generally speaking, relate to all sorts of objects; but they are chiefly worthy of attention when they relate to ourselves, that is to say, when it is our own merit or demerit that we judge of; and the motion of the spirits which causes them is then so manifest that it shows itself in the whole bearing, the gestures, the walk, and, in general, in all the actions of those who conceive a better or a worse opinion of themselves than common.

Article CLII.

The ground of self-esteem.

And inasmuch as one chief part of wisdom is to know in what degree and on what ground one ought to esteem or contemn himself, I will now attempt to state my opinion. I observe within ourselves but one thing which can afford just ground for self-esteem, namely, the use we make of our free-will, and the control we have over our desires; for it is only the actions which depend upon this free-will for which we may, with reason, be praised or blamed; and it makes us in a certain way like to Deity, by making us masters of ourselves, provided we do not, by a base remissness, lose the rights which it confers.

Article CLIII.

In what high-mindedness consists.

Accordingly I think that true high-mindedness (*générosité*), which makes a man esteem himself as highly as it is legitimate for him to do, simply consists, in part, in his being persuaded that there is nothing which truly belongs to him but this free control over his desires, and that there is no reason why he should be praised or blamed, except because he has used this power well or ill ; and, in part, that he is conscious within himself of a firm and steadfast determination to use it well, that is to say, never to fail willingly to undertake and to carry out all things which he shall judge to be the best: which is to follow virtue perfectly.

Article CLIV.

That it keeps one from despising others.

Those who have this knowledge and sentiment concerning themselves are easily persuaded that any other man may have it also of himself, because there is nothing in it which depends on other persons. It is for this reason that they never despise anyone ; and although they see that others commit faults which betray their weakness, they are nevertheless more inclined to excuse than to blame them, and to believe that it is more from want of knowledge than from want of will that they have done these things ; and while they do not think themselves much inferior to those who have greater possessions or honors, or even to those who have more intellect, more learning, more beauty, or, in general, who surpass them in any other perfections, so, on the other hand, they do not esteem themselves much above those whom they surpass, because all these things appear to them quite inconsiderable in comparison with the good will, for which alone they esteem themselves, and which they assume to be, or at least may possibly be, in every other man.

Article CLV.

In what virtuous humility consists.

Thus the most high-minded are usually the most humble; and virtuous humility consists simply in this, that reflecting on the infirmity of our nature and upon the faults which we have committed in the past, or are capable of committing, which are not less than those of others, we do not prefer ourselves above anyone else, mindful that others have free-will as well as we, and may make as good use of it.

Article CLVI.

The characteristics of high-mindedness, and how it serves as a remedy for all the disorders of the passions.

Those who are high-minded, after this sort, are naturally led to do great things, and yet not to attempt anything of which they do not think themselves capable ; and because they do not esteem anything greater than to do good to other men, and to think lightly of their own advantage, for this reason they are always perfectly courteous, affable, and obliging toward everyone. And at the same time they have complete control of their passions, particularly of the desires, of jealousy and envy, inasmuch as there is nothing the acquisition of which does not depend on themselves, that they think worth sighing for ; and they are able to control the passion of hatred, because they think well of all men ; and of fear, because the confidence they have in their virtue gives them assurance ; and finally, of anger, because, esteeming but lightly all things which depend on others, they never give so much advantage to their enemies as to show that they have been offended. . . . .

Article CLXXXV.

Of pity.

Pity is a species of grief, mingled with love or good will toward those whom we see suffering some evil which we think they have not deserved. It is thus contrary to envy, by virtue of its object, and to ridicule, because it regards that object in a different way.

Article CLXXXVI.

Who are the most compassionate.

Those who are keenly sensible of their infirmities, and of their exposure to the adversities of fortune, appear to be more inclined to this feeling than others, because they represent the evil which happens to another as something which might happen to themselves; and they are thus moved to compassion rather through the love which they bear themselves than that they have for others.

Article CLXXXVII.

How the more generous are affected by this sentiment.

But, nevertheless, those who are more noble and who have the greater fortitude, so that they fear no evil for themselves, and thus place themselves beyond the power of fortune, are not devoid of pity when they look upon the infirmities of others and hear their complaints; for it is the mark of the noble mind to desire the happiness of everyone. But the sadness of this pity is not bitter, and, like that caused by the tragic scenes which one witnesses in a theater, it is rather an external affair and more a matter of the senses than of the mind itself,* which, nevertheless, has the satisfaction of thinking it has discharged its duty in that it has sympathized with the afflicted. And there is this difference, that whereas most people feel pity for those who complain, because they think that the evils they suffer are very serious, the principal object of compassion on the part of greater minds, on the other hand, is the weakness of those whom they see complaining, because they consider that no adversity that can possibly occur is so great an evil as the pusillanimity of those who cannot endure it with constancy ; and, although they abhor vices, they do not abhor those whom they perceive to be subject to them, but simply regard them with pity. . . . .

ARTICLE CCXII.

That upon the passions alone depend all the good and the evil of this life.

To conclude : The mind may indeed have its own pleasures apart from the body, but as for those which it has in common with the body, these depend entirely

* "Not always. A man of great fortitude and nobleness of character may at the same time possess great constitutional sensibility, with a lively imagination. Now the latter will represent to him the distresses of another, whether known by verbal description, or by the usual signs and visual language of pain or grief, with great vividness and distinctness of impression, and thus produce in his own passive life perhaps even more acute feelings and stronger sentiments of grief than the actual sufferer's nature is susceptible of—while he cannot take for granted an equal share of fortitude with himself. He fancies himself suffering the distress without the power of enduring it—and apart from the alleviations and compensations with which it would be accompanied in his own instance—and this may be a very painful sympathy.—S. T. C."
Marginal jotting by Coleridge.

upon the passions, insomuch that the men whom they can most deeply stir are capable of tasting most sensibly the sweetness of this life, but it is true also they may experience most keenly its bitterness, in case they know not how to regulate them, or fortune be contrary ; but in this very thing appears the principal use of wisdom, that it teaches a man how to become master of himself, and so skillfully to regulate his passions that the evils they cause shall be quite endurable, while from every one of them he shall extract its due delight.

ETHICS.
LETTERS ON THE HAPPY LIFE AND THE HIGHEST GOOD.

ON THE HAPPY LIFE.*

WHEN I decided upon Seneca's book *De Vita Beata* to propose to your Highness as an agreeable subject for correspondence, I had in mind merely the reputation of the author and the importance of the subject, without considering the treatment he had given it, which, when I did consider afterward, I did not find to be quite careful enough to deserve to be followed. But in order that your Highness may the more easily judge of it, I will endeavor to explain in what manner it seems to me that this subject should have been treated by a philosopher such as he was, who, not being enlightened by faith, had only natural reason for his guide. He says very well at the beginning : *Vivere omnes beate volunt, sed ad pervidendum quid sit quod beatam vitam efficiat, caligant.* But we need to know what *vivere beate* is. I would say in French *vivre heureusement*, if it were not that there is a difference between *l'heur* and *la béatitude*, namely, that *l'heur* depends merely on things external to us, whence it comes about that those are rather to be esteemed fortunate than prudent (*sages*) to whom some good happens which they have not themselves procured, whereas *la béatitude* consists, as it seems to me, in a perfect contentment of spirit and an interior satisfaction which the most favored of Fortune do not commonly have and which the virtuous (*les sages*) acquire without her aid. Accordingly, *vivere beate*,

*Letters to the Princess Elisabeth, *Œuvres*, t. ix, pp. 210-249.

vivre en béatitude, is nothing else than to have the mind perfectly content and satisfied.

Considering next what *quod beatam vitam efficiat* means, that is to say, what the things are which are able to yield us this supreme contentment, I observe that they are of two kinds, namely, those which depend upon ourselves, such as virtue and wisdom, and those which do not depend upon ourselves, such as honors, riches, and health; for it is certain that a man well-born, who is in health, and in want of nothing, and who, besides that, is as wise and virtuous as another man who is poor, sickly, and deformed, can enjoy the more complete contentment. Still, as a little vessel may be as full as a larger one, although it hold less liquid, so, taking the contentment of each to mean the fulfillment and satisfaction of his desires regulated according to reason, I do not doubt that the poorest and most disgraced of fortune or of nature may be as entirely content and satisfied as others, although they may not enjoy so many advantages. And it is this sort of contentment only which is here considered; for since the other is in no wise within our power, inquiry regarding it would be superfluous. Now it seems to me that everyone has it in his power to secure contentment from himself alone, without seeking for it elsewhere, provided only he will observe three things, to which relate the three rules of conduct which I have laid down in the Discourse on Method.*

The first is that he always endeavor to use his mind in the best way possible to him, to find out what ought to be done or not to be done in all the occurrences of life. The second is that he maintain a firm

---

* *Œuvres*, t. i, pp. 146–153. See above, pp. 50–55.

and constant resolution to carry out everything which his reason dictates, without being turned aside therefrom by his passions or his appetites ; and it is this firmness of resolution which I believe should be taken for virtue, although I am not aware that anyone hitherto has so defined it ; but it has been divided into many species, to which different names have been given, in view to the different objects to which it relates.

The third, that, while he is thus conducting his life so far as possible in accordance with reason, he consider all advantages which he does not possess as being one and all entirely beyond his power, and that he thus accustom himself not to desire them ; for there is nothing but desire or regret or repentance which can prevent us from being contented. But if we always do as our reason dictates, we shall never have any occasion for repentance, because, although in the event we may see that we were deceived, it could not be through our own fault. And the reason why we do not desire to have, for example, more arms or more tongues than we do, but desire rather to have more health and more riches, is merely that we imagine that these latter may be acquired by our effort, or perhaps that they are due to our birth, and in the other case it is not so. We ought to rid ourselves of this opinion, by considering that, in case we have always followed the dictates of our reason, we have omitted nothing of that which was within our power, and that maladies and misfortunes are no less natural to man than prosperity and health.

Finally, not every sort of desire is incompatible with true happiness (*la béatitude*) but only those which are accompanied with impatience and sadness. It is not necessary, also, that our reason never deceive us; it is enough that our conscience give its inward witness that we have never been wanting in the resolution and the virtue to perform everything which we have judged to be the best ; and thus virtue alone is sufficient to make us contented in this life.

But nevertheless, inasmuch as our virtue, when it is not sufficiently enlightened by the understanding, may be false, that is to say, the resolution and the will to do right may take us to things which are bad when we believe them to be good, the contentment which results from it is not secure ; and inasmuch as this virtue is ordinarily opposed to pleasures, to appetites, and to passions, it is very difficult to put in practice ; whereas the right use of reason, affording a true knowledge of the good, prevents virtue from becoming false ; and also, by bringing it into accord with lawful pleasures, it renders the practice of it so easy, and, by making us understand the limitations of our nature, so limits our desires that it must be admitted that the highest happiness of man depends on this right use of reason, and consequently that the study which leads to its acquisition is the most useful occupation in which one can engage, as it is also, undoubtedly, the most agreeable and pleasant.

Accordingly, it seems to me that Seneca should have taught us all the principal truths the knowledge of which is requisite to facilitate the practice of virtue and to regulate our desires and our passions, and thus to secure our natural happiness, which would have made his book the best and the most useful that a pagan philosopher could have written. . . . .

. . . . . I observe, in the first place, that there is a difference between true happiness (*la béatitude*), the highest good, and the final aim or end to which our actions should be directed ; for true happiness is not the highest good, but it presupposes it, and is the contentment or satisfaction of mind which results from its possession. But by the end of our actions we may understand both ; for the highest good is undoubtedly that which we ought to propose to ourselves as the end in all our actions ; and the contentment of mind which springs from it, being the attraction which makes us seek it, is also with good reason called our end.

I observe, further, that the word pleasure was taken in a different sense by Epicurus from what it was by those who disputed with him ; for all his opponents restricted the meaning of this word to the pleasures of the senses, while he, on the contrary, extended it to all satisfactions of the mind, as may readily be seen from what Seneca and others wrote about him.

Now there were three principal opinions held by pagan philosophers touching the highest good and the end of our actions : to wit, that of Epicurus, who said it was pleasure ; that of Zeno, who decided it to be virtue ; and that of Aristotle, who made it consist of all the perfections as well of the body as of the mind. These three opinions may, as it seems to me, be taken as true and accordant with one another, provided they are favorably interpreted. For Aristotle, having in view the highest good of our whole human nature taken in general—that is to say, that which the most perfect of mankind may attain—is right in making it consist of all the perfections of which human nature is capable ; but that does not serve our turn. Zeno, on the other hand, took it to be what each man in his own person may possess ; that is why he was quite right in saying, also, that it consists only in virtue, because it is that alone among all the goods we can possess which depends entirely upon our free will. But he represented this virtue as being so severe and so opposed to pleasure, by making all vices equal, that, as it seems to me, only melancholy persons, or those whose minds were entirely detached from the body, could have been his followers.

Finally, Epicurus was not wrong, when, considering the nature of true happiness and the motive or end of our actions, he said it was pleasure in general, that is to say, contentment of mind ; for although the simple knowledge of our duty may oblige us to perform good actions, that, nevertheless, would not cause us to enjoy any happiness, if no pleasure came to us from it. But inasmuch as the name pleasure is often attributed to false delights, which are accompanied or followed by disquietude, *ennui*, and repentance, many persons have thought that this opinion of Epicurus inculcated vice ; and, indeed, it does not inculcate virtue. But just as when there is a prize offered for shooting at a mark, those to whom the prize has been shown have a desire to shoot, but yet cannot gain it if they do not look at the mark ; and those who look at the mark are not thereby induced to shoot at it, unless they know that there is a prize to be gained ; so virtue, which is the mark, does not excite desire when seen by itself alone, and contentment, which is the prize, cannot be gained, unless the virtue be practiced.

This is why I think I may rightly conclude that true happiness consists solely in contentment of mind (that is to say, in contentment taken in general ; for although there are forms of contentment which depend upon the body, and others which do not depend upon it, there, nevertheless, is none which does not exist within the mind) ; but to have a contentment which is secure, one must follow virtue, that is to say, one must have a firm and constant will to perform all that he judges to be the best, and employ the whole force of his understanding to secure a right judgment.

. . . . But in order that we may know precisely how much each thing may contribute to our contentment, the causes which produce it must be considered, and this is one of the main things to be known to facilitate the practice of virtue. For all acts of the soul which lead to the acquisition of any perfection are virtuous, and our whole contentment consists only in the interior witness that we have acquired some perfection. Accordingly, we never shall practice any virtue, that is to say, do anything which our reason persuades us we ought to do, without receiving therefrom satisfaction and pleasure. But there are two kinds of pleasures, the one pertaining to the mind alone, the other to man, that is to say, to the mind in its union with the body ; and the latter, presenting themselves confusedly to the imagination, often appear greater than they are, especially before they are possessed—which is the source of all the evils and of all the errors of life. For, according to the rule of reason, each pleasure should be measured by the greatness of the perfection which produces it, and it is thus that we measure those the causes of which are clearly known by us ; but, frequently, passion makes us believe certain things much better and more desirable than they are ; afterward, when we have taken great trouble to acquire them and have lost meanwhile the opportunity to gain other things which are really better, the enjoyment of them makes us aware of their defects; whence come disgust, regret, repentance. Hence the office of reason is to examine into the true value of all the goods the acquisition of which depends in any manner upon our conduct, in order that we may never fail to use all our diligence in the endeavor to acquire for ourselves those which are in reality the most desirable: in which, if fortune oppose our designs and hinder our success, we shall at least have the satisfaction of losing nothing through our own fault, and we shall not fail of enjoying all the natural happiness the acquisition of which was within our power. Thus, for example, anger may excite in us such violent desire for revenge as to lead us to imagine more pleasure in punishing our enemy than in preserving our honor or our life, and imprudently to imperil both for this end.

Whereas, if reason inquire what is the good or perfection upon which is founded this pleasure which proceeds from revenge, it will find no other (at least when the revenge does not serve merely to prevent a fresh offense), than that it makes us imagine that we have some superiority or some advantage over him upon whom we take vengeance: which is often only a vain imagination not worth considering in comparison with honor or life; nor even in comparison with the satisfaction that one would have in seeing himself master of his anger and in abstaining from revenge. And the same is true of all the other passions: for there is none of them which does not represent the good to which it tends in brighter colors than it deserves, and which does not make us imagine its delights far greater, before we possess them, than we find them to be afterward, when they are ours. This is why pleasure is commonly condemned ; because this word is used to signify false delights which often deceive us by their appearance and cause us meanwhile to neglect other far more substantial ones, the aspect of which does not affect us so much, as is ordinarily the case with purely intellectual pleasures ; I say ordinarily, for not all pleasures of the mind are praiseworthy, since they may be founded on some false opinion, as the pleasure which one may find in detraction, which is based solely on the notion that one must be so much the more esteemed as others are less so ; and they can also deceive us by their appearance, when some strong passion accompanies them, as is seen in one who yields to ambition. But the principal difference between the pleasures of the body and those of the mind consists in the fact that the body being subject to perpetual change, and its very preservation and its welfare being dependent on this change, all its pleasures are of short duration ; for they proceed only from the acquisition of something which is useful to the body at the moment that it receives it, and as soon as it ceases to be useful to it, the pleasure ceases also ; whereas, those of the mind may be as immortal as itself, provided they have a foundation so solid that neither knowledge of the truth, nor any false persuasion, may destroy it.

Finally, the true use of our reason for the conduct of life consists simply in the examination and dispassionate estimate of the value of all perfections, as well those of the body as of the mind, which can be acquired by our own effort, in order that, being commonly obliged to do without some in order to have others, we may always choose the best ; and since those of the body are the least, it can, in general, be said that without them one has the means of making himself happy. Still I am not of the opinion that they should be entirely slighted, nor even that one should be exempt from passions; it is enough that they be made amenable to reason, and when they have thus been made tractable, they are often the more useful in proportion as they incline to excess. . . . .

. . . . There can be, I think, but two things requisite to our always being disposed to judge rightly; one is knowledge of the truth, the other the habit of reminding one's self of this knowledge, and of conforming to it whenever occasion requires it. But since it is God only who perfectly knows all things, we must content ourselves with knowing those which most nearly concern us; among which is first and chief that there is a God upon whom all things depend, whose perfections are infinite, whose power is unlimited, whose decrees are infallible; for this teaches us to receive in good part whatever happens to us as being expressly sent to us from God. And since the true object of love is perfection, when we raise our minds to think of him as he truly is, we find ourselves naturally so inclined to love him that we extract joy even from our afflictions, when we think that his will is being done in our receiving them.

The second thing to be known is the nature of the soul, inasmuch as it exists without the body, and is much more noble than it, and is capable of enjoying an infinitude of pleasures which are not found in this present life; for this rids us of the fear of death, and so detaches our affection from earthly things that we look with mere disdain upon all that is within the power of fortune.

It will also be of much advantage to us to take worthy views of the works of God and entertain that vast idea of the extent of the universe which I have endeavored to unfold in the third book of my *Principles.** For if we suppose that beyond the heavens there is nothing but empty space (*des espaces imaginaires*), and that the whole heavens were made only for the sake of the earth, and the earth only for man, we are led to think that this earth is our principal abode, and the present life our best ; and instead of recognizing the perfections which we truly have, we attribute to other creatures imperfections which they have not, in order to exalt ourselves above them ; and going on in our impertinent presumption, we would enter into the counsels of Deity and undertake with him the management of the world—a source of vain disquietude and vexation without end.

When we have thus taken into account the goodness of God, the immortality of our souls, and the greatness of the universe, there is still one truth more, the recognition of which seems to me to be very useful, which is this, that although each one of us is a person separate from others, whose interests, consequently, are in some degree distinct from those of the rest of the world, it must still be remembered that one cannot exist alone, that he is in reality a part of the universe, still more particularly a part of this earth, a member of the state, the society, the family, to which he is joined by his abode, his oath of allegiance, his birth ; and he must always prefer the interests of the whole of which he is a part to those of himself in particular, yet with measure and discretion : for it would be wrong for one to expose himself to a great

* *Œuvres*, t. iii, p. 180.

evil in order to secure a trifling advantage to his family or his country; and if a man is worth more, himself alone, than all the rest of his town, he would not be right, were he willing, to sacrifice himself to save the town.

But if one refers everything to himself, he will not shrink from doing considerable harm to other men, when he thinks he may gain some small advantage from it, and he will have no true friendship, nor fidelity, nor any virtue at all; whereas, by considering himself a part of the public, one takes pleasure in doing good to everybody, and even does not fear to expose his life for the welfare of others when occasion presents itself; as one might be willing even to lose his own soul, if it were possible, to save others: so that this way of looking at things is the source and origin of all the most heroic human actions. But as for those who brave death through vanity, because they hope to be applauded; or from stupidity, because they do not perceive the danger; I think they are rather to be lamented than approved. But when one imperils his life because he believes it to be his duty, or, indeed, when he suffers any other evil to the end that some good may accrue to others, although he may not do this with distinct recognition of the fact that he owes more to the public of which he forms a part than to himself as an individual, he nevertheless may act from this consideration obscurely present to his mind; and one is naturally led to it, if he knows and loves God as he ought; for then, entirely surrendering himself to his will, he divests himself of his own individual interests, and has no other desire than to do what he believes to be agreeable to the will of God. Such an one experiences an inward satisfaction and content worth incomparably more than all the petty fleeting joys of sense. . . . .

Finally, I said above that, besides knowledge of the truth, habit is also necessary to make one disposed always to decide correctly; for inasmuch as we cannot give our attention constantly to the same thing, however clear and convincing may have been the reasons which have hitherto persuaded us of any truth, we may afterward be turned aside from our belief in it by false appearances, unless by long and frequent meditation we have so impressed it upon our minds that it has become a habit; and in this sense they are right in the school in saying that virtues are habits; for in fact one does not fail in duty from the lack of a theoretical knowledge of what he ought to do, but from the want of a practical possession of it, that is to say, from the want of a fixed habit of conviction. . . . .

ON THE HIGHEST GOOD.*

I HAVE learned from M. Chanut that it pleases your Majesty that I should have the honor of laying before you my views concerning the highest good, considered in the sense in which the ancient philosophers discussed it; and I esteem this command so great a favor that the desire to obey it diverts my mind from every other thought, and leads me, without deprecating my incompetency, to put down here in few words all that I may know on this subject. One may consider the goodness of each thing in itself without relation to other things, in which sense it is evident that God is the highest good, since he is incomparably more perfect than the creatures; but the good may also be considered in respect to ourselves, and in this sense I see nothing which we ought to esteem good but that which may belong to us in some manner, and be such as should render our possession of it a perfection.

Thus the ancient philosophers, who, unenlightened by the faith, knew nothing of supernatural blessedness, took into account only the goods we may possess in this life, and it was among these that they asked themselves what was the sovereign, that is to say, the principal and the greatest good. But in order that I may answer this question I hold that we ought to esteem as goods in respect to ourselves those only

* Letter to Catherine, Queen of Sweden, *Œuvres*, t. x, pp. 59-64.

which we possess, or rather those which we have the power to acquire ; and this granted, it seems to me that the highest good of mankind in general is the sum or assemblage of all the goods, as well of the mind as of the body and of fortune, which may exist in any men ; but that the highest good of each one in particular is quite another thing, and that it consists simply in a steadfast will to do right, and in the satisfaction which it produces ; the reason of which is that I do not know of any other good which seems to me so great, or which is so entirely within the power of each person. For, as for the goods of the body and of fortune, they do not depend absolutely upon ourselves : but those of the mind all turn on two principal ones, which are, the one, to know, the other, to will, that which is good ; but the knowledge of the good is often beyond our ability ; there remains, therefore, our will alone, which we may absolutely control. And I do not see that it is possible to make a better disposition of it, than for one to have always a fixed and steadfast determination scrupulously to perform everything which he shall judge to be best, and to make use of all the powers of his mind to discover it ; it is in this alone that all the virtues consist ; it is this alone which, properly speaking, merits praise and honor ; finally, from this alone results the greatest and the most solid satisfaction of life : accordingly, I conceive that in this consists the highest good.

And by this means I think I can bring into accordance the two most opposed and most celebrated theories of the ancients, namely, that of Zeno, who placed it in virtue or honor, and that of Epicurus, who placed it in that form of gratification to which he gave the name of pleasure. For as all vices proceed only from the uncertainty and the weakness which follows ignorance, of which the offspring is repentance; so virtue consists only in the resolution and the energy with which one is borne on to the doing of things which he thinks to be good; provided this energy does not spring from opinionativeness, but from the fact that he is conscious of having, to the extent of his moral ability, examined into the matter; and although what is then done may be bad, he is nevertheless assured that he did his duty; whereas, if one performs a virtuous action, and yet means to do evil, or even does not take pains to know what he is doing, he does not act as a virtuous man.

As for honor and praise, they are often bestowed upon the gifts of fortune; but, as I am sure that your Majesty thinks more highly of your virtue than of your crown, I do not hesitate to say here that it seems to me there is nothing but virtue which can rightly be praised. All other goods deserve simply to be cherished and not to be honored or commended, except on the presupposition that they are acquired, or obtained from God, by the right use of our free will; for honor and praise are a kind of reward, and nothing but that which depends upon the will can be the subject of reward or punishment.

There remains still to show that from the right use of free will results the greatest and most solid satisfaction of life; which does not seem to me to be difficult, for considering carefully wherein consists pleasure or delight, and in general all the forms of gratification there may be, I observe, in the first place, that there is none which does not exist entirely within the mind, although many of them depend upon the body; just as it is the mind which sees, although it be through the medium of the eyes. I observe, next, that there is nothing which can afford satisfaction to the mind but the thought that it is in the possession of some good, and that frequently this idea is nothing but a very confused representation, and also that its union with the body is the cause of the mind's commonly representing certain goods as incomparably greater than they are ; but that if it should distinctly recognize their just value, its satisfaction would always be proportioned to the greatness of the good whence it proceeds.

I observe, further, that the greatness of a good in our esteem should not be measured simply by the value of the thing in which it consists, but mainly also by the manner in which it is related to ourselves ; and besides, free will being in itself the noblest thing which can exist within us, inasmuch as it renders us in a certain manner equal to God, and appears to exempt us from being subject to him, and by consequence its right use is the greatest of all our goods— it is also that which is most peculiarly our own, and is of the highest importance to us ; whence it follows that from it alone can proceed our highest satisfactions ; as witness, for example, the peace of mind and interior delight of those who know that they have never failed to do their best, as well in the effort to know what is good, as in the gaining of it—a pleasure beyond comparison more sweet, more lasting, and substantial than all that come from any other source. . . . .

INDEX.

Abelard, cited, 155.
Absolute and relative, defined, 74, 75.
Acids, action of, 218.
Air, 218, 219, 224, elements of, 227.
Algebra, 46, 68, 74.
Anaclastic, the, 82.
Analysis of the Ancients, 46.
Anger, 336.
Animal spirits, 276 ff., 296.

A priori demonstrations of natural events, 246.
Aristotle, 333.
Arithmetic and geometry, the most certain sciences, 63.
Arts, method in, 88.
Attribute, 194, ff.
Augustine, cited, 117.
Automata, bodies compared to, 280.
Automatism of brutes, 280 ff.
Axioms, 193.

Bacon, Lord, cited, 86.
Blood, circulation of the, 295.
Body, meaning of term, 120; extension its essence, 176; divisible, 183; distinguished from mind, 293; living and dead, 294; pleasures of, 337.
Brain, impressions in, 184, 186.
Brutes, *automata*, 281 ff.; do not think, 282; have no proper language, 283; have no souls, 285.

Catherine, Queen, letter to, 342.

Cause and effect, 76; reality in, 132.
Chance, no such power, 316.
Chaos, 235.
Circular, all movements, 222.
Clearness and distinctness in conception, test of truth, 126, 154, 165, 169, 176, 179, 191.
Cogito, ergo sum, 115.
Coleridge, cited, 292, 297, 325.
Colors, in objects, 203.
Comets, 230, 251 ff.
Compassion, 324.
Composite and simple objects, 85, 97.
Conarium, 299.
Conception, distinguished from imagination, 169.
Concurrence of God, 156, 194.
Connection, contingent and necessary, 100.
Contempt and esteem, 320.
Contentment, 329, 330; rules for securing, 330 ff.
Contradiction, test of impossibility, 169.
Corporeal things, ideas of, 135; proof of their existence, 178.

Death, cause of, 293.
Deduction and intuition, the paths to knowledge, 64, 79; how related, 90.
Definitions, logical, 118, 119.
Desire, defined, 311; where the issue depends upon ourselves, 314; and upon other things, 315; what sort is compatible with happiness, 331.

Diophantes, mathematician, 70.
Discipline of the mind, the end of studies, 61.
Distinct and clear conceptions true, 126.
Doubt, not for doubt's sake, 56; the starting-point, 119, 187.
Duration, 195.

Earth, element of, 227; the, 230; motion of the, 260.
Elements, their number, etc., 226, 228, 229.
Eloquence, nature of, 39.
Eminently, 133, 137, 178.
Emotions, interior, 317.
End of action, 333.
Energy, active and passive, 95.
Enumeration, methodical, 77; or induction, 78, 79; sufficient, 79, 80.
Epicurus, 333, 334, 343.
Erdmann, reference to, 99.
Error, nature and source of, 148, 150; in judgments based upon the senses, 174.
Esteem and contempt, 320.
Existence of God not separable from his essence, 162.
Extension, 159; essence of body, 176, 200, 236.

Faculties, employed in knowledge, 83, 85, 92; active and passive, 177; of mind, not parts, 183.
Faith, verities of the, 55; an act of will, 65.
Feeling, nature of, 172.
Final cause, not to be sought in nature, 149, 184.
Fire, element of, 226, 229, 231.
Fischer, K., references to, 58, 84, 139, 144, n.
Flame, 211, 217, 219, 228.
Fluids, 215, 216, 217, 220.

Gassendi, reply to, 116.
General notions, 192.

Geometry and arithmetic, the most certain sciences, 63.
Gland, pineal, 276 ff., 298 ff.
God, proofs of existence of, 126 ff., 144; idea of, 132, 135, 137, 195; first of innate ideas, 165; all other knowledge dependent on the knowledge of, 166, 168; the only substance, 194; concourse of, necessary to perception, 194; immutable, 239, 243; author of all movements in the universe, 248.
Good, the highest, 333, 342, 343.
Goods, of the body and of the mind, 343.
Gravity, theory of, 259 ff.

Habit, necessary to virtue, 338, 341.
Happiness, true, 331; distinguished from the highest good, 332, 333.
Harvey, reference to, 295.
Hatred and love, defined, 310.
Heart, structure and action of, 295; not the seat of the passions, 301.
Heat, nature of, 211, 213; of the heart, 224, 280, 296.
Heavens, nature of the, 230; movements of, the cause of the motions of the stars, etc., 251 ff.
Highmindedness, 315, 321 ff.
History, defects of, 39.
Hobbes, cited, 154.
Honor and Praise, how rightly bestowed, 344.
Humility, 323.
Hyperaspistes, reply to, 128 n.

I—a thing which thinks, 142.
I think, therefore I am—a necessary truth, 115; not the conclusion of a syllogism, 116; not identical with reasonings of Augustine, 117.

INDEX.   349

Idea, a first, 134.
Ideas, 94, 127, 135; received by the senses, 173.
Imagination, aid to intellect, 83; part of the body, 94; nature of, 169.
Immortal, brutes not, 285.
Immortality of the soul, 337, 339.
Inertia, law of, 239.
Infinite, a positive idea, 138; God actually so, 140.
Intelligence, the first thing to be known, 61, 83.
Intuition, conditions of, 90; and deduction, the path to truth, 64, 104.

Joy, defined, 311.
Judgments, from impulse, conjectures, deduction, 103; the source of error, 127.

Kant, references to, 84, 180.
Knowledge, only certain, to be sought, 62; what it is and how far it extends, 84; intellect alone capable of, 85; whether it may increase to infinity, 139.

Language, belongs to man alone, 282.
Life, the happy, 329.
Light, nature of, 207, 250, 262; ff.; properties of, 265 ff.
Logic, opinion of, 45, 67, 89.
Logical distinction, 198, 199.
Love and hatred, defined, 310.

Mahaffy, reference to, 154.
Man, the body of, 275 ff.; compared to a machine, 278.
Mathematics, love of, 39; meaning of term, 71; the universal science, 72.
Mathematical truth, why we may doubt it, 112.
Matter, primary, 234; essence of, its extension, 236; its tendency to move in straight lines, 243 ff.
Memory, employed in knowledge, 83, 85, 92; explained, 303.
Method, necessity of, 66.
Mind, always thinks, 128 n.; its essence, thought, 176; indivisible, 183; receives impressions solely from the brain, 184; power over the body, 302; pleasures of, 336.
Miracles, not wrought in the new world, 246.
Modal distinction, 198, 199.
Modes, 192, 196.
Motion, heat and light, modes of, 211, 213; forms of, 215; always circular, 222, 243, 247; of matter at creation, 235, 238; three rules of, 239 ff.; simplest form of, 240.
Moral code, 50.

Natural phenomena, all are modes of motion, 245.
Nature, light of, 130, 132, 136, 140, 142, 146, 155; the order established by God in creation, 179; truth of its teachings, 179, 180; falsity of its teachings, 181, 187; sense of the term, 179, 181, 238.
Negation and privation, 99, 156.
Nerves, origin in the brain, 94, 184.
Notions, simple, 192; common, or axioms, 193.
Number, 197.

Object and idea, 131.
Objective reality, 132.
Ontological argument for the being of God, 162 ff.

Pain and pleasure, sensations of, 209.

Pappus, mathematician, 70.
Particular truths known before general, 117.
Particles, into which matter is divisible, 216, 219.
Passion, is action, 291 ; distinguished from bodily functions, 292 ; effect of, 302, 335, 336, 338.
Passions, primary causes of, 307 ; their service, 307, 310, 313 ; how their number is determined, 307 ff.; due to the motions of the blood and spirits, 312; upon them depend all the good and evil of this life, 325.
Perceptible, what objects are, 224.
Perception, is thought, 122 ; the self known in, 124 ; dependent on motion, 224.
Perfection, of the universe, 150, 157; pleasure measured by, 335 ; true object of love, 335.
Perspicacity, how cultivated, 87.
Philosophy, opinion of, 40.
Pineal gland, 276, 298 ff.
Pity, 324.
Planets, 230, 251 ff., 255 ff.; scintillations of, 272.
Pleasure, senses of the term, 333 ; as end of action, 334 ; measure of, 335 ; kinds, 335 ff.
Poetry, 39.
Preservation, continued creation, 141.
Privation, 99, 155.
Probable opinions, when to be followed, 52.
Providence, divine, 315, 316.

Real distinction, 198.
Reason, intuitive and discursive, 99 ; office of, 336, 337.
Regret, how avoided, 331.
Relative and Relations, defined, 75.
Revenge, 336.

Sadness, defined, 312.
Sagacity, how cultivated, 87.
Science, nothing but the human intelligence, 61.
Sciences, all bound together, 62.
Self, existence of, undeniable, 114.
Self-esteem, ground of, 321.
Seneca, reference to, 329, 332, 333.
Sense, perceives passively, 93 ; the common, 93, 94, 184.
Senses, deceive us, 108.
Sensations, 172, 202, 213.
Sensible qualities, 136.
Simple and composite things, 85, 97.
Sleep, illusions in, 109.
Society, interests of, to be preferred to those of self, 339 ff.
Solids, 215, 216, 217, 220.
Soul, united to the body, 297 ; and body, how they act on one another, 301 ; conflict of inferior and superior parts, 305 ff.
Sound, nature of, 208.
Space, not empty, 221.
Stars, fixed, 230 ; scintillations of, 270.
Substance, 136 ; infinite and finite, 138 ; defined, 194; two forms of, 194, 200, 207.
Sun and stars, formation of, 247 ff.
Syllogism, of no use in discovery, 90.

Theology, reverence for, 40.
Thinking substance, the mind, 176, 200.
Thought, what it is, 115, 121.
Time, distinguished from duration, 196.

Understanding, not the source of error, 151 ; should precede will, 155.
Uniformity of motion and fig-

ure, tendency of matter toward, 247 ff.
Universal and particular notions, 75.
Universals, 197.

Vacuum, 220, 221, 223, 247.
Veitch, references to, 58, 125, 126, 127, 129, 132, 133, 144, 153, 177, 178, 193, 207, 220.
Verities, eternal, 245.
Vices, source of, 343, 344.
Virtue, the remedy for the passions, 318 ; depends upon ourselves, 330 ; defined, 331, 344 ; alone worthy of praise, 344.

Volition, effect of, on the body, 304.
Voluntary, term defined, 310.

Will, its range, 152, 156 ; cause of error, 153 ; understanding must precede, 155.
Wisdom, depends upon ourselves, 330.
Wonder, 308.
Words, as symbols, 207.
World, description of a new, 233 ff.

Zeno, reference to, 333, 343.

www.ingramcontent.com/pod-product-compliance
Lightning Source LLC
Chambersburg PA
CBHW031426230426
43668CB00007B/451